MW01280212

Becoming Entitled

ABIGAIL TROLLINGER

Becoming Entitled

Relief, Unemployment, and Reform
during the Great Depression

TEMPLE UNIVERSITY PRESS
Philadelphia • Rome • Tokyo

TEMPLE UNIVERSITY PRESS
Philadelphia, Pennsylvania 19122
tupress.temple.edu

Library of Congress Cataloging-in-Publication Data

Names: Trollinger, Abigail, 1982– author.
Title: Becoming entitled : relief, unemployment, and reform during the Great
   Depression / Abigail Trollinger.
Description: Philadelphia : Temple University Press, 2020. | Includes biblio-
   graphical references and index. | Summary: "Becoming Entitled examines the
   Depression-era political and intellectual shifts that occurred at the city and
   state levels and ultimately enabled the passage of unemployment insurance in
   the United States, and the role played by local reformers and settlement leaders
   in bringing about these changes"—Provided by publisher.
Identifiers: LCCN 2019057720 (print) | LCCN 2019057721 (ebook) |
   ISBN 9781439919521 (cloth) | ISBN 9781439919538 (paperback) |
   ISBN 9781439919545 (pdf)
Subjects: LCSH: Unemployment insurance—United States—History—20th
   century. | Unemployment—United States—Public opinion—History—20th
   century. | Unemployed—Services for—United States—History—20th century. |
   Social settlements—United States—History—20th century. | Social reformers—
   United States—History—20th century. | Unemployment insurance—Illinois—
   Chicago—History—20th century. | Unemployment—Illinois—Chicago—Public
   opinion—History—20th century. | Unemployed—Services for—Illinois—
   Chicago—History—20th century. | Social settlements—Illinois—Chicago—
   History—20th century. | Social reformers—Illinois—Chicago—History—
   20th century.
Classification: LCC HD7096.U6 T75 2020 (print) | LCC HD7096.U6 (ebook) |
   DDC 368.4/40097309043—dc23
LC record available at https://lccn.loc.gov/2019057720
LC ebook record available at https://lccn.loc.gov/2019057721

Printed in the United States of America

9 8 7 6 5 4 3 2 1

For Millie and Eloise

Contents

Acknowledgments

B ecoming Entitled started as a dissertation and grew into this book, so I have accumulated many debts of gratitude over its years of existence. It began at Northwestern University with a recommendation from Henry Binford, an enthusiastic and thoughtful adviser who supported me in moments of doubt and steered me away from the pitfalls of overly simplistic analysis and unsubstantiated arguments. The members of my dissertation committee, Michael Sherry and Susan Pearson, read countless drafts and offered valuable feedback time and again. More recently, editor Aaron Javsicas championed Becoming Entitled as a book, and he and Ashley Petrucci patiently and expertly guided me through the publishing process at Temple University Press.

Becoming Entitled rests on the work and expertise of the archivists who made available to me the rich world of settlement work in the 1930s. I particularly want to thank Kevin Leonard and Janet Olson, who introduced me to the Northwestern University Settlement archives and warmly welcomed me day after day. At the University of Minnesota's Social Welfare History Archives, David Klassen offered financial assistance and critical insights into my research. I am also grateful to numerous archivists who helped me navigate settlement collections in the Chicago History Museum, the Special Collections and University Archives of Marquette University, and the Sophia Smith Collection at Smith College.

While I was in graduate school, many colleagues and friends graciously read and responded to drafts of my work. The two years I spent in the Newberry Library's Urban History Dissertation Group were invaluable; in the basement of the Newberry, I found camaraderie and benefitted from this group's wealth of knowledge on cities and their people. I also remember with great fondness a series of weekend workshops held by a group of Jane Addams scholars called the Interdisciplinary Jane Addams Society (IJAS), including Marilyn Fischer, Kristen Gwinn-Becker, and Lucy Knight. Friends, including Rebecca Marchiel and Neal Dugre, provided laughter and support, not to mention feedback on drafts. Finally, I am indebted to Genevieve Carlton and Anne Koenig, Europeanists who befriended me when I was the lone remaining female Americanist in our cohort, and with whom I have shared much of my adult life. A special thanks to Anne Koenig, who read late drafts, offered critical feedback, and proved to be a master indexer.

I am also fortunate to have found an academic home at St. Norbert College (SNC), which is peopled by many whom I admire and enjoy spending time with. Members of the history department, particularly Vicky Tashjian, Marti Lamar, and Bob Kramer, welcomed me to SNC and encouraged me throughout this project. Leah Hennick, our history teaching assistant extraordinaire, demonstrated intelligence and problem-solving skills beyond her years when she researched the cover image for this book. Over summers working in the Mulva library, I was glad to have the quiet punctuated by conversations with Amy Lewis, David Bosco, Connie Muelemans, and Sarah Titus. And my friends here in the frigid North are some of the warmest and most intelligent individuals I have met. Thanks to Kathleen Gallagher Elkins, Anna Antos, Raquel Lopez, Becky McKean, and Carrie Larson for the love, memes, and inspiration.

During the years that I worked on this project, my family changed significantly, but I found that its purpose remained much the same, so I offer profound thanks to the members of my family who buoyed me in work. My father, William Trollinger, indoctrinated me into the cult of history when I could hardly form the words "Donner Party," and for that, I thank him. From long conversations about poverty to last-minute feedback on my work, his enthusiasm, generosity of time, and sharp mind greatly improved this project. He and Susan Trollinger cheered me on every step of the way. I am beholden to my mother, Gayle Trollinger, for providing me with a seemingly bottomless well of encouragement, intellectual fortitude, and resilience. As an academic and a mother, she is a model whom I try my best to emulate in life. She and Mike Malone offered unwavering support.

I do not have enough words to thank the two pillars in my life: Rebekah Trollinger and Dan Hatch. Bekah, my best friend since before I can remember, has long been an intellectual inspiration to me. She is the funniest, most insightful person I have ever known, which is lucky for me, because I have known her longer than anyone else. And I am fortunate to share a life with Dan—he gives our children massive amounts of time and energy, models for all of us a balanced work ethic, and reminds me to be aware of the built and natural world. Finally, this book is dedicated to Millie and Eloise, who grant me an endless supply of creativity, weirdness, and love every day.

Becoming Entitled

Introduction

Entitlement in Historical Context

I n 1934, a group of unemployed workers, organized as the Workers Committee on Unemployment (WCOU), published a pamphlet for their jobless brethren, declaring, "You are entitled to live. . . . We can not beg all the time. We must ask and demand. Join our demonstration Nov. 24, and raise your voice for decent relief."[1] Noteworthy in many ways, not least because it draws attention to the fact that the unemployed were organizing during the 1930s, the pamphlet's use of the word *entitled* stands out. Although *entitlement* as a term today connotes an unwarranted sense of deservedness, in the 1930s, the term meant something very different. When jobless workers in the 1930s called themselves "entitled," they were claiming their right to a new kind of government protection—the protection from undeserved unemployment and the financial straits that such unemployment created. To workers and their supporters, *entitlement* was a word that indicated their lack of culpability in the economic crisis and allowed them to shed the shame of joblessness. In other words, the term *entitlement* in the 1930s restored workers' dignity as they sought relief (including work relief) during the Great Depression and unemployment insurance afterward.

This book is about the emergence of worker entitlement in the 1930s and the people who cultivated it, with a particular focus on the city of Chicago, where the settlement house and labor movements both flourished. Most notably, settlement workers were instrumental in the shift toward entitlement. The settlement house movement had emerged in the Progressive Era as a way to combat the social disloca- tion, chaos, and inequality of rapid industrialization. Such reformers as Jane Addams bought houses in industrial neighborhoods, where they could live and work among poor, often immigrant, populations. With the assistance of wealthy (often Protestant) supporters, settle- ment workers like Addams moved into what began as stand-alone houses and often grew into large complexes. Although the reformers who resided in these houses periodically sheltered families threat- ened with eviction, it was rarely for more than a night; the houses were really homes only for the reformers. By 1910, as many as four hundred operational settlement houses existed in the United States. In a wave of urban reform, among other efforts, settlement work- ers set up some of the first day nurseries for urban laborers; hosted classes and discussion groups on a variety of topics; demanded that cities undertake sanitation efforts, such as garbage pickup; and facili- tated conversations between reformers, labor organizers, and intel- lectuals. By that time, settlement workers also welcomed the work of regular volunteers or interns from local universities, many of whom would shape social policy in the decades to come.

Settlement workers lived in a world defined by economic precari- ousness and inconsistent, complicated forms of aid. Looking at the options available can help parse out the terminology and policies. In 1928, a white working man in Chicago who found himself un- employed and needy could turn for support to a variety of places. Certainly, he could visit one of the city's many charitable institutions, privately funded organizations (such as Catholic Charities) that of- fered assorted forms of assistance. Because these charities could vary widely in type, generosity, and accessibility, our jobless worker might instead turn to a publicly funded welfare agency, such as a Bureau of Public Welfare, which was usually based in the worker's county of residence and offered similar forms of assistance as chari- ties. Charities and welfare agencies historically offered either indoor relief, forms of assistance that required that the recipient move into an institution, such as a poorhouse, or outdoor relief, forms of assistance that the recipient could take home, such as groceries, coal, or clothing. By the 1930s, these local forms of charity and welfare also often included casework, the "scientific" assessment of need that involved individuals visiting the home of the impoverished to determine whether they truly were needy and deserving. Although settlement houses offered small forms of outdoor relief, such as free milk and crackers for children every morning, most settlement workers saw themselves as an alternative to charity workers; therefore, our worker would likely look to a settlement house to fill his newly acquired leisure time with socialization or classes, but not to survive.

It is also possible that our worker would think outside these local systems of aid. In 1928, the United States was developing a more complicated and extensive system of social policy, or the collection of laws and programs that influence people's everyday lives and well-being. Social policy, as it was understood in the interwar period, included forms of "public assistance," those programs that are publicly funded, distributed by the state or nation, and intended to aid the vulnerable and helpless. Pensions for widowed mothers were a widely supported form of public assistance in the 1920s. Modern public assistance programs are often associated with "welfare," a connotation that leads many to view them suspiciously at best. In the 1930s, the term *welfare* did not have such negative implications, and Aid to Dependent Children was a relatively uncontroversial part of the 1935 Social Security Act. Still, use of public assistance indicated dependence, so our worker would likely hope to access some form of social insurance instead of public assistance. Publicly funded programs for social insurance, which were still largely theoretical in 1928, were modeled on private insurance programs and intended to provide workers with protection against a wide range of social problems, such as unemployment, old age, and death. Unemployment insurance was one form of social insurance, and although policy experts proposed several forms of unemployment insurance, all were monetary, and they all specifically protected workers against job losses.

These public assistance and social insurance programs were understood, by their nature, to be somewhat permanent, but because of the economic crisis of the 1930s, all kinds of assistance were closely tied to *relief,* a term that usually described a form of aid given to people rendered needy by an acute crisis or disaster. In 1930, many people understood relief as being distributed to victims of major fires and floods, but as the country's economic crisis worsened, our job-less man would likely make the case that unemployment could be as damaging as a natural disaster.[2]

Whether he appealed to the city's charities or sought unemploy-ment insurance, our unemployed man would try to establish himself as being poor through no fault of his own—in other words, he would likely argue that he was not a pauper. In this period, *paupers* (whether real or imaginary) were frequently part of conversations about so-cial welfare because they were a cautionary tale: individuals who accepted assistance without wanting or trying to work, the kind of people who could be self-sufficient but instead loafed and depended on the charity of others or the state. Our unemployed man, calling on the city's charities and the county's public welfare agencies for relief and social insurance, would again and again have to prove that he was not a pauper.

Settlement workers were keenly aware of the perceived threat of pauperism, and in the 1930s, decades-deep into their social project, they recognized early signs of growing unemployment. They thus be-lieved that their relationships with laboring communities positioned them to promote a program of social insurance. Reformers (such as those in the American Association for Labor Legislation [AALL]) and policy experts (including such economists as John Commons) had long advocated for social insurance. Yet by the 1920s, unemployment insurance still had not caught favor with the American public, an is-sue that settlement workers aimed to rectify.[3] They were also well con-nected in the urban North, which positioned them to be influential in the region. Their long history in progressive reform work nurtured relationships with policy makers, city leaders, and state and national legislators. At the state and national levels, before, during, and after the Great Depression, settlement workers mobilized a campaign for unemployment insurance and sharing personal stories from unem-ployed workers to exonerate them from the stigma of poverty.

As the national economic crisis set in, settlement workers part-nered with people in every part of Chicago society: the unemployed, city relief officials, and state legislators. Therefore, they provide a win-dow to a city strained by poverty but marked by creativity, contest, and compromise. Working in the urban communities most affected by unemployment, settlement leaders created coalitions throughout the city and through them developed the concept of entitlement: the idea that the unemployed were not at fault for their poverty and that the government owed it to them to ameliorate the consequences of unemployment. At the city and state levels, settlement workers and the jobless exposed a faulty relief system and recommended state legislation as the solution—and, perhaps inadvertently, established an enduring framework for distributing public relief in Illinois. In doing so, they created the space for the adoption of a previously sidelined definition of poverty, one that maintained that some poor workers had the right to claim federal assistance and one that did not view poverty and pauperism as being synonymous.

Although the New Deal era and subsequent years often loom large in narratives of the emergence of worker entitlement, a study of settlement workers repositions this view.[4] Settlement activism highlights the many campaigns for state social insurance that began in the 1920s and the subsequent reforms made in cities including Chicago, New York, and Philadelphia, all before Franklin Roosevelt was elected president. In the mid-1920s, members of the National Federation of Settlements (NFS) argued that social insurance was a necessity for modern workers. In 1931—two years before President Herbert Hoover left office and four years before Congress approved federal unemployment insurance—settlement worker Lea Taylor informed her suburban supporters that "unemployment insurance of some sort seems only a sane protection against a similar disaster to individual families."[5] Settlement workers, then, were well ahead of the curve in advocating for social insurance.

Examining settlement work in the 1930s also uncovers the ways in which social welfare policy stemmed from collaboration between local figures and state governments, a process that prepared workers, officials, and lawmakers for federal involvement. Settlement leaders worked at the city and state levels to change public opinion on unemployment insurance and to pass legislation that would distribute relief funds from the government to the unemployed. Local actors turned to policy and legislation at the state level to acquire the help that they could not get from Washington. Settlement research, articles, and protests pressured state governments to engage in direct relief, and local and state governments drafted legislation that attended to struggling laborers and created a template for New Deal programs. Together, this coalition drastically changed how workers could protect themselves from the vulnerabilities of labor.

Just as significant, though, is what did not change: long-held relationships between the city's charities and their needy neighbors. A study of settlement houses reveals the persistence of neighborhood institutions and relief agencies, suggesting that class consciousness and neighborhood identity were frequently mutually affirming during the 1930s. Chicago's relief officials and settlement workers engineered drives for relief funds that ultimately preserved local systems of relief in the city; when the state stepped in, local institutions funneled state money to workers' neighborhoods through largely familiar means and institutions. Unemployed workers' groups, many established before the introduction of state assistance, also frequently organized along neighborhood and ethnic lines. In other words, neighborhood institutions facilitated class consciousness, and new social policies bolstered these neighborhood institutions.

At the center of this work were settlement leaders who were ideally situated to reach out to laborers and relief officials. The centrality of settlement workers in the creation of the ideology of, and policies related to, worker entitlement is a key argument of this book, a departure from New Deal historiography that describes major changes as occurring at the federal level[6] or at purely the grassroots level.[7] Thus, this work could be called a history from "the middle," which takes seriously the achievements made by reformers working on city- and nationwide issues. As neighborhood workers and activists, settlement leaders were practiced in responding to problems through interpersonal conversations and protests. Chicago's thirty-plus active settlements reached into many of the city's neighborhoods. On the national level, members of the NFS had access to settlement workers (and their neighbors) across the country. And perhaps more importantly, settlement workers in the 1920s and 1930s were devoted to the issue of unemployment. Unemployment became central to settlement workers, and settlement workers are central to my study of unemployment.

In the 1920s, settlement workers and social policy theorists looked to European precedents for inspiration. At international conferences, progressives argued that European governments had proven the effectiveness and necessity of programs for social insurance. In the NFS, leaders were campaigning for social insurance in the 1920s—well before the Great Depression forced laborers, city social workers, and Roosevelt to support federal intervention. Thus, when it became clear that localities could not sustain their unemployed workers, settlement leaders already had a solution in mind. As inheritors of a reform tradition, moreover, settlement workers were poised to cooperate with left-leaning laborers and right-leaning relief officials. They proposed a pragmatist's solution to the problem of unemployment; after witnessing firsthand the needs of the unemployed, settlement workers embraced social insurance while engaging with (rather than rejecting) capitalism.[8]

Their work among the unemployed led settlement workers to challenge notions that unemployment was indicative of a person's moral failings, so their solution depended on changing the public's perception as well. Although it may be easy to assume that widespread poverty brought with it an equally widespread sense of empathy, the mainstream embrace of relief was fairly slow in coming.[9] Years after the 1929 stock market crash, settlement workers battled a persistent belief that joblessness was usually a consequence of sloth. Even more striking was the guilt that many workers felt, year after year, as they were unable to provide for their families. The public (politicians, average Americans, and the unemployed themselves) needed to be convinced that the poor might not be to blame for their condition. Settlement workers thus actively strove to redeem the reputation of the unemployed in their campaigns for public relief funds and in their dealings with unemployed workers.

When considering historical shifts in the interwar period, many scholars have discounted the role of settlement houses in the 1930s. Some perceive settlement workers as reformers-turned-caseworkers, who embraced professionalism during the 1920s. Professionalism was a shift from the reform spirit of the Progressive Era, which seemed to many to have died with the brutality of the World War I and the consumerism of the 1920s. As has been usefully charted by such historians as Roy Lubove, the profession of social work (propelled by schools of social service) had emerged in the first decades of the twentieth century, and by the 1920s, many professional social workers had developed highly systematized systems of casework.[10]

Although some settlement workers embraced professionalization, many historians have been too quick to assume that settlement houses faded from significance in the 1920s. Such arguments suggest that settlement work in this decade became indistinguishable from the emerging profession of social work, as settlement workers abandoned reform for casework.[11] Some scholars argue that, in the face of professionalization, the significance of settlements lay in their ability to incubate great reform talent, which then became relevant at the level of policy and governance. As Michael Katz puts it, settlements "had their greatest impact on the stream of young men and women who passed through them."[12] These scholars rightly describe settlement workers' broader impact in the 1920s and 1930s, yet they also imply that settlement workers had lost their drive to reform.

However, research into unemployment reveals that settlement workers became increasingly invested in reform as the 1920s went on. Moreover, in 1930s Chicago, settlement caseworkers were actually noteworthy for their *lag* in professionalization. While their counterparts in Catholic Charities, for instance, had developed extensive systems for cataloguing and keeping track of clients, settlement workers were just beginning to experiment with streamlining casework and saw themselves as auxiliaries to such relief agencies.

Likewise, settlement leaders in the 1930s were noteworthy for talking about poverty as being the result of environmental conditions (such as overcrowding and poor pay) rather than individual moral failings. In this view, they echoed Progressive Era leaders, who had attributed urban poverty to industrialization and called for reform legislation. At the turn of the twentieth century, leading figures in Chicago's early settlements, including Jane Addams from Hull House, Mary McDowell from the University of Chicago Settlement, and Graham Taylor from Chicago Commons, claimed that with changes to workers' environments, such as when the Tenement House Act of 1901 mandated air shafts and sanitation, these urban workers could escape the grinding poverty to which they seemed doomed. Addams described how early social workers "tended more and more to discuss the economic conditions underlying the poverty, disease, and overwork they were seeking to ameliorate."[13] In this approach, settlement workers challenged a historic tendency among some charity workers and policy makers to blame poor individuals for their moral failings—or, at the very least, to assume that they should recover with minimum government intervention.[14]

During the interwar period, settlement workers seemed to directly mimic their forebears by focusing on unemployment and calling for labor-related legislation. Many Progressive Era settlement workers (and former settlement house residents) maintained that labor legislation was imperative for improving lives of urban residents. Florence Kelley, for example, argued that "low wages produce more poverty than all other causes together."[15] Linking poverty and labor, Kelley exemplified settlement leaders' tradition of identifying the structural causes of urban poverty, many of them related to working conditions. As the Depression set in, Chicago's settlement leaders, including Lea D. Taylor and Harriet Vittum, joined jobless workers to assess neighborhoods' and individuals' deterioration, access better relief funds, and agitate for relief and social insurance. In much of their work, settlement workers and their allies underscored that the poverty they witnessed was the result of social problems rather than individual moral failings. In an NFS study on unemployment, Helen Hall explained, "Experience has taught us to recognize broken work not merely as a symptom of financial crises, but as a recurring fault of modern production."[16]

Settlement workers in the 1920s and 1930s drew on arguments for the environmental roots of poverty—in other words, unemployed workers suffered not because of their own failings but because of external circumstances (such as changing trends in consumer habits, capricious employers, or poor health care). In their 1929 campaign for social insurance, settlement workers held American industry liable for undervaluing labor and underestimating the human cost of an unpredictable economy. During open hearings with the unemployed and meetings with unemployment committees, Chicago's settlement leaders characterized the unemployed as victims, thus exonerating them from pauperism and its accompanying shame. They assured the unemployed that they were not alone and encouraged them to seek assistance with their pride intact. As Chicago's relief funds dried up, the city's settlement and relief leaders took their case to Springfield, Illinois, and Washington, DC, and suggested that the state or federal government should buoy those sinking into destitution. The newly poor, they argued, should be able to turn to the government for relief.

Yet settlement work in the 1930s was multifaceted, and it forces historians to consider labor history and social welfare history as intersecting and influencing each other. Caseworkers, attempting to mitigate the more immediate problems of the Depression, were forced to think more about material concerns. At the end of the 1920s, settlement casework increased exponentially, and caseworkers dealt less frequently with family conflict and delinquency, problems that had allowed them to turn to the courts and rarely required long-term material aid. Instead, caseworkers began to respond to higher numbers of families suffering from loss of income and destitution. As buildings fell apart and evictions became common, settlement neighborhoods became marked by transience and disrepair. Caseworkers hoped to dam the rising tide of poverty but found few options. Chicago's financial state was a mess, and the local relief system was wholly unable to meet increased need. Therefore, settlement workers joined in the task of distributing aid.

The irony of settlement work at this time was that caseworkers, the colleagues of the pioneers of such progressive measures as unemployment insurance, frequently lapsed into using well-worn language to describe the poor. The mounting pressure for settlement workers to contribute to the growing relief crisis taxed their already strained budgets and tested inexperienced caseworkers. Home visitors, expected to allot limited funds to their many unemployed neighbors, struggled to establish parameters for assessing need and distributing aid. Their reflections, jotted down on small pieces of paper or elaborated on casework forms in settlement archives, reveal the all-too-easy slippage between need and worth, as visitors evaluated cleanliness and characterized some applicants as more "deserving" than others. Perhaps not surprisingly, when settlement workers participated in direct relief, they began to resemble the charity workers whom they had decried in the Progressive Era. Settlement leaders and caseworkers hardly had the time to consider the ways in which relief affected their settlements, but their relief work uncovered the persistence of ideas that linked worth and poverty.

Crucially, settlement workers and their allies constructed a campaign for relief and social insurance around gendered concepts of work and family. Their attention to the breadwinner model of the family stemmed from their close ties with the unemployed themselves and with settlement workers' sense that unemployment undermined gender roles and family self-confidence. The 1929 NFS study on unemployment noted female and child employment in families but categorized unemployment as joblessness among male breadwinners. Settlement workers tackled the weight of unemployment in Chicago along gendered lines, by organizing separate departments and distinct programming for men and women. Men's Department settlement workers worried that neighborhood men might not be able to manage their "enforced leisure," so they offered discussion groups and reading rooms; Women's Department settlement workers offered classes on cooking within the constraints of a tight relief budget and opportunities to discuss homemaking.

On the one hand, settlement workers reflected a marketplace in which women and children could rarely earn enough to support a family and a society in which their employment was a last (albeit common) resort. On the other hand, by relying on consistent employment to prove legitimacy, settlement leaders prepared their neighbors, legislators, and Americans to accept a system of welfare in which certain groups (traditional breadwinners) were categorized as entitled, while others (the group called "unemployables" included single women, the disabled, and anyone unable to sustain steady employment) were looked upon with suspicion. Perhaps unwittingly, settlement workers' focus on relief and social insurance for regularly employed men reinscribed popular gender roles and facilitated a further codification of gender inequality in American welfare policies.

In the 1920s and 1930s, therefore, settlement workers and the jobless called for a specific form of entitlement: legitimate access to a program of social insurance that prioritized unemployment. While anti-poverty workers had long considered the vulnerable (including children or the blind) to be entitled to protection, settlement workers in the 1930s argued that a different form of entitlement should extend to jobless workers, whom they saw as victims of industry and the economy. While entitlement for children and widows was bound up in Christian notions of mercy and protection of the weak, entitlement for jobless workers implied deservedness that came from hard work. Settlement workers were not opposed to other elements of insurance, such as old age insurance or universal health care, or programs of public assistance, such as pensions for the blind or single mothers.

In fact, despite the common separation of public assistance and social insurance, settlement workers in the 1930s collapsed the distinction, instead demanding good assistance (through relief) *and* social insurance. Whether discussing relief or social insurance, though, settlement workers committed themselves to easing joblessness and ultimately preserving the breadwinner family economy and the legitimacy of a safety net for workers who had fallen prey to corrupt or unpredictable economic forces.[17]

Their attention to jobless men is especially noteworthy, considering what Linda Gordon describes as the bifurcation of social security in the United States. By the middle of the twentieth century, it was clear that while recipients of social insurance received assistance with dignity, recipients of public assistance were subjected to what she calls "personal supervision of [their] private lives; and [with it] a deep stigma."[18] European precedents demonstrated that social welfare and social insurance could be united into one program that protected workers *and* removed the stigma from relief, which was considered a backup to the safety net. Settlement workers, though, ignored those possibilities, functionally reserving entitlement for breadwinners—male heads of household.

Indeed, although it was codified in New Deal policy, settlement work foreshadowed what Robert O. Self calls the "breadwinner consensus."[19] When settlement workers met with groups of frustrated unemployed men and then founded a workers' committee, they articulated an argument for state intervention that emphasized prior participation in the labor market. In publications, at open hearings, and in correspondence with legislators, settlement and relief workers argued that the unemployed laborers who deserved relief and social insurance were typically hard working but forced into joblessness by the economy.

Settlement workers proposed a transformation in how people should see unemployment by suggesting that the unemployed were not at fault for their poverty. Whereas social workers in the 1920s proposed that a jobless person make changes (whether in lifestyle or morality, which was often one and the same), settlement workers charged the government to change to reflect jobless people's needs. Their arguments for social insurance also expanded the category of "employable" to include people who were without work because of the economy. Yet by proving that the unemployed were "employable," based on their history of work, settlement leaders effectively maintained the category of "unemployable" as well. As such, settlement workers bolstered their argument for social insurance while also maintaining the two-tiered welfare state.

Considering their position in workers' communities and among city leaders, it is not surprising that settlement workers played a key role in legislating state relief and federal unemployment insurance. In Illinois, their campaign succeeded in establishing a state commission for providing relief to the unemployed. Out of Chicago came a chorus of varied interests calling for state funds: settlement workers, relief officials, and the unemployed themselves. A few years after the state granted assistance to the unemployed, Chicago's persistently jobless finally saw the federal government establish a program of social insurance. Although the Social Security Act proved to be less generous or immediate in its funding than they had hoped, it was a symbol of worker entitlement. Through casework and club work, worker organizing and legislating, settlement leaders and unemployed workers created a public conception of unemployment and poverty that would define American welfare policy for the rest of the twentieth century, one that legitimized aid for the jobless and maintained boundaries around the "worthy" poor.

This book is divided into five chapters. Chapter 1 centers on settlement work in the 1920s and positions settlement workers at the vanguard of a movement for social insurance. Settlement house workers were concerned with unemployment numbers even before most people realized that it was a national problem. In 1929 the NFS undertook a nationwide study of unemployed Americans, by which its members collected first-person accounts of families on temporary relief due to joblessness. This research, published in two forms, attempted to disprove the widely held belief that social insurance created dependency and rewarded indolence. In *Some Folks Won't Work*, a popular press argument for social insurance published in 1930, and the more academic *Case Studies of Unemployment*, published the following year, settlement workers charge that the U.S. economic system was capricious and economic prosperity untenable. Settlement workers like Helen Hall and social reformers like Paul Kellogg were not the first or only voices that had called for social insurance since the turn of the century. Yet unlike the economists and reformers who lamented unemployment during economic slumps, the settlement campaigns argued that, even in prosperity, American industry left some workers unable to find work. This chapter ultimately argues, however, that despite their efforts, their campaign did more to reveal many Americans' persistent resistance to unemployment insurance than to enlist anyone to their cause. At the start of the Depression, settlement workers still found that most Americans (even workers themselves) had not developed a sense of entitlement for employed and unemployed workers.

The crisis of the Great Depression finally spurred others to recognize the need for unemployment insurance. Chapter 2 outlines the steps that relief officials took in Chicago to raise much-needed funds and, they hoped, preserve a system of private, local relief. As the relief system collapsed under intense demand, relief officials organized a series of much-publicized campaigns for private donations. They attempted to integrate their campaigns for relief into Chicago society, arguing that it was the city's responsibility to provide relief funds and preserve a system of charity based on noblesse oblige more than governmental intervention. Even though relief officials were unable to raise sufficient funds for relief, their efforts revealed the resilience of the concept of local charity and its ineffectiveness in the face of economic disaster.

While relief officials led failing drives for funds, caseworkers in the city's settlement houses embarked on a new path for their work. Chapter 3 investigates settlement workers in the Depression to access their narrative on unemployment and their resulting arguments about social insurance. The intensity of the Depression ultimately led residents and staff to accept their responsibilities as relief-giving organizations, and settlements around the city developed hastily assembled departments for assessing need and distributing aid. At the same time, settlement leaders attended to the nonmaterial needs of their neighbors by expanding clubs, discussion groups, and activities that might ease the pain of unemployment. In giving relief, settlement workers insisted on the necessity of material relief *and* came to employ distinctions between the "worthy" and "unworthy" poor. In noncasework programming, they maintained the dignity of the unemployed, even in a cultural climate that attempted to dethrone jobless men from their posts as breadwinners. At the same time, settlement workers subtly endorsed a definition of masculinity that preserved gender-based family roles and expectations. In all these efforts, social reformers constructed an intellectual framework that would influence them (and their allies) throughout the decade: a framework that associated masculinity with employment, called on the government to right the economic crisis, and entitled some poor people to federal subsidies.

As Chapter 4 reveals, settlement leaders took these ideas into their work with unemployed workers, who began to consider their own entitlement to federal social insurance. In 1932, settlement workers and other community leaders supported the unemployed in forming the WCOU. Through public hearings and public unrest, the WCOU engineered a shift in self-perception among jobless workers. Those who had been isolated and embarrassed by their condition at the beginning of the Depression came to understand themselves as victims of the economy and deserving of aid. Mimicking strategies of labor organizing, WCOU members orchestrated a social movement in which workers called on the federal government for more than just relief: they demanded aid in the form of paid work, release from a condescending system of casework and relief, and security from the economic system. By the early 1930s, the notion of entitlement had been planted, and it began to grow in the minds of Chicago's workers and settlement leaders.

Chapter 5 examines the embrace of partial entitlement: first in the battle for state funding of relief and then in the failed Lundeen bill. In Illinois, early relief bills simultaneously introduced state-sponsored aid and upheld the integrity of local/private care for the poor. The Illinois state legislature created a framework for funding public relief that, a few years later, became the infrastructure for New Deal programs, including the Federal Emergency Relief Administration (FERA) and, ultimately, unemployment insurance. An unlikely coalition comprising relief officials, settlement leaders, social workers, and Chicago's leading business owners first suggested the necessity of publicly funded relief, and in so doing they paved the way (materially and intellectually) for federal unemployment insurance. Three years later, Congress failed to pass the Lundeen bill, a progressive bill for social insurance backed by the Chicago WCOU and settlement workers in Chicago and New York. This chapter demarcates the limits of worker entitlement, which would characterize entitlement through the twentieth century.

This book tells the story of a group of reformers who joined workers and relief officials to redeem the unemployed and secure for them government-funded social insurance. In the 1920s, a settlement committee on unemployment combined appeals for empathy with seemingly objective social science research, a technique that appealed to the educated middle class, academics, and policy makers. In 1930s Chicago, settlement workers created programs that, on the individual level, helped the unemployed escape the demoralizing effects of poverty. In the city, settlement workers joined unemployed organizers to demand public relief—not charity.

Settlement workers helped create entitlement before the New Deal. They drew on their experiences with the unemployed in poor communities as well as their historic commitment to reform to make claims for social insurance. Although economists had been writing about social insurance for a decade, settlement workers argued that only personal stories would convince the American public of its benefits. Their campaigns for social insurance were shaped by the Great Depression itself, which made people want to hang onto old systems *and* forced them to accept new ones. In the end, settlement workers and the jobless successfully established a limited form of entitlement for workers. The entitlement of the New Deal maintained that the unemployed were still workers and deserved government assistance, but it adhered to the ideals of the breadwinner family. Settlement workers and the jobless, in large part because of the Great Depression, clung to the notion that entitlement should only be extended to the right kinds of workers.

This story focuses on settlement workers and their role in creating a specific sense of entitlement among American workers, but it also intersects a number of key historical discussions. It benefits from earlier examinations of settlement workers by such scholars as Clarke Chambers, Allen Davis, and Judith Trolander, although it departs from their characterization of the movement and its works by examining settlement houses in the decades following their Progressive-Era heyday; by focusing on lesser-studied settlement houses and agencies within Chicago; and by examining settlement workers across the spectrum of their work, from national organizing, to local community work, to the very private process of casework.[20] It offers a critical reappraisal of New Deal social and economic changes by suggesting that the transformations of the 1930s came from the "middle" (reformers, community leaders, and state governments) as much as from "above" or "below."[21] And this story brings together bodies of research in labor history and social welfare history, which have largely overlooked the interconnectedness of these fields, especially considering that the caseworker was a very real part of workers' lives.

Because of its focus on settlement leaders and on the work done in the city of Chicago, this story is not a comprehensive study of all conceptions of entitlement as they developed in the early twentieth century. It is not able, for instance, to trace the ways in which entitlement was received or altered in other major cities, or in much of rural America—although given Chicago's centrality in the movement and the national level at which much of this story plays out, many of the experiences that this story conveys and the conclusions that each chapter makes can be applied more broadly than my research specifically shows. Most notably, however, the story this book tells says uncomfortably little about race. Settlement workers were, generally speaking, slow in addressing racism and race-based inequality in their cities, and their notion of entitlement and their focus on "the right workers" had a clear racial bias that largely ignored African American laborers.

Therefore, even though this study focuses on a decade when African American laborers gained new prominence in the Communist Party (CP), African American voting hugely shifted party politics, and (despite their newfound affection for the Democratic Party) African Americans were pointedly left out of important New Deal programs, the settlement workers described in this book almost never spoke explicitly about race or racism, nor did they demand entitlement for African American workers. That said, such scholars as Elisabeth Lasch-Quinn and Ruth Crocker have done good work to uncover the significance of settlement houses in African American neighborhoods in the urban North as well as settlement-like institutions among communities of color in the South. Yet the settlement movement (especially as led by the NFS) was woefully unwilling to adjust to growing communities of color in the North, and Lasch-Quinn has demonstrated the ways in which the NFS's decision to exclude sectarian settlement houses and organizations drew racial boundaries around the settlement movement, largely because African Americans were fiercely denominational.[22]

Similarly, from my research on Chicago settlements, it is clear that although settlement workers in the Chicago Federation of Settlements (CFS) were happy to ally with black-led organizations like the Urban League and to host an unemployment hearing at an African Methodist Episcopal church in Chicago, they maintained an eerie silence on the issue of race in their city. This silence might in part have been driven by the fact that these settlement workers were largely attuned to the needs of white laborers in the city. White workers often saw it in their interest to exclude African Americans from their organizing.[23] Moreover, the very concept of male breadwinner liberalism, which motivated workers and settlement leaders to advocate for the entitlement of laboring men, was a fundamentally racial concept. The entitled breadwinner was implicitly coded as white, and organizers and settlement workers in Chicago did little to extend the new sense of labor entitlement beyond the white, able-bodied, male worker. Indeed, black laborers would struggle to claim entitlement well into the twentieth century, during the decades when welfare was being coded as black and policy makers on all sides of the political spectrum turned their attention to the problems of absentee fathers and African American female–headed families.[24] It is my hope, however, that future research will interrogate the ways in which African American laborers contributed to the embrace of entitlement, even as the concept often excluded them.

Ultimately, this book tells the story of workers who at the beginning of the Depression were considered paupers—by their government, their neighbors, and themselves—but who by 1934 were becoming entitled. *Becoming Entitled* reveals the constructed nature of entitlement and the moment when some people shed the stigma that came with unemployment and demanded that the government do the same. They were successful in acquiring government relief and, eventually, unemployment insurance for workers, and they were hugely successful in implanting the concept of worker entitlement in the American public and among American workers. Yet the material benefits were harder to come by. While the Depression (and the activism of workers and their allies) forced the hand of state and federal legislators, the architects of the Social Security Act exploited fears of radicalism to pass a limited bill for entitlement.

Yet even a limited entitlement was not a given, and the unemployed clearly had to earn it. Thus, this book also reminds us of the extent to which claims for assistance in the United States depended (and still depend) on personal evaluations. Settlement workers who argued for social insurance were almost defensive in their repeated insistence that *these* unemployed men were not paupers. Instead, they contended, these were, and had always been, good men—and hard workers. When workers proved their inherent worth, they moved into a category of people who no longer had to defend their character: from being poor, they became entitled. In a country where the poor were scrutinized at every turn, for workers, entitlement was a great achievement.

1

Revealing the "Social Consequences of Unemployment"

"It is going to take a great deal of educating," settlement worker Helen Hall wrote to Pennsylvania governor Gifford Pinchot, "to clear away the fog in the public mind caused by that one small word 'dole.'"[1] Hall's lament was unsurprising. After spending years working with other reformers on the issue of unemployment, Hall was intensely aware that suspicions of jobless workers were entrenched in American society. Moreover, Hall's concern reflected a collection of ideas on unemployment that was common among settlement workers at the beginning of the Great Depression. Even before the economic crash, members of the National Federation of Settlements (NFS) argued that the plight of the unemployed was thoroughly misunderstood by the American public and that by changing public opinion, settlement workers could affect social welfare policy. Hall's sentiments were the outgrowth of years of work on doing just that.

Beginning in 1927, the NFS had committed funds and time to study unemployment and to advocate for the regulation of the labor market and the relief of the unemployed. Through the NFS Committee on Unemployment, settlement workers and their allies proposed an argument in favor of unemployment relief, regulation, and insurance that was accessible to average Americans and that explicitly connected changes in industry with changes in workers' lives. Their research rested on a survey of more than three hundred unemployed families across the nation and was showcased in two books and a series of articles. The first book, published in 1930, was *Some Folks Won't Work*, a popular-press account of unemployment written by a nonfiction writer named Clinch Calkins. The second was *Case Studies of Unemployment.*[2] Published in 1932, *Case Studies* presented the study's research findings for an intended audience of social scientists. Two members of the Unemployment Committee contributed to *Case Studies*: Hall wrote the introduction, and Paul Kellogg, the editor of the landmark social welfare journal *Survey Graphic*, wrote the foreword.

Members of the Unemployment Committee entered a debate over social policy that had developed at the beginning of the century and centered on what was called "social insurance." Social insurance, as reformers discussed it, included health insurance, old age insurance, workers' compensation, and unemployment insurance. Economists, labor leaders, and policy experts all debated the extent to which programs for social insurance would be funded publicly, by worker contributions, or by employers. Yet while policy experts and reformers had been debating specific proposals to protect the unemployed, many Americans had only recently begun to consider unemployment to be an involuntary condition. Settlement workers on the Unemployment Committee believed that although economists, policy experts, and reformers had long been discussing unemployment, their arguments were largely esoteric to average Americans.

Settlement workers proposed to change how social policy experts and American voters talked about unemployment in several ways. First, the NFS Unemployment Committee offered "average" Americans a digestible argument for regulating labor and providing for the unemployed. Second, it aimed to humanize unemployment to persuade American voters and policy makers. Settlement workers offered personal stories that introduced their readers to the plight of the jobless, a strategy intended to prove the pervasiveness of joblessness even in good times and to persuade average Americans of the need to protect—rather than condemn—unemployed workers.

In these two features of the Unemployment Committee, a look into their campaign offers a path to understanding social and policy change. Examining settlement workers, more than other reformers, offers a look at social policy change that can be described as "history from the middle." Many narratives place the engine for policy change either at the level of government or at the level of organized workers, but settlement work serves as a reminder that policy change was a dynamic process and that the impetus for change often came from the middle—a tier of society "in between" workers and policy makers made up of community leaders, low-level bureaucrats, academics, upper-middle-class reformers and the like. Settlement workers in the 1920s drew on their direct daily experiences with workers to influence voters and policy makers on the need for unemployment legislation. Thus, these reformers demonstrate policy as being shaped by people who understood the demands of workers and the priorities and abilities of legislators. This process can best be seen in their campaign for unemployment regulation and relief.[3]

Settlement workers also aimed to provoke change on unemployment by drawing on traditional conceptions of family and work. Members of the Unemployment Committee bolstered their defense of unemployment regulation by echoing popular arguments for a "family wage"—a wage for a male breadwinner that could support the whole family—and thus reflected gendered conceptions of labor and family. The NFS Unemployment Committee argued that the labor regulations and unemployment insurance championed by prewar reformers and economists would primarily protect hardworking families that were headed by male breadwinners. In their study on the home life of the unemployed, these reformers drew on maternalist descriptions of female dependency to placate readers who might otherwise have bristled at the thought of government support for the unemployed.

The NFS Unemployment Committee offers a complicated look at maternalist reform, which dominated the Progressive Era. Maternalist reformers like Grace and Edith Abbott, many of whom began their reform work in settlement houses, frequently used women's dependency as justification for federal and state protection, such as legislation that limited the number of hours women could work in a day. In the process, they built careers on women's dependency. Indeed, well-known settlement workers like Chicago Commons's Lea D. Taylor supported arguments for unemployment insurance that emphasized the dangers of female employment, all while nurturing a successful career in reform. And the Unemployment Committee unabashedly described women's work as "makeshift," the unfortunate product of intense economic need.

Yet although settlement workers echoed the ideological defenses for the family wage, the Unemployment Committee's work suggests a more complicated interplay between ideology and pragmatism. In the height of the Great Depression, settlement workers acknowledged that women's labor was not rewarded sufficiently and contended that the most effective way to ensure that entire families could survive the crisis was to bolster the labor market for men. Moreover, because of widespread unemployment, the NFS Unemployment Committee took on the unusual task of defending relief for men. Relief and charity had long been considered the safety nets of paupers, women, and children, but in the 1930s, NFS participants and settlement workers around the nation claimed that relief was the right (albeit temporary) of men victimized by industrial confusion. Settlement workers hoped that, whether through relief or unemployment regulation, men might be able to again earn enough to ensure that their wives would not have to work multiple jobs and care for their families. It is certainly true that members of the Unemployment Committee espoused an ideology of essential female dependency, but it must be acknowledged that they did so in response to intense practical concerns.

In the end, settlement workers like Hall proposed that the most effective strategy to protecting the unemployed was to induce the voting public to demand a change in policy. As members of the Unemployment Committee put it, their task was "to have material ready in order to create public opinion and stimulate public action."[4] Thus, they used their research first to educate American voters on the plight of the jobless (and in this goal, they rarely discussed specific policies) and second to educate policy makers and call for relief and social insurance. In the process, they redeemed unemployed workers from the stigma of pauperism and reinvigorated a long-popular defense of family wage and the male breadwinner household. Through their work on the Unemployment Committee, these settlement workers established new priorities for the settlement movement and took an active role in reshaping the debate on unemployment legislation and social policy.

Changing Public Opinion on Unemployment

In 1928, settlement workers and other reformers (such as the writers and editors of *The Survey* and *Survey Graphic*, a journal of social work that often took on issues related to social reform), many of whom had long made urban working neighborhoods their homes, determined that their next project should be centered on the growing number of unemployed workers. Like many reformers, these settlement workers believed that reaching voters was a crucial step in achieving legislative change and presented themselves as the group most equipped to understand unemployment and to recommend its solution. Although the NFS ultimately endorsed plans for unemployment insurance, its primary goals at first were to generate empathy for the unemployed and create a demand for unemployment relief and labor regulation. The NFS Committee on Unemployment, created at the 1928 NFS conference, orchestrated a nationwide survey regarding unemployment in U.S. industrial centers and promised to position workers at the center of the conversation. With research and writing, settlement leaders promised to humanize unemployment, prove the pervasiveness of joblessness in good times, and persuade Americans that workers deserved large-scale and federally administered measures to prevent and deal with unemployment.

Other reform organizations had already established campaigns for unemployment insurance and regulation, but settlement workers hoped to shift the conversation to unemployed workers themselves. The most notable was the American Association for Labor Legislation (AALL), which by 1913 was, according to Daniel Rodgers, "the most active and important social insurance lobby in the United States."[5] Established in 1906, the AALL initially drafted model legislation for government-funded unemployment insurance. By the 1920s, AALL leader John B. Andrews had turned to an alternate model of regulation that emphasized prevention and enjoined employers to lead the way in stabilizing the labor market.[6] Through the 1920s, the NFS supported the AALL's work (Jane Addams served as a vice president for the association), and NFS members likely concurred with AALL leadership's contention that reform workers could mitigate class conflict by working with labor and industry. Yet when the NFS committed to studying and campaigning for unemployment legislation, its leaders created a campaign that was solely committed to advocating for, and speaking from the perspective of, workers themselves.[7]

Moreover, although settlement workers were new to the conversation on unemployment, they argued that their close experience with vulnerable workers made them an especially good fit for the task. They were the descendants of a Progressive-Era movement that was famous for establishing community-based houses in cities throughout the urban North (the most famous being Hull House in Chicago). Locally, settlement workers moved into these houses and established themselves as "good neighbors" to the economically disadvantaged, largely immigrant populations among whom they lived. On the national level, settlement leaders from Jane Addams to Lillian Wald successfully pushed for municipal and labor reforms in the early twentieth century.[8]

In the wake of World War I, settlement workers led by Philadelphia's Helen Hall asserted that NFS members should use their intimate knowledge of workers and connections to policy makers to address the issue of unemployment. Hall led the NFS as an experienced neighborhood worker. A graduate of the New York School for Social Work, she served as the director for the University Settlement, a large settlement house in Philadelphia. At the University Settlement, Hall witnessed the frequency with which her neighbors reported joblessness and the increasing difficulty that many of them had in finding work. The "closeness of the settlements to their neighbors," Hall reflected in 1959, "made them aware of mounting unemployment even in 1927–28, . . . a time supposedly of wide prosperity."[9] As Hall explained to the NFS, settlement workers were ideal for carrying out two lines of action: "one to stir up governmental thought and action along the lines of unemployment insurance, and second to bring out the human effect of the lowering of the standard of living and various methods of relief."[10]

The establishment of the Unemployment Committee indicated that the NFS would shift its priorities while maintaining strategies for engaging in social issues. Members of the NFS voted the Unemployment Committee into action on the same day that they halted the work of the Prohibition Committee, yet they also voted that the Unemployment Committee would take "as a model the organization and procedure of the Prohibition Committee."[11] By securing money for research on joblessness, Hall shifted the attention of the NFS from vice to jobs. Moreover, the Unemployment Committee became so significant to the NFS that it was ultimately transformed into the Unemployment Division, which housed various efforts related to unemployment throughout the 1930s. Hall and members of the Unemployment Committee believed that if they could educate the public and policy makers about pervasive joblessness, then surely legislation to protect the unemployed would follow.[12]

Their daily interaction with poor workers and their history of relating structural problems to personal consequences rendered them ideal to make real headway on the issue of unemployment insurance. Kellogg, who was the editor of the popular social work journal *Survey Graphic*, served on the Unemployment Committee as an ally of the settlement movement. In a letter to a fellow writer, Kellogg declared, "While various agencies, from the Senate Committee on Education and Labor to the Industrial Relations Counselors, are tackling the problem from one angle and another, the settlement study has distinction in its canvass of consequences in terms of intimate household and family experience."[13] In short, settlement workers and their allies believed settlements to be the optimal place to carry out such a study.

To change public opinion, the committee undertook a large-scale research project of the unemployed in settlement neighborhoods. Its research was grounded in a series of three hundred household "pictures" collected by settlement workers at 104 settlements from thirty-two cities and towns in twenty-one states and supplemented by analyses of group discussions and an unemployment-themed essay contest. These resources would, committee members hoped, offer a more human-centered description of the economic system than most Americans had seen. In the Unemployment Committee members' presentation to the NFS Executive Committee, they were clear about the purpose of the study: to create a domino effect, from stories, to education, to action.

Hall and other committee members[14] relied on a strategy of presenting personal stories in the packaging of social science research to make the case for social insurance. The committee began with an extensive survey of unemployment in the nation. Between 1927 and 1930, members developed a research plan, recruited settlements and community organizations to participate, collected their findings, and assembled those findings into publishable material. In 1928, Hall and the ten-member Executive Committee began writing a survey, which they hoped settlement workers around the country would fill out and send back to them.[15] These surveys asked settlement workers to each transcribe the stories of at least five families suffering from unemployment, to lead and take notes on settlement discussion groups on unemployment, and to collect from their neighbors essays on life with unemployment. To acquire such materials, the Executive Committee set up a Field Committee, comprising nineteen workers who identified settlements at which to fill out surveys, and then reminded, cajoled, and pressured leaders in these settlements to collect and return research materials. In the end, the committee had around three hundred case studies, a substantial body of research on which to base its arguments about unemployment and social insurance. In 1929, Albert Kennedy, a member of the NFS Executive Committee, explained that this study would "reveal the social consequences of unemployment as found in certain neighborhood families which have been intensively studied."[16]

By focusing on stories and anecdotes telling the "social consequences of unemployment," settlement workers hoped to make their arguments resonate with the kinds of Americans who were unmoved by economists. The household pictures they offered depended on a specific relationship common between settlement workers and their neighbors, in which settlement workers considered their neighbors to be research subjects and delved into their personal lives. These were consensual interviews, and unemployed families often demonstrated an appreciation for such a study, but settlement workers' methods also relied on a system that filtered and at least partially assessed the unemployed. The committee was upfront about this strategy, even in publication. "It is common to regard the unskilled laborer statistically," Calkins lamented in *Some Folks Won't Work*. "He is not a person," she continued. "He is a unit of production. . . . Yet if we see them in their homes, making the struggle which differentiates us from the earthworm, can we still regard them without empathy?"[17] Writing to a public audience, Calkins framed settlement workers' quasi-scientific methods as an especially appealing part of their work, because they allowed stories of the unemployed to reach a previously untouched audience.

Calkins's work exemplified the part of the unemployment study that aimed to galvanize popular opinion, yet the committee hoped that it could reach two distinct audiences: an educated, middle-class readership and social science researchers. The committee's two books were thus aimed at these two groups of people, who settlement workers believed were necessary in the project of establishing social service legislation. The more general work, with the catchy (and perhaps misleading) title *Some Folks Won't Work*, guided readers through a description of unemployment: its causes, the "makeshifts" used by its victims, and its long-term consequences. Even though the aptly titled *Case Studies of Unemployment* incorporated far less interpretation than did *Some Folks Won't Work*, Hall and Kellogg each provided an introduction that spelled out their arguments about unemployment. In the years following its publication, moreover, Hall and the NFS aimed to use *Case Studies* to influence legislators at the state and federal levels to pass legislation for the unemployment relief and insurance. Hall also wrote numerous articles based on NFS research for journals with an educated, middle-class readership, including *Survey Graphic* and *The New Republic*.[18] By using relatable language, by focusing on the workers and their families, and by drawing on gendered ideas of family organization, settlement leaders suggested that the unemployed were not to be viewed with suspicion and that the government was not exempt from the problem.

The Settlement Case for Social Insurance

The public debate over unemployment insurance emerged in the beginning of the twentieth century and captivated reformers, economists, and industrialists into the 1920s. Although policy experts and reformers frequently used the term *social insurance*—an umbrella term encompassing health insurance, old age insurance, compensation for injury on the job, and unemployment insurance—all of them addressed unemployment specifically and drove the debate over unemployment legislation. The concept of unemployment itself, which implied that some people were jobless involuntarily rather than paupers or loafers by nature, was fairly new to most Americans. Yet beginning in 1909, especially as European systems of social insurance emerged, economists and social scientists began to question the wisdom of expecting low unemployment in a healthy market. Many social scientists and settlement workers were influenced by European (most notably German, British, and French) systems of social insurance, which offered comprehensive insurance against sickness, unemployment, spousal loss, and death.[19] By the 1920s, a small but significant group of intellectuals had studied European social policy and produced studies of unemployment that suggested that it was an endemic problem of industry.

Settlement leaders argued that the ideas put forth by established economists and social policy experts were too esoteric to reach the kinds of average Americans who, they said, could sway public policy. Such economists as William Beveridge and William Leiserson proposed that organized labor markets, state-administered labor exchanges, and public works projects would be able to predict and manage periods of unemployment. For economists and policy makers who had long understood unemployment to be sporadic and unexpected, Beveridge's and Leiserson's recommendations included solutions that were far more interventionist than had previously been favored.[20] Leiserson argued that economic measures, such as labor exchanges, unemployment insurance, and targeted public works projects, could go a long way in regulating employment and making the most of the labor market.[21] NFS campaigners echoed these proposals, but Unemployment Committee members also recognized that their arguments were largely inaccessible to nonexperts. Beveridge's *Unemployment: A Problem of Industry* was an intimidating 317 pages long, and its eleven chapters and four appendixes included the titles "The Sources of Information: The Unemployed Percentage" and "Cyclical Fluctuation: Alternate Rise and Fall of Average Unemployed Percentage in Periods of Years."[22] Some specialists were captivated by Beveridge's recommendations, but many Americans likely struggled to even understand them.[23]

The Unemployment Committee aimed to reshape the kinds of proposals put out by Beveridge and his contemporaries to make them accessible and compelling to American voters and policy makers alike. Written for audiences who had been slow to embrace social insurance, *Some Folks Won't Work* and *Case Studies of Unemployment* were based on the premise that the U.S. economic system, even when functioning smoothly, contained cracks through which hardworking and well-intentioned workers and their families could easily fall. Their authors argued that too many Americans believed that unemployment was only a problem of "hard times," a sign of a faltering economy from which workers would recover when the market righted itself. With that knowledge in mind, the committee members structured their research and writing with an attention to "the inadequacy of our scheme of protecting such families against the hazard of unemployment in normal times."[24] While the encroaching Depression certainly gave purchase to their books, the crux of their argument was that unemployment was an unavoidable side effect of the American economic system, one that industrial and political leaders had thus far not dealt with. In other words, as Hall would later describe, the significance of their research "was not that it was a measure of the mass unemployment which has roused our American communities to action in hard times, but of an evil to which, for the most part, they have been blind when times were good."[25]

The subtext of this argument was that the escalating Depression was not the only (or primary) instigator of unemployment, so the solution to unemployment needed to address regular, systemic bouts of joblessness.[26] In his foreword to *Case Studies of Unemployment*, Kellogg explicitly differentiated between the big crisis—which he said was complicated and would attract the attention of economists, financiers, and legislators—and regular, cyclical unemployment. "We should distinguish," he wrote, "between the grand strategy of overcoming the causes of business depression (and its resulting mass unemployment) and the tactics of closing in on unemployment as a recurring and measurable risk of modern production."[27] Unemployment as experienced by workers and their families was, he argued, simpler and more manageable than the economic crisis, and it warranted immediate action. Although the Unemployment Committee's recommendations would not solve the economic crisis, Kellogg wrote, they would "cut down the bulk of unemployment . . . and bring an orderly easement to wage-earning households which now bear the brunt of this recurring and measurable risk over which they have no control."[28]

Beyond characterizing unemployment as part of a functioning economic cycle, Kellogg actually described it as the product of modern industrial development and as warranting equally modern solutions. In a 1929 letter, he explained that "the settlement group is the only body of social workers to as yet face the fact that we are dealing with something different from the old unemployment of hard times—we are dealing with the new unemployment of technical change and progress."[29] Hall echoed Kellogg's sentiments in her introduction to *Case Studies*, writing, "Experience has taught us to recognize broken work not merely as a symptom of financial crises, but as a recurring fault of modern production."[30] Kellogg's and settlement workers' attention to modernity fit in with the settlement movement's tendency to advocate for reforms of the system rather than calling to overthrow it, and it is striking that Kellogg offered less a criticism of industrial capitalism than a recommendation for safeguards to protect workers from it.

It is noteworthy that settlement workers focused so heavily on modernity, because that focus carried racial implications. In the 1930s, the industrial workplace was still controlled by white workers (a category that included descendants of immigrants from Southern and Eastern Europe, although those groups were only in the process of "becoming white"), while African American workers, many of whom had recently migrated north, faced unequal pay and serious discrimination. What is more, Kellogg and the NFS ignored the economic crisis that was facing traditionally black workers, especially in agriculture. In *Some Folks Won't Work*, Calkins erroneously describes the farmer as an independent laborer who could prepare for the seasonal ups and downs of his work, overlooking the fact that farmers, whether landowners or sharecroppers, had been struggling since the early 1920s and were some of the hardest hit laborers during the 1930s. Thus, while defending the right of jobless industrial workers to government protection, NFS members perhaps inadvertently excluded rural agricultural workers (many of them nonwhite) from their study and thus the conversation.[31] As discussed below, they seemingly more deliberately excluded African American industrial workers as well, choosing to include only a handful of African American families in their broad survey of the "worthy" unemployed.

If unemployment was a side effect of modern production, as committee members claimed, a modern system should be able to manage it. Just as industrial leaders protected their raw materials, they should not allow their labor supply to rot in a down cycle. Kellogg wrote satirically, "If we were to take a leaf out of the modest proposal of Dean

Swift and organize a Society for Wasting Labor Power and Gutting the Wage-Earning Market, it would promote exactly our present-day policies of irregular employment and would set its cap for an occasional cyclical depression."[32] Working for corporations that had used scientific management to boost wages while still making a profit, laborers had every reason to expect their employers (or the government) to manage periods of high unemployment. And modern business, Kellogg and Calkins claimed, should have the capacity to manage their labor power through predictable lulls in demand.

Above all, the NFS Unemployment Committee's books placed the responsibility on employers and the government—rather than the unemployed—to ease the effects of joblessness. The ultimate burden of unemployment, Calkins declared, "falls upon men least able to bear it and frequently upon those in no way responsible for its incidence."[33] Referencing the widely popular workmen's compensation legislation, which at that time had passed in most states, Calkins described industrial unemployment as a parallel problem to industrial accidents: like industrial accidents, unemployment was a problem that employers should attempt to prevent and respond to. The solution, she proposed, would be a combination of economic planning, stabilization, and "some form of protection for families caught by the dislocations of work which we fail to control."[34]

Disregarding what they saw as an unwarranted faith in political leaders, members of the Unemployment Committee called for change in social policy. A temporarily unemployed worker, they argued, should be able to count on the government, employers, and private agencies to make the best use of their labor. In their books, Hall and Calkins called for three steps to safeguard workers: (1) the regularization of production as enacted by employers, (2) a system of public works projects that could step in when private industry failed, and (3) a federal employment system that could coordinate and modernize state and municipal employment agencies. This line of action, Hall explained, was necessary "to modernize our public employment services, to lift the standards of private agencies, and to weed out the abuses and inefficiencies of our present haphazard methods of labor placement."[35] In addition, Hall called on the NFS to push for greater legislation related to unemployment insurance and relief, as in 1932, when it published a resolution stating that it "expresses its conviction that unemployment insurance is essential to preserve a minimum standard of economic security; and that it urges the governor of every American state to press for the enactment of . . . measures to protect American standards of living at their most vulnerable point."[36] Although the committee's recommendations were often somewhat unspecific, the main goal was to catalyze business and government involvement.

When Hall made her case, she reflected the hallmarks of the settlement campaign for social insurance:

> No one who scans the ups and downs of American business enterprise, our changes in techniques and styles and markets, the shiftings of industry from one region to another, can but see that there will still be need for protection of some sort against unprevented or unpreventable unemployment over which the worker himself has no control.[37]

Workers were helpless in the face of technological change, consumer demand, and standard economic cycles, the committee argued, and thus deserved the protection of the state. Perhaps most importantly, though, settlement campaigners for social insurance insisted that this social policy was about workers themselves, not the labor market.

Unemployment in Families

To persuade their readers that economic cycles warranted legislative change, Unemployment Committee members humanized the plight of the jobless by shifting the conversation away from the workplace and positioning it in the home. Anticipating readers who perceived of unemployment as an impersonal issue of job placement that should be left to labor and business analysts, Calkins wrote a narrative about good families trying to survive a catastrophe and suggested that unemployment's real victims were families, not industrial leaders or even individual laborers. In so doing, the committee reconstituted the jobless: once perceived as paupers and loafers, workers (and their families) in this telling were the hapless victims of changes outside their control.

A central goal of the committee's work was to exonerate the unemployed for their condition, a difficult task given that American readers were fundamentally suspicious of the jobless. *Some Folks Won't Work* directly challenged the popular myth that "if a man really wants to work, he can find it."[38] This myth was echoed even by other settlement workers. Irene Nelson quoted one settlement caseworker as saying, "These spells of unemployment don't last; if a man amounts to anything he can always get work."[39] Nor did they believe that it was possible to be unemployed and employable at that time. Hall, unphased, brushed off this skepticism as the reaction of a "Case Hardened" family caseworker, someone who had seen enough dishonesty to distrust anyone requesting aid.[40] To Hall and other Unemployment Committee members, the presence of dissention within the NFS was not surprising and indicated the extent to which average Americans misunderstood joblessness.

Others evinced a faith in the federal government, which the NFS study proposed to challenge. In Columbus, Ohio, workers at the Gladden Community House opted out of participating in the study because of their faith in the current system of managing unemployment—in which the jobless relied on private agencies and spurts of state and federal assistance, often channeled through private agencies or public bureaus of charity. C. H. Bogart, the Gladden head resident, informed Irene Nelson that "President [Herbert] Hoover will undoubtedly conduct through governmental channels a study of unemployment in which settlements are in a unique position to cooperate."[41] Bogart and his allies seemed to maintain faith in ad hoc government responses to poverty and implied that the committee was stepping out of line in its work.[42]

To further disassemble misunderstandings about unemployment, Calkins and the NFS introduced secure Americans to a category of deserving poor: the unnecessarily jobless. In *Some Folks Won't Work*, Calkins argued that the poor families they aimed to protect were hardworking and worthy of assistance. "There are many of these who would rather starve than accept charity," Calkins informed the reader. "Unfortunately, physical laws break down their natural hauteur, and charity makes its hateful entrance through sick relief, perhaps."[43] Charity, Calkins stated, was far from a first solution. Over numerous chapters, she described a sequence of "makeshifts," steps that the unemployed took to get by. The jobless were tireless at "hunting the job": answering ads in the paper, walking miles in search of work, and paying often untrustworthy private employment agencies to find work for them. At home, they sold such valuables as furniture and engagement rings, moved into cheaper housing, and even split up the family among extended family members or invited additional renters to help offset housing costs. Charity was often a last resort. These makeshifts formed the bulk of Calkins's popular press argument about unemployment: the unemployed and their families were not sitting around and waiting for the government to bail them out. They were thrifty, industrious—and barely surviving.[44]

The task of finding and highlighting "worthy" poor families became central to the Unemployment Committee's strategy for changing popular opinion about unemployment insurance. Believing that unemployed families—especially those who had not previously relied on charity—represented an invisible or misunderstood segment of the poor population, committee members made it their duty to expose the nation to these men and women. "I am convinced," Nelson confessed to Hall, "that there is a whole stratum of the population who are really having the devil of a time and about whom absolutely nothing is known—they have kept it all under their hats, or at least within the circle of a few obscure and inarticulate friends."[45] By characterizing the study's subjects as formerly unseen and as previously unknown to social service agencies, Nelson preemptively excused any future forays into charity as unusual and necessary—these families acted from blameless desperation and not from a place of dependence.

The committee members' research strategy reflected their commitment to exonerating the "right" kind of jobless individuals, and they thus chose to publish only the stories of the "blameless poor"—men who were capable and willing to work—and their families. When the committee requested case stories from settlement workers, they offered this suggestion: "Cases should be chosen in which the wage-earner through suffering from continuous or intermittent unemployment, is still considered employable."[46] Over and over, they articulated what kind of family they wanted to present. As Hall counseled Taylor:

The test I applied was simply this: is or was the unemployment due to causes entirely outside the family's control and are there definite consequences which can be set down and described as fact? As you say, we shall have to search for families in which unemployment is not interwoven with other factors in producing their present situation.[47]

This specific targeting of the "best" of the unemployed reveals that despite their progressive understandings of persistent unemployment, members of the Unemployment Committee mobilized some rather traditional notions about the poor to defend jobless workers. They demonstrated the deservedness of jobless workers by highlighting their lack of dependence on charity. When Nelson described to Hall the five "best" families she had run into, she commented that "it is interesting that not one of my five is known to any charitable organization, and this without my having specified that we should prefer the sort."[48] Thus the committee paradoxically contributed to a discourse about poverty that associated accepting relief with failure, a seemingly unintentional by-product of arguing that poor workers in the 1930s were not to blame for their predicament.[49]

If one of the features of faultless poor workers was that they had never relied on charity, then committee members connected being independent with deserving aid. In a letter to a discouraged Nelson, Hall offered words of consolation that revealed her strategies and beliefs about relief. Nelson had written to complain of the resistance she faced from caseworkers at family-centered social service agencies, who argued that their clients did not fit the requirements that Nelson was looking for. "In taking the Family Case Workers reaction," Hall counseled, "we must realize that they get the type of family which we do not want particularly to include in our work."[50] In other words, family caseworkers, who were more likely to see domestic disputes, juvenile delinquency, and other "behavioral" issues, would likely not see many of the "worthy" poor who would make solid cases for study.[51]

Hall's subsequent thoughts more clearly indicate the intellectual consequences of shaping the committee's study around the "best" unemployed families: "I think that we of the Settlements feel that almost the keenest suffering and the greatest change of standards come often in the family which does not resort to the relief giving agencies."[52] The committee's strategy, then, required that its members establish markers for this kind of person, such as prior requests for aid or a relationship with a family service agency. "Our settlement study," Kellogg explained to readers of *Case Studies of Unemployment*, "sought to disentangle the unemployed from the unemployable by dealing only with families whose predicament was due to industrial causes outside their control."[53] The Unemployment Committee intentionally structured its research project to defend the unemployed against judgment and to show that such families accepted charity only as a result of a systemic failure. In effect, it was distinguishing between the kinds of people who should be supported by unemployment insurance and those who should not, and Calkins carried these implications into the published work.

Those "best" kinds of families were almost entirely white, which certainly shaped the committee's argument about relief. Of the 150 case studies that appeared in *Case Studies of Unemployment*, only 4 of them were categorized as "American (Negro)." These families came from settlement houses and institutions from around the nation: the Robert Gould Shaw House near Boston, Massachusetts; Hiram House, in Cleveland, Ohio; and several centers in Louisville, Kentucky. The notes from the Hiram House offer a quick look into the realities of being unemployed while black. The caseworker described the family:

> The father, a carpenter by trade, was forced to join the union in 1923. Then because union wages were as high for Negroes as for others, his white employers dropped him from their pay roll and hired white men instead.[54]

Yet this look into the racial dimensions of the Depression was rare: the entries on the other three African American families did not discuss discrimination, and the vast majority of the case files had little reason to. Although it is likely that the NFS Unemployment Committee actively excluded African Americans from its study, the realities of the data set meant that their arguments about unemployment centered on the "default" worker: white, male, and industrial.[55]

The NFS Unemployment Committee turned its attention to families to persuade its readers of the importance of unemployment regulation. By focusing on families rather than just the labor market, Calkins compelled readers to acknowledge and respond to the plight of the unemployed. The economic system (seasonal slackness, technological innovation, and periodic downturns) rendered individuals unemployed, and they and their whole families struggled to survive. "Clearly whether unemployment is controllable or uncontrollable," Calkins stated by way of conclusion, "its ultimate burden falls upon men least able to bear it and frequently upon those in no way responsible for its incidence. Most of the great modern nations have provided their workers with some form of insurance against such unemployment. We have not."[56] Moreover, the NFS Unemployment Committee suggested that a breadwinner's joblessness carried consequences for the entire family and perceived of the family as the social unit in which people experienced unemployment, not as individuals, collections of workers, or communities.[57] With this idea, the Unemployment Committee humanized jobless workers, in the process recasting them as victims rather than paupers.

Preserving the Male Breadwinner Family

Beyond merely emphasizing families, the Unemployment Committee proposed a specific definition of *family* that would have been amenable to its readers and that established employment as fundamentally male. By emphasizing widely accepted conceptions of the male breadwinner family structure, the committee could argue for government intervention in dealing with unemployment (social insurance) without alienating its audience. This rhetorical strategy likely reassured readers of the nonradical nature of the NFS's campaign and demonstrated that federal insurance would preserve rather than revolutionize the American social fabric. Thus these reformers drew on Progressive maternalist policies, which emphasized female dependence and the state's obligation to preserve the male breadwinner family structure.[58]

For settlement researchers, the right kind of family was also one that affirmed a family structure centered on a male breadwinner. In a recorded roster of 150 case studies, the researchers organized each around that family's breadwinner. Each family was titled according to its (male) breadwinner and catalogued by nine categories: name, case number, nationality, sex, age, vocation, last occupation, others earning (like children or women), and dependents. The study only included ten female breadwinners, even though forty-three wives were categorized as "others earning." It is perhaps a given that none of the women who were listed as breadwinners had husbands as dependents, and it would be anachronistic to expect married women to be listed as breadwinners. The structure of this roster, though, proves the narrative that Hall and settlement workers were trying to tell: that whole families were suffering because of an economic condition that attacked (male) breadwinners specifically. In presenting this narrative, they set up a social ideal—that men were breadwinners even in families in which wives and children worked—that did not necessarily reflect the reality of increased female employment throughout the 1920s or the economic hardship that occurred when those women then experienced unemployment.[59]

The settlement study echoed a long-standing discourse in the United States about motherhood and wage labor. In the nineteenth and early twentieth centuries, many laborers and reformers concurred that families benefited most from a breadwinner model, in which fathers worked and mothers were able to focus on caring for the family. Much of maternalist social welfare work simultaneously reflected and shaped a labor market that gave preference to male labor, a pattern that bolstered calls for a family wage. Progressive reformers influenced by maternalism partnered with such labor leaders as Samuel Gompers of the American Federation of Labor (AFL) and John R. Commons of the American Association for Labor Legislation (AALL) to establish a wage by which a man could earn enough to support his wife and children. As Martha May argues, family wage advocates worked to challenge "the ideology of working-class poverty" by removing women from the workforce, thus simultaneously (in theory) boosting wages and allowing women to practice "true womanhood."[60] The product of reformers' emphasis on the male breadwinner family was that their policies codified dependency among working-class women. By the 1920s, minimum wages tended to be higher for men than women, while working or working-class women were expected to rely on charitable aid (the kind of aid that was considered legitimate for the "vulnerable" or "helpless") when their circumstances prevented them from receiving the security of a male breadwinner family.[61]

The NFS study of unemployment echoed the maternalist preference for male breadwinner households. From the study's framing,

NFS researchers advocated for a system of employment that centered on men and discouraged women's work. In the chapter "Makeshifts" in *Some Folks Won't Work*, Calkins positioned a mother's employment as virtually the last makeshift that a family might turn to during times of unemployment—listed after selling goods, borrowing, living on credit, and even eating less. At a 1932 conference, Hall suggested the same. After describing how families cut down on food, she explained, "There is still another reserve that the family found within itself [that comes after cutting down on food]. The mother goes to work—for she can often get a job when the man cannot." What is interesting here is that Hall connected this seemingly cultural argument about women working with the NFS's larger argument regarding the nation's industrial and financial structure. "When the bankers and industrialists, the engineers and managers have not, in their organization of industry, enough work for the men," Hall continued, "enter Mrs. Jenkins, Mrs. Levy, Mrs. Carbino and the rest."[62] Women worked as a last resort, and their employment indicated a failure in the economy rather than a successful adaptation to new conditions.

In part, the Unemployment Committee's work reflected a common assumption among working-class families themselves: that the male breadwinner model was preferable. One of Nelson's favorite family stories, that of the Clark family from Philadelphia, nicely illustrates the role of gender in conversations about unemployment. In *Case Studies of Unemployment*, Frank Clark described his life without work for a caseworker: "You see it's because I've always worked so steady that I've got nervous about being out of work now," making him a perfect candidate for the committee's study. Clark emphasized his resistance to letting his wife work but acknowledged that it may be necessary. "I don't believe in my wife working," he said, "although she did when I didn't know it during the year I was away, and paid the first money on our house out of what she saved." Nelson understandably hoped that the Clarks might find some relief, but interestingly, she expressed this sentiment to Hall by writing, "Poor Mrs. Clark!— let's hope her story may stir people to do something about unemployment."[63] In one sentence, then, Nelson laid out her belief that women unfairly bore a significant portion of the burden of unemployment, even though they were not expected to be breadwinners. Moreover, by positioning Mrs. Clark as the victim, Nelson's lament suggested that a woman's employment was part of the problem rather than a possible solution.

Reformers had long used many ideological arguments to defend male breadwinner households. As Florence Kelley said in 1912, "It is the American tradition that men support their families, the wives throughout life, and the children at least until the fourteenth birthday."[64] Maternalist policies for social welfare and labor reform thus expressed an ideology rooted in perceived innate gender roles and positioned women as fundamentally domestic and dependent.[65]

Reformers advocating for male breadwinner households, moreover, cautioned that when women worked, they upset gender norms and put their families at risk. For instance, Catholic thinkers, such as Father John Ryan, and Progressive reformers, such as John Spargo and Annie Daniel, argued that women's work could be blamed for a range of evils, including child malnourishment, infant mortality, and juvenile delinquency. Settlement workers were certainly not immune to maternalist sensibilities. In 1910, Jane Addams decried that "the long hours of factory labor necessary for earning the support of a child leave no time for the tender care and caressing which may enrich the life of the most piteous baby."[66] Such language reveals the extent to which these reformers—often single, often childless, always professional—expected poor women to embody long-standing traits of "true" womanhood for the sake of their children.

In many ways, the NFS's Unemployment Study reflected the opinions of these advocates for maternalism and the family wage. The stories presented in *Some Folks Won't Work* offered harrowing examples of what could happen to hardworking, faultless families when the job market shifted and their male breadwinners were rendered jobless. In an article for the *Chicago Daily News*, Graham Taylor warned that men without work would inevitably lose the respect of their families and their own self-respect. "Faith in him changes to hope, to fear, to suspicion, to judgment that he is no good," Taylor lamented. "He grows sullen, curses, begins to drink, turns against the good, the law, the government—and before he knows it he drifts into crime."[67] Moreover, in *Some Folks Won't Work*, Calkins argued that without the regulation of unemployment, women and children were vulnerable to overwork, exhaustion, and even serious ailments. Expecting women to bear the financial burden of unemployment, she argued, was akin to sending them to their graves and their families to the poorhouse.[68]

The NFS's support of a male-centered household, though, came from practical concerns and as such suggests the complicated interplay between ideology and material reality. Its members clearly knew that in working-class households, women regularly supplemented (or solely provided) the family income, but they cautioned against it for practical reasons. As she described women's tendency to earn less than men, Calkins offered the common explanations for paying women less: "Her physical inferiority made her less widely useful when arm power counted, for there were fewer kinds of things she could do. Her physical cycles made her emotions unsteady. And most of all she had, even if only a legendary one, a husband or a father to support her. She could work for pin-money."[69] Here, Calkins relied on common stereotypes about women's abilities and temperament not to justify their limited wages but to explain to readers why a family could not (and should not have to) rely on a female breadwinner. But without protections and social insurance for the unemployed, women would have to continue to work for miserly compensation, only perpetuating the income disparity. Calkins lamented that "novels could be written about this particular period in unemployment—the almost invariable shift of wage-earning from the man's to the woman's shoulders because women will work for less pay."[70] Thus, a working mother indicated a drop in family income—a very material problem that warranted action.

The NFS Unemployment Committee drew on the widespread commitment to a male breadwinner household to advocate for regulation on unemployment. As these statements demonstrate, committee members echoed ideas of difference to rectify a real practical problem: that the labor market prohibited women from earning enough to make the difficult work worthwhile. Members of the Unemployment Committee recognized that women were paid less (largely because employers thought women were less suited to industrial labor than their husbands), which rendered them the primary beneficiaries of a generous policy for social insurance. While *Some Folks Won't Work* at times emphasized women's natural suitability for domestic life, the reality that an employed mother would not earn enough for her family was the impetus for the Unemployment Committee to position

men as breadwinners and the male-centered family as ideal. Therefore, it is a mistake to assume that supporters of the male breadwinner household did so for purely ideological reasons.

Some Folks Won't Work also made claims to the dangers of women
working, but it did so without emphasizing women's responsibility
to care for their families. Rather than focusing solely on the dangers
that female employment bore for children, according to Calkins, the
dangers posed by a family's dependence on female labor went beyond
the family economy to a mother's health. Because working mothers
frequently remained responsible for much of the housework, settlement workers rightly suggested that a working mother was likely a
wearied woman. Through its books, the committee tried to deal with
the very real, physical consequences of a woman working—that she
found herself cleaning at nights and cleaning, cooking, and child-
rearing during the day. Hall said that "the stories abound in the results of the double load on their shoulders": exhaustion, illness, and
sometimes death. One working mother, described in *Case Studies
on Unemployment*, was only able to sleep by resting her head on the
kitchen table between work and cooking, while her son sat beside her.
The problem of the double load faced by working women led settlement workers to focus on social insurance policies that would bolster
male breadwinners, seeing getting help for male workers as the best
solution to the problem of the overworked wife.[71]

These books reflected the practical reality that women bore the
burden of domestic care and seemed to confirm that a working
mother endured alarming physical ramifications. Almost every time
that Calkins described a working wife, the story ended with the wife
becoming extremely exhausted and sick. In *Some Folks Won't Work*,
mothers forced to work told of the horrors that came from doing so.
A settlement worker described one Polish woman who was "driven
out to do cleaning," causing her health to spiral. Calkins's writing
provided a warning to any woman considering work and a confirmation to stalwart supporters of male-centered households: "The blood
in her veins shone blue through her ghostly skin, and her eyes, a pur-
plish blue, seemed fixed upon a point in space where the Philadelphia
courts, squalor, starvation, and the kindness of neighbors were all as
one. She was too tired to hear."[72] Exhaustion was but an inconvenience
compared to what other mothers suffered. Mrs. Shanti, who came

from Russia, was forced to work long hours to support her family. But "overwork and nerves wrecked Stacia's health," Calkins wrote, "and a tumor developed in her breast." According to *Some Folks Won't Work*, Mrs. Shanti was not alone in suffering from job-related ill health. Mrs. Daly, according to Calkins, found herself in bed with cancer that developed after she worked as a nighttime janitor: what began as a lump from hitting her head in an office she was cleaning developed into a tumor that then threatened her life. The very physical act of working as a cleaner caused Mrs. Daly to develop cancer.[73]

In the end, the members of the NFS Unemployment Committee offered a narrative for unemployment that cast women as dependent and thus defenseless in the face of joblessness. The circumstances of the Depression and the insufficiency of women's work to provide for a family prompted these reformers to push the boundaries of relief by charging that the failures of the relief system put families at greater risk for destitution and suggesting that relief not be reserved solely for women. In the process, the Unemployment Committee confirmed and challenged research on maternalism, demonstrating that ideology and material need often went hand in hand in defending the male breadwinner household. In other words, the solution that committee members proposed was intended to improve the conditions of women, but it cemented in unemployment regulation the prerogatives of the male breadwinner family and the ultimate dependence of women and mothers. By calling for sweeping yet nonradical responses to cyclical unemployment, the Unemployment Committee articulated a position that could catalyze change without scaring off middle-class, educated Americans.

Reception and Outcomes

In the wake of finishing their survey of and publications regarding the plight of the unemployed, settlement workers embarked on the dynamic process of bringing workers' voices to legislators and policy experts. Their priority was to translate the difficulties of unemployment to lawmakers, so they focused their attention more on personal stories than on specific policies. By reaching out to the voting public, contacting politicians, and continuing to work with the unemployed, settlement workers created a "middle-out" method for policy change.

Among the voting public, the Unemployment Committee's research was received quite well, and *Some Folks Won't Work* certainly made its way onto the nightstands of educated, reading Americans. Reviews by sympathetic readers emphasized the positive impact that such a study could make on the campaign for unemployment insurance. Paul Douglas, an economist whose research also dealt with unemployment, aimed at such a readership in this ad:

If the settlements and Miss Calkins do not cut through the stiff hide of middle-class indifference with these moving chronicles of heroism and human loss, then there is no hope for the improvement of the world by pity.[74]

The *Chicago Daily Tribune* echoed Douglas's description, if much more briefly, and in 1930, *Some Folks Won't Work* made it onto the *Tribune*'s best book list (it should be said, along with 136 other books).[75] By 1931, *Some Folks Won't Work* was in its fourth edition and, according the Unemployment Committee, "selling steadily."[76]

Settlement leaders also took their research to the voting public through various other mediums. Although he was not a member of the Unemployment Committee, Graham Taylor (the father of Chicago Commons head resident Lea D. Taylor, a central figure in Chapters 3 and 4) published a compelling piece in the *Chicago Daily News*, simultaneously advertising and explaining the arguments presented in *Some Folks Won't Work*. For a largely conservative readership, Taylor described the pitiable state of joblessness and warned of the danger of inaction: "A man respected by wife and children gradually loses their respect and his own self-respect as he fails to be their bread-winner."[77] In January 1932, Hall gave a public lecture in Detroit, Michigan. As the *Detroit News* described it (in an article that also expanded her audience), Hall explained to the audience that the first job of industry and the government was "stabilization of employment," and she continued by advocating for "long time planning of public works."[78] In these approaches, Taylor and Hall thus acted on the settlement workers' commitment to translating their knowledge of the unemployed to a middle-class, voting audience.

The committee used a few methods to convey this knowledge to policy makers and politicians. In 1931, Congress debated the Wagner bill (S. 3060), which would create a federal employment exchange to regulate unemployment, and the Unemployment Committee worked feverishly to lobby for its passage. The committee's meeting minutes reveal that its members believed that "only sufficient pressure from [the] country will bring [the bill] to a hearing before March 1st," and soon after, committee members exhorted settlement workers from around the country to press their representatives for action on the bill.[79]

Members of the Unemployment Committee also directly appealed to legislators and policy makers. After the publication of *Some Folks Won't Work*, Hall sent a copy to Frances Perkins, the commissioner of the New York State Department of Labor; soon after, she met with Samuel Joseph (of the City College of New York), Frances Perkins, and Paul Kellogg to work in favor of Wagner's bill.[80] Then, in 1932, Hall and other members of the Unemployment Committee traveled to Madison, Wisconsin, to support the passage of the Wisconsin Unemployment Compensation Law of 1932 (the nation's first), recognizing that, as Hall said to the NFS, "It is not a model bill, indeed its chief virtue is that it could be passed. Its terms had to be conservative."[81] A few months later, Hall testified before a commission in Columbus, Ohio, that aimed to pass a more robust bill for unemployment insurance.[82] By the end of 1932, the NFS was clear on the role that settlement workers could take in securing legislation, stating in a resolution:

> Whereas, the National Federation of Settlements, Inc. has already endorsed the principle of unemployment insurance, be it resolved that we now re-affirm this stand and urge all our members at this time to throw the weight of their conviction toward expediting the passage of appropriate laws in their respective states.[83]

Hall personally positioned herself to make recommendations to policy makers. Early in 1931, she used her newfound position as an expert on unemployment to urge Pennsylvania governor Pinchot to organize a state committee on unemployment, and she pushed for statewide labor exchanges.[84] Hall also served on a Philadelphia task force that made recommendations for long-term structural reforms and advised New York senator Robert Wagner as he wrote a series of bills calling for public works for the unemployed. A strongly worded letter written by Hall on behalf of the NFS to President Roosevelt received warm reception. Perhaps most significantly, in 1934, when the president issued an executive order creating the Committee on Economic Security (CES), Hall and Kellogg both sat on its advisory council. In these capacities, Hall was able to convey the experiences of the unemployed to policy makers.[85]

Most settlement workers on the Unemployment Committee, however, maintained their intimate connection with unemployed workers themselves. At the city level, committee member Lea D. Taylor spearheaded efforts to manage unemployment in Chicago. She helped orchestrate citywide public hearings on unemployment, in which hundreds of individuals affected by joblessness testified to the deprivation and social disorganization they experienced. In concert with Chicago's Workers Committee on Unemployment (WCOU), reformers and labor activists orchestrated a successful campaign for state funding for the unemployed.

Through the NFS study on unemployment, then, settlement leaders shaped the character and purpose of settlement work in the nation and on national efforts toward the implementation of social insurance. The actions of settlement workers in the 1920s and 1930s thus demonstrate that policy change did not come primarily from below (although the unemployed workers' movement was quite significant) or from above (for instance, policy makers and the federal government). Rather, social policy change was something that happened in the middle—among reformers who could translate the experience of laborers for the voting public and political leaders. Hall herself was at least tangentially related to many of these economics departments, as she had close relationships with Douglas and Kellogg. Settlement workers like Hall also played a role in social reform even while providing support in the form of casework, which embraced gendered notions of work, the family, and the role of the federal government.[86]

It would be a mistake to overstate settlement workers' influence on policy details, as they were not primarily invested in shaping

specific pieces of policy. Settlement workers like Hall understood
their purpose to be providing a link between jobless workers and
legislators, for their specialized knowledge lay in the personal experience of the unemployed, not the nuances of social policy. Thus,
they worked less on crafting legislation than on educating policy
makers on the very human issue of joblessness and tried to persuade
more people (voters *and* legislators) to support social insurance. To
be sure, settlement workers had opinions on policy—for instance, in
a 1935 report regarding their work on the Advisory Council, Hall
and Kellogg reflected dismay that they were not able to shape the
Social Security Act to include stronger state standards and a greater
federal contribution.[87] But settlement workers' primary interest was
in presenting the human picture of unemployment to those people
who might look askance at the jobless.

Yet their work nevertheless significantly played a role in ensuring
the passage of, broadly speaking, policies to protect the unemployed.
So, for instance, while they clearly favored the Ohio plan over the
Wisconsin plan, settlement workers threw their weight behind both,
because each was intended to arrest destitution among the unemployed. And their weight proved to be influential. As NFS meeting
minutes report, committees in Wisconsin, Ohio, and Congress (such
as the La Follette–Costigan committee) all asked for and drew on the
Unemployment Committee's research in crafting policy. This influence fit their goals: it is striking that Hall (and Kellogg and Douglas,
for that matter) believed that a project to change public opinion was
crucial for gaining legislation on unemployment.

Because its members recentered debates for unemployment insurance onto (largely white) jobless workers' families, the Unemployment Committee was able to introduce to economically illiterate
readers the natural cycles of a capitalist economy. At the same time,
they catalyzed the creation of empathy among the voting public, enabling voters to fully understand the plight of the jobless. Yet their
argument came at a cost, for it relied on a distinction between the
jobless who deserved unemployment insurance and those who had
long relied on charity. Well before the New Deal, settlement workers
recommended that some poor Americans were "entitled" to government assistance and thus contributed to the creation of the two-tiered
welfare state.[88]

By holding the economic system to task while mobilizing the rhetoric of male breadwinner families, settlement workers presented fairly radical recommendations for dealing with unemployment (social insurance) alongside traditional and widely accepted conceptions of social structures, which reassured readers of the nonradical nature of their campaign and demonstrated that the distribution of federal insurance would preserve rather than revolutionize the American social fabric.

2

Charity, Relief, and Localism in Depression-Era Chicago

I n 1931, just after Christmas Day, Chicago's well-to-do rang in the holiday season in style, at a gala in Chicago's Auditorium Theatre. A *Chicago Tribune* society reporter, writing under the pen name Cousin Eve, breathlessly chronicled the event's finer points: terraces and hedges creating an "outdoor supping-in-the-garden effect," an evening playbill featuring Paul Whiteman's and Ted Weems's orchestras, and decorated servicemen and their wives, who had traveled all the way from Fort Sheridan to grace the partygoers with their presence. The hosts of this holiday ball offered a celebration of Chicago society. Perhaps surprisingly, they also promised that an evening of music and socializing could offer salvation to the city's destitute, for this party's purpose was to raise funds for the city's many unemployed. Cousin Eve mused, "Nobody yet knows the exact sum raised—somewhere between ten and twenty thousand, perhaps," and followed this comment with a description of the Auditorium's decorations. In so doing, she suggested that, although the well-to-do had a responsibility to support the jobless, society events need not be curtailed by the worsening economic depression.[1]

The Great Depression was indeed a force to be reckoned with. Unemployment was on the rise before the stock market crash, but after 1929, a cascade of economic disasters reverberated through the country, and through Chicago. As banks failed and prices fell, Chicago's leading industries began cutting hours and wages, leaving the city's workers scrambling for fewer jobs and less pay. County welfare agencies, incapable of shouldering the burden of relief, rendered private charities the primary distributors of relief funds, which was a scary prospect for the city's jobless. The city itself could not support the unemployed, as Chicago could hardly afford to pay its own municipal employees, so a group of city leaders made it their job to fund local charities.

The coalition of businesspeople-philanthropists and social service leaders who organized the gala did so under the auspices of the Joint Emergency Relief Fund (JERF), one of a series of fundraising ventures launched in the early 1930s to meet growing relief demands in the city. JERF committee members built a model of charity in Chicago, declaring that employers, industrialists, workers, and relief officials together could rescue Chicagoans from the crisis. Their forum was the *Chicago Daily Tribune*, a conservative newspaper with society reporters (like Cousin Eve) who lived and socialized among Chicago's elite. Before the intervention of the New Deal, these city leaders artfully expanded on nineteenth-century strategies for dealing with social crisis and poverty by merging that philanthropic tradition with the culture of welfare capitalism and professionalization. As such, Chicago's relief drives (populated by industrialists and relief officials) reveal the persistence of welfare capitalism into the 1930s and the close cooperation between industry and charity and their complementary goals and strategies. Moreover, in Chicago's drives for relief, officials prioritized localism, or the notion that the city should care for its own. In all, officials complicated an easy distinction between private charity and public relief and set firm limits on relief giving.[2]

The massive drives for relief were a testament to the serious commitment to rescuing the newly unemployed that many Chicagoans demonstrated. Yet relief officials worked within financial and conceptual limitations. The weight of unemployment was too much for the city's systems of relief to bear, and many relief agencies buckled. Moreover, the city's relief leaders functioned under a sense that the need for relief itself was fundamentally disdainful, and they bristled at the prospect of widespread efforts. A city that was too generous, they worried, would only degenerate into a city of tramps. In the city of Chicago, relief officials and industrialists threw their weight behind the idea of voluntarism, couched in the language of localism. In other words, they asserted that Chicago's well-to-do could buoy their sinking neighbors through acts of generosity, negating the need for outside assistance. Through galas, clothing drives, and industrialists' matching gifts, relief officials desperately tried to save local charity. In the process, they instead proved the limitations of voluntarism and localism.

The Depression Arrives

In Chicago, some knew that the economy was faltering long before the market slump of 1929 confused investors and observers. In September 1928, Lea Taylor, the head resident of the Chicago Commons settlement house, reported that unemployment had been plaguing its neighborhood for a year. "A quick survey . . . in March," she described, "showed a considerable number of the breadwinners out of work, and the fact that we were making the inquiry stirred up many requests for jobs that we in no way could meet."[3] Laborers in Chicago confronted intense unemployment, but the city faced a crisis even beyond the lack of work. In the city, unemployment combined with the county's financial insecurity, taxing a system of relief that was even less prepared than usual to manage increased joblessness.

As economic uncertainty transitioned into a nationwide depression, the Chicago workforce was particularly decimated. In a nation beset by unemployment and a state facing a decline in mining and agricultural prices, Chicago's workers faced the highest rate of unemployment. Joblessness in Chicago hit 30 percent in 1931, which dwarfed the national rate and made up almost 60 percent of the state's unemployed men and women. Payrolls in Chicago shrank by 25 percent between 1927 and 1933, and manufacturing jobs declined by 50 percent between 1929 and 1932. These circumstances hit Chicago's African American population especially hard, and their unemployment rates hit 40–50 percent in 1932.[4]

Manufacturing jobs did not pick up over the following years, and those who were lucky enough to find work could expect a cutback in hours as industrial employers tightened their belts by transitioning workers to part-time, leading to a 70 percent drop in payrolls in manufacturing. Newspaper reporter Lorena Hickok reported that in 1934, the Pullman Company "was employing about 10 per cent of its normal payroll, with the prospect of raising it temporarily to 25 per cent while doing some air conditioning, which, according to George A. Kelly, vice president, would be 'negligible in relation to our capacity.'" Moreover, she reported, at that time only 10,000 of the 125,000 members of the Chicago Building Trades Council were regularly employed.[5]

Vulnerable Chicagoans were greatly enfeebled by their city's disastrous financial affairs. A deficit in county property tax payments left the city teetering on the edge of bankruptcy even before the 1930s. Chicago is situated in Cook County, a sprawling county that also includes suburbs and rural regions. In the 1920s, Cook County's tax assessments and property valuations were infested with corruption and graft, and so a 1928 reassessment order declared that Cook County could not collect property taxes based on the 1927 assessment. The county had almost $3 billion worth of taxable property; that order, combined with declining property values in downtown Chicago and a "tax strike" called for by the Association of Real Estate Taxpayers in 1929, produced a fiscal crisis that jeopardized city employees and the growing ranks of poor Chicagoans. Moreover, the city did not escape the nation's banking crisis. Of the 228 Chicago banks that stood at the close of the 1920s, only 51 survived until the fall of 1931.[6]

City employees, at the mercy of Chicago's insolvent municipal government, went unpaid for months at a time. Teachers in the public-school system were perhaps hit worst of all. Chicago's schools depended heavily on property taxes for funding. Whereas schools in New York City, for instance, could count on the state to pay around one-third of their budgets, Chicago schools relied on local property taxes to pay for more than 90 percent of operating costs.[7] Beginning in 1931, the Chicago School Board began defaulting on payrolls, and teachers who until then had been paid in cash received scrip, an official form of IOU that served as a substitute for legal tender and a promise of future payment. In the spring of 1931 alone, the board owed more than $15 million in salaries and bills and issued $5 million in scrip. Yet its value was unstable. Between May 1931 and May 1933, Chicago's fourteen thousand teachers received pay for four months in scrip that was, at best, redeemable for ninety cents on the dollar. As the months went by, area businesses, concerned that they might never receive cash for scrip, forced teachers to accept greater and greater discounts. In the process, the city's already shoddy payment system became virtually worthless.[8] William Leuchtenburg limns the municipal disaster: "In Chicago, where teachers, unpaid for months, fainted in classrooms for want of food, wealthy citizens of national reputation brazenly refused to pay taxes or submitted falsified statements."[9]

The county's insolvency reverberated into social welfare efforts. Cook County did not typically offer much in the way of public relief, but even the usual amount was slashed. The Cook County Bureau of Public Welfare spent millions between 1929 and 1931, but most of that went toward pensions for widows, the blind, and veterans. Anything leftover went toward items that would be distributed (mainly by private agencies) for outdoor relief, a type of assistance granted without the requirement that recipients enter an institution. Such items included coal, groceries, milk, and clothes. Although the Bureau of Public Welfare did at times give direct relief to needy families and individuals, its ability to do so in 1930 was hampered by the county's tax delinquencies, and the state was hardly prepared to step in.[10] In 1928, the bureau spent 64 percent of all money on public and private relief in Chicago—more than $1.7 million—but three years later, the ratio had nearly reversed, and private agencies were spending almost 64 percent of welfare funds, their budgets skyrocketed to $12.5 million. In Springfield, Illinois, representatives were hesitant to supply funds for a county that could not collect its own property taxes.[11]

Cook County could hardly hang on, so private agencies attempted to make up the difference, but Chicago's relief and social welfare systems were unable to deal with escalating demand. The city's private relief agencies increased their budgets by some 700 percent between 1928 and 1931, yet they could not keep up with ever-higher rates of poverty. The city's largest private charitable agencies—Catholic Charities, Jewish Charities, and United Charities—were inundated with requests for aid. Catholic Charities set up a series of St. Vincent de Paul Societies around the city in an attempt to make outdoor relief more accessible, but those quickly ran out of goods. One St. Vincent de Paul Society, located at St. Adalbert Church on Fridays at 7:00

P.M., reportedly ran out of goods in its first hour open every week. As Taylor described to a Philadelphia settlement worker, "The relief agencies have been simply swamped."[12]

By 1930, Chicago's workers faced rates of unemployment that were beyond what the city and county could manage. Business and relief leaders in the city, confident in the ability of voluntarism and welfare capitalism to manage downturns, turned to their own community to manage the crisis.

Relief Is a Party: Creating a Culture of Charity in the Depression

In a county unable to fund its own relief efforts, Chicago's welfare and relief officials aspired to create a culture of relief giving that might save the unemployed and local charities. If they could persuade the city's well-to-do that giving was de rigueur, relief officials hoped, the relief drives might just inspire a frenzy of gifts and save the city's charities. If they could convince industrialists that it was their obligation as benevolent capitalists, they could keep the job of city maintenance in the hands of industrial leaders. And finally, relief officials hoped that if they could compel employed workers to offer a hand to their unemployed neighbors, they could preserve the integrity of their city in the face of transience and unrest.

During the first years of the 1930s, then, Chicago's industrial and community leaders drew on the obligations of noblesse oblige, voluntarism, and welfare capitalism to compel employers and workers alike to buoy their unemployed neighbors. In so doing, they created a lively culture of relief that reveals their persistent faith in long-standing relationships between work and charity as well as the reality that those relationships could not solve the crisis of unemployment.

Meeting Chicago's Relief Officials

For much of the decade, the Chicago business owners who came together to manage the city's dwindling relief budgets organized specific, annual relief drives with the goal of engendering a spirit of giving in Chicago. Their first iteration, in 1930, was the Chicago branch of Illinois governor Louis Emmerson's Governor's Commission on

Unemployment and Relief (GCUR). By 1930, the GCUR had discovered that the state's, and especially Cook County's, social service agencies (including Catholic Charities and United Charities) were incapable of carrying on such an assault against unemployment, at least without financial assistance. The agencies dealing with unemployment, they discovered, were "swamped by appeals" and "spending as much in one week as was formerly spent in an entire month,"[13] according to Philip Clarke, who chaired a GCUR campaign to raise $5 million for unemployment relief in Cook County. The GCUR was Governor Emmerson's attempt at stimulating donations to local, private relief, with the intention of staving off government intervention.[14] Within the GCUR, such men as George Getz and Philip Clarke orchestrated a wide variety of benefits, fundraisers, and incentives intended to give Chicagoans of all means the opportunity to donate funds for relief.

These were Depression-era practitioners of a nineteenth-century philanthropic tradition. In the nineteenth century, it became common for elite members of society to return some of their fortune through a kind of philanthropic impulse that is often termed *noblesse oblige*. In part, many in the elite believed that it was their Christian duty to contribute to charity, as nineteenth-century evangelical Protestantism required a demonstration of piousness through benevolence. Moreover, especially for women, philanthropy could provide a route to strong public standing, for charity was a crucial part of society. "Charitable work conferred membership in a philanthropic elite," historian Ruth Crocker explains of philanthropist Olivia Sage, "earning in the words of Thomas Jefferson, 'the approbation of their neighbors, and the distinction which that gives them,' and it demonstrated self-sacrifice, a necessary precondition for winning esteem in this life and salvation in the next."[15]

Philanthropy took on a new light in such a crisis, which city and state leaders were quick to point out, and burgeoning philanthropists saw themselves as the figures to solve it. In 1931, Governor Emmerson described the plight of the unemployed and the mission of relief officials: "The maintenance of families who through no fault of their own are unable to maintain themselves is not only a humanitarian duty but is absolutely essential to the restoration of normal and healthy conditions."[16] The *Chicago Daily Tribune* underscored Emmerson's plea just a few months later. In the aptly titled article "Jimmy Goes without Lunch and Breakfast, That's Why He Lags in School Work," a University of Chicago professor of physiology, Anton J. Carlson, employed a similar strategy when he declared, "Chicago cannot afford to maim thousands of its future citizens by starvation now." Carlson paired the threat of disaster with an appeal to protecting the helpless: "There is no 'dole,' no 'charity' for the child; the best we have is his by right, by any aspect of social prudence. When the parents cannot give this, the public must."[17] This crisis, he suggested, warranted the invigoration of widespread giving.

Like their predecessors (friendly visitors, benefactors, and "Good Samaritans"), the members of the GCUR in the 1930s expressed an obligation toward civic stewardship in the early days of the Great Depression. They believed, as did Samuel Insull Jr., that "every man owes something besides his taxes to the community in which he lives."[18] Insull compelled his colleagues to meet a "dual obligation" to commit money and time to the city that had given so much to industrial development, and many therefore gave widely of their time and talents. Members of Chicago's relief drives made no small matter of the fact that they received no compensation for grueling, often thankless work. Insull, for one, insisted that he was not making a cent. The JERF offices, he declared, had "no fat, lazy, sanctimonious paid secretaries or loquacious 'managing directors'—too often only a stylish name for racketeers."[19]

Yet for all their harkening to nineteenth-century ideals of noblesse oblige, relief officials were fundamentally rooted in the professionalization of the interwar period, arguing that their experience ensured success. Described as "45 outstanding bankers, industrialists, sociologists, and charity workers,"[20] the figureheads of the relief drives were presidents of companies and utility magnates who professed to be running "an economic and economical project organized and personally operated by Chicago business men on a business basis."[21] Relief officials were also preaching to a choir made up of what Kathleen D. McCarthy calls the "Donor Generation." In the wake of the Jazz Age and in an increasingly professionalized world, active voluntarism had given way to financial contribution. Depression-era relief drives, likewise, called for donations of money and sometimes material goods, but rarely time.

The men (and a few women) who ran Chicago's relief drives also benefited from a social scene defined by inside knowledge and practices. JERF members knew each other from their financial exploits, creating a network within relief organizing. E. V. Thayer, for instance, sat on the JERF with Insull Jr. and was appointed receiver of Samuel Insull Sr.'s Mississippi Valley Utilities Investment Company until 1936. Business leaders in Chicago were, as the Chamber of Commerce's Committee on Business Ethics explained, "to function as socially conscious 'trustees'" for interest groups broader than their stockholders, obligated "to employees, [and] to the public."[22] The irony of this conviction rested in the fact that although some of these business leaders could rightfully claim a commitment to public betterment, a few had themselves peddled the kinds of overpriced shares that had ruined millions of Americans at the start of the 1930s. Insull Jr., a prominent member of the JERF, sat as chairman of the board for two such operating companies and had witnessed their stocks rise at a precipitous and artificial rate between 1926 and 1929, thanks to average Americans' faith that buying on margin would eventually pay off. All the while, Insull's family's holding company borrowed millions from banks and investors to secure control over the city's utilities.[23]

As successful business leaders, relief officials were driven to run efficient private welfare programs, but their past successes proved to be a liability at the beginning of the Depression. Accustomed to the business trends of the 1920s, many were hesitant to accept the crisis. In 1934, Edward Ryerson looked back on the first years of the Depression with a keen self-awareness, admitting:

> We paid little heed to our friends among the intelligent social workers who spoke frequently of the increased load of family relief organizations, . . . [and] might have been more intelligent in our planning and avoided many mistakes if we had paid more attention to the signals of distress so clearly seen by the relief agencies.[24]

As Ryerson's confession indicates, the business owners at the helm of Chicago's relief drives were handicapped by their own hubris; the confidence that they had developed in the 1920s precluded their acting on the early warnings of the city's social workers and social reformers.

Moreover, as the Depression worsened, some relief officials were self-conscious about their own prosperity. Ryerson, the figure connecting these relief officials to the poor, was a member of the business elite and head of the Council of Social Agencies (CSA). The Ryerson family owned a steel company that merged with Inland Steel manufacturers in the mid-1930s, and at the start of the decade, Ryerson was climbing a ladder that would eventually take him to a seat as chairman of the board for Inland Steel. Ryerson's reflections on the decade reveal his sense that appearances did indeed matter in the world of relief and welfare. "We did more for ourselves," Ryerson told Studs Terkel decades after the Depression had lifted. "I did away with my chauffeur and so forth. I drove my own car, and my wife did and all that sort of thing. We had to cut ourselves down so that it would not look too far out of line. After all, I was in the midst of a very close relationship with a lot of people who had nothing."[25] Ryerson evinces a sense that, as head of the CSA, any show of wealth would have seemed gauche at best and downright hypocritical at worst. Ryerson's self-awareness indicates the conviction that some relief officials held toward buoying the poor—and their equally powerful conviction that the social hierarchy was not to be tampered with too seriously.

Chicago's relief officials also departed from the impulse behind nineteenth-century philanthropy in their emphasis on short-term, immediate relief. At the turn of the twentieth century, the newly wealthy had moved away from charity and toward larger goals: to attack problems at their roots and find long-term solutions. As Olivier Zunz explains, "Charity had been for the needy; philanthropy was to be for mankind."[26] But the conditions in the early 1930s prohibited Chicago's relief officials from thinking long-term; their field of vision narrowed, and they returned to charity. Moreover, while relief officials approached their city's collapse with enthusiasm and some optimism, it is clear that they abandoned the sense that they might be changing mankind, a lofty and impractical goal.

Ryerson, particularly, developed a sense of personal obligation and guilt as a relief official. In 1934, he reflected on the personal nature of the collapse: "Our business interests demanded immediate curtailment of employment in order that we might continue to operate at all, and our relief activities demanded that we find new ways to maintain the lives of those for whose unemployment we were responsible." He continued:

> Day after day the conflict and unavoidable inconsistency of our actions were repeated, while the tide of distress rose swiftly and steadily, with no adequate relief in sight either for those who lacked the necessities of life or those who were attempting to provide them.[27]

As his words indicate, Ryerson certainly approached the collapse with a sense of obligation to somehow stem misery.

Ryerson also expressed his embrace of welfare capitalism, a system of labor-capital relations that emerged in the early twentieth century and involved businesses providing such services as financial assistance and legal aid in return for loyalty at the workplace.[28] Welfare capitalists, such as the managers of General Electric in the 1920s, were often perceived as "enlightened capitalists," who understood that caring for their workers was moral *and* good for business. Although many welfare capitalists lost the ability to provide for workers during the Depression, it seems that for some, this approach to labor relations continued to shape their outlook.[29]

The combination of cultural logics—noblesse oblige, professionalization, welfare capitalism, and monetary voluntarism—produced a specific set of narratives that emphasized not only civic obligation and neighborliness during the Depression but also the professional knowledge and obligation that business leaders brought to relief drives. These narratives, then, combined with a catastrophe so encompassing that Ryerson describes it as "nothing but chaos at every turn."[30] As business owners and relief officials, Ryerson and his cohort saw the Depression as a threat to their effective and necessary system of private relief and charity, and they threw themselves into raising funds for the unemployed. Relief officials used the *Chicago Daily Tribune* as the vehicle for their relief drives; on its pages, officials compelled Chicagoans of all means to contribute while also confirming social hierarchies and popular disdain for the system of charity they hoped to preserve.

"The Best We Have Is His by Right": Funding Charity in the Depression

At the start of the Great Depression, while social workers struggled to assess need and unemployed laborers began to demand more from the government, Chicago's relief officials reconfigured nineteenth-century ideals for the economic crisis. As the city's messy system of charity and public welfare struggled under the weight of rising demands and declining resources, members of the GCUR made it clear that those Chicagoans who had the means also bore a duty to contribute to the relief efforts. Chicagoans, they argued, could take care of themselves. In part, relief leaders counted on the city's wealthiest residents to achieve this goal, and in 1930, relief leaders hoped to capitalize on an elite who in the decade prior had donated almost $45 million to the city's cultural centers, educational programs, hospitals, and charities.[31] At the same time, relief officials drew on the ideas and methods of welfare capitalism and recast them for city relief. Relief officials charged employers and industrial leaders with carrying the burden of the relief drives; in turn, these elite compelled their employees to do their part.

Chicago's relief officials made public their sentiment that the city's wealthiest residents should (as they had long been expected to do) keep Chicago's charities functioning. As the first winter of the Depression bore down, Clarke (chairman of the GCUR Fundraising Committee) announced that the GCUR was increasing the "quota" that the city's wealthy residents were expected to meet. The commission, he announced, had formerly asked $1 million of them but needed an additional $650,000 in individual gifts. "The cold weather seems to have chilled the spirit of giving," Clarke told the *Tribune*, for "only forty-three of the well to do citizens have responded to the mercy appeal. The others must feel a sense of shame when they face the 125,000 ordinary citizens who have contributed. The wealthy are facing a challenge they must meet."[32] Clarke's public statements contributed to a discourse on philanthropy that assumed the obligation of the wealthy to uphold private charity.

Even though relief officials expected Chicago's elite to contribute, Clarke and the GCUR insisted that charity should not hamper society. In the 1930s, Chicago's benefactors flitted from party to party and gave generously to an assortment of institutions and issues. During 1931–1932 alone, Chicagoans were invited to a wrestling match between world champions, a night of vaudeville and stage stars (featuring jazz legend Louis Armstrong) at the Aragon Ballroom, a Civic Opera House benefit, a "Tennis Battle for Charities," a week of charity parties in December 1931, and a French American benefit concert by French sensation Maurice Chevalier.

In August 1931, the Chicago subcommittee of the GCUR geared up for another drive labeled the JERF, and its members continued with many of the same tactics that they had used in 1930. For instance, the JERF hosted a 1932 Spring Horse Show "for needy families," a three-day benefit featuring Chicagoans' equestrian skills. As with many of the JERF fundraisers, the advertisements evinced a connection to Chicago society, describing pictured participants by their outfits: "Grace Byrnes," one caption read, "wearing tan jodhpurs with felt English riding hat, and Jeane Harris wearing green tweed coat, tan cavalry breeches, and green felt hat."[33] In advertising pages, relief officials acknowledged and capitalized on the machinery of Chicago consumerism that persisted even in the midst of economic collapse. At the very bottom of advertisement pages marketing fur coats, pajamas, and Parisian-style hats, department stores Carson Pirie Scott and Company and Marshall Field and Company announced their participation in the drive. Their appeals called on patrons to send any old clothing to a collection center, and from December 1–6, 1931, both stores sold "inexpensive serviceable garments," which their patrons could purchase for the GCUR.[34] Shoppers could spend money at Foster Shoes for Women and know that every purchase contributed one dollar to the joint campaign.[35] Relief events and offers projected specific ideas about the obligations and expectations of Chicago society during the economic crisis. In endless benefits and society events, relief officials suggested that, although the wealthy bore a civic obligation to give, it was not their responsibility to engage directly with the problems at hand. Leisure activities and conspicuous consumption, rather, could right the economic crisis.

While elite benefactors participated in a kind of charity based on philanthropy rather than on volunteering, relief officials also produced narratives about employer giving that promoted a welfare capitalist model of employer/employee relationships. The ideas behind welfare capitalism—that employers could gain labor's goodwill and loyalty by providing for workers' welfare—had roots in the preceding decades. Progressive-Era industrialists tinkered with ways of keeping workers happy and under control, from company towns to medical services. By the 1920s, welfare capitalism was far more measured than at the turn of the twentieth century. In the 1920s, which Lizabeth Cohen describes as the "era of welfare capitalism," "the enlightened corporation, not the labor union or the state, would spearhead the creation of a more benign industrial society."[36] Employers in the 1920s looked with a paternalistic eye toward their employees and the community at large, offering benefits and wage incentives and hosting events like picnics.

By the 1920s, however, welfare capitalism had also developed a darker side. Employers exploited ethnic divisions among workers to minimize union organizing; one Chicago employment manager explained, "We have Negroes and Mexicans in a sort of competition with each other. It is a dirty trick."[37] While propagandizing through company newsletters or intentionally separating immigrant groups to keep them from organizing, employers in the 1920s understood themselves to be the fathers of their industrial families: in charge, but looking out for their workers. But at a more basic level, welfare capitalism never succeeded at supplying workers with their needs and benefits. In lieu of effective employer-based aid, during the first decades of the twentieth century, it fell on ethnic and neighborhood associations to dependably provide assistance in emergencies, policies for insurance against injury and old age, and community.

During the early years of the Depression, even the best welfare capitalists failed to take care of their workers. Ethnic and neighborhood institutions buckled under increased economic strain, but Chicago's relief efforts suggest that these employers toiled to preserve their close relationship with the workforce. Employers worked to preserve welfare capitalism by implicating employers and workers in the project of supporting jobless workers and by making relief a local effort.

Relief officials undergirded their drives for money and the tenets of welfare capitalism by encouraging employers and industrialists to raise the bulk of relief donations. In 1930, relief officials assessed employer giving in twenty-six trade groups, which they called "Trade

Teams." On a regular basis, the GCUR ranked the teams by contribution and published the list in the *Tribune*. On December 14, for instance, GCUR officials congratulated five teams (including "Leather, rubber, and shoes"; "Advertising, newspapers, etc."; and "Men's clothing") for exceeding their $5 million relief quota. The remaining twenty-one, however, were publicly shamed for having "not yet completed their solicitation."[38] Business and industrial leaders, they were told, bore a responsibility to aid relief efforts, for they were, as Insull Jr. declared, "Chicago's leading citizens—men with reputations for accomplishment."[39] Relief officials echoed and attempted to preserve a cultural logic that positioned employers as being responsible for the welfare of their city and able to fix its economic woes. In so doing, they declared that private, local sources (rather than state or federal government) would be their city's salvation.

In the spirit of welfare capitalism and corporate voluntarism, relief officials made it clear that workers should be a central part of the relief effort and championed the employed workers who would, with the encouragement of their bosses, sustain their jobless brethren. Relief officials assigned to employers the responsibility to enable and encourage their employees to contribute and pressed corporations to offer matching grants for their employees. By early December 1930, the GCUR announced that the "bulk of the contributions . . . have come from corporations and their employés [*sic*]."[40] A few weeks later, the *Tribune* announced that manufacturing giant U.S. Gypsum Corporation had contributed $42,390 to the campaign, "raised under the pay-deduction plan recommended by the Commission, whereby the corporation matched dollar for dollar the contributions of the workers."[41] The next year, Chicago's postal workers followed suit: in the first months of the JERF campaign, postal workers each agreed to donate between $2 and $4 a month for six months, amounting to a $100,000 donation for the joint campaign.[42] Relief officials during the Great Depression expanded noblesse oblige to include Chicagoans of modest means, but by attaching workers' contributions to their employers, they espoused a paternalistic relationship between the two groups. When Charles S. Dewey, who headed the drive for funds from the division of trades, assured *Tribune* readers that "employés [*sic*] of firms will, of course, be asked to do their part along with their employers,"[43] he subtly confirmed a workplace hierarchy in which workers gave because their generous bosses asked them to.

Through the combined logics of noblesse oblige, philanthropy, and welfare capitalism, Chicago's relief officials constructed a narrative and method of relief giving that argued that the city could take care of its own (whether as an act of benevolence or within the expectations of a close employer-employee relationship). The relief drives were built on the concepts of voluntarism and localism, which gave shape to fundraising efforts and, in the end, proved to be of greater benefit to employers than to the unemployed. For in the end, voluntarism cast a distrustful eye on the jobless, rendering the victims of the Depression fundamentally suspect.

Chicagoans for Chicagoans and the Failure of Localism

Throughout Chicago's efforts to stem the economic tide, relief officials and political leaders celebrated the concept of localism—the obligation and feasibility that Chicagoans' could care for their own and thus save their city in a moment of crisis. Relief officials used the concept of localism as a final, effective device for calling on their city's financially stable to contribute to their drives. While the concept was insufficient in overcoming the city's monetary deficits (the process of raising relief funds), relief officials and city journalists found it useful in delineating the boundaries around relief giving. In the end, although localism proved to be materially untenable, it gave relief officials the language to identify undeserving recipients of relief, thus drawing strict boundaries around relief giving.

Early on, relief officials emphasized that their drives would be *local* efforts—fundraising by and for Chicagoans. Relief workers articulated a connection between place and philanthropy and championed a system of charity rooted in locality. The sense that the maintenance of the poor was a local obligation was deeply rooted in Western (especially British and American) systems of welfare and poor law, and it simultaneously bred generosity toward one's neighbors and undergirded the notion that, as Michael Katz puts it, "the public owed nothing to strangers."[44] By the 1930s, localism seemed firmly rooted in American philanthropic efforts. In a 1932 statement on the JERF relief drives, committee president Ryerson gushed about his people: "This high percentage of collections in the face of present conditions is truly remarkable and is a splendid testimonial to the loyalty, self-sacrifice and cooperative spirit of the people of Chicago."[45] The relief drives, Ryerson suggested, proved that Chicagoans wanted to take care of their city.

Others, such as United Charities superintendent Joel Hunter, drew on ideas about local character to defend unemployed Chicagoans who needed relief. In a *Tribune* article titled "Sure There Are Unemployed, but Idle? Not Many, Thousands Look for Work" he described "how Chicago's jobless men and women are helping themselves" and informed the reporter that he had "heard of no family head who didn't want work instead of charity and strove to find it."[46] Hunter's defense of the city's unemployed simultaneously pardoned certain unemployed workers and identified the unpardonable. Relief workers' insistence on a sense of duty to one's place thus functioned to set up limits to relief and giving. Relief drive organizers created boundaries around giving and implied that there were people (outside the community) to whom Chicagoans had no obligation.

Unfortunately for many Chicagoans, localism was ultimately only partially successful. On the one hand, the drives for relief funds— led by Chicago business and social service leaders who proclaimed the sanctity of the city's privately funded charities—were seen as a model for other cities. During multiple drives, Chicago's leading industrialists, along with workers, churchgoers, and society members, met their goals (in one drive alone, they raised $5 million), and their efforts were "highly commended by President [Herbert] Hoover."[47] The city seemed to have come together around the issue of unemployment, perhaps proving Chicagoans' commitment to their locality. On the other hand, as early as 1931, it became clear that Chicago's relief drives were beset by financial limitations, a reality that city reformers recognized before relief officials did. That year, settlement house leaders and social service workers realized that, even if officials could meet their fundraising goals, the local drives for relief would not sustain the unemployed. In January 1931, Taylor reflected that "there is an increasing feeling that no great improvement is in sight and that we may have to plan for another winter of distress."[48]

Despite public commendations, reformers and the distributors of relief spent 1931 in a deficit. Accustomed to a decrease in need during summer months, the city's social and charity workers were dismayed to find an increase in the summer of 1931. Even worse, the summer surge foreshadowed an even heavier load in the rest of 1931 and through 1932. Settlement workers at Chicago Commons reported that while 649 families requested aid in 1929 and 813 sought help in 1930, by the end of the summer of 1931, they had seen 1,159 requests for material aid.[49] In August 1931, members of the GCUR reorganized (with some changes in leadership) as the JERF for Cook County.[50] By the time JERF leaders initiated the next relief drive, "at least one-third of the population of Chicago, or well over a million people, were with out a source of income." By December 1931, officials reported that the relief load on average was 400 percent larger than it had been in 1930, and JERF officials confessed that although they had raised nearly $10 million, the funds would hardly last four months.[51] Local systems of relief, it seemed, were not strong enough to weather the storm.

Yet despite its material failure, localism successfully conveyed for Chicagoans and outsiders the ideal boundaries around relief giving in the city. JERF leaders emphasized localism and reassured residents by exploiting the notion of the "tramp," a wandering hobo who, with no intention of finding proper work, would arrive in Chicago to steal legitimate workers' hard-earned relief funds. Certainly, relief officials did not invent the idea of the tramp; by the early 1930s, generous cities like Chicago were seeing waves of out-of-towners moving in to make use of their relief policies. So, while defending public funding and large drives for private funding, relief officials attempted to control where their money went by keeping relief funds out of the hands of nonresidents and those who had not gone through the correct channels.

Relief workers (with the help of *Tribune* reporters) publicly drew the line at giving outside Cook County, reassuring donors that their funds would remain in the community. As JERF chairman, Ryerson responded to stories of transients by asserting, "Every effort possible is being made by the JERF to give relief only to regular residents of Chicago and Cook county."[52] Ryerson's statement to the *Tribune* certainly reflected the limited funds and great need in the county and tapped into a suspicion of transience that loomed large in the social imaginary of Chicago. The *Tribune* alone showed a culture that was protective of the city and its funds, a culture reflected in the statements made by leaders of relief drives. Most notably, city leaders and residents evinced a serious concern about nonresidents who might be trying to take city funds. "The need for relief among the destitute of Chicago," Ryerson explained, "is that it would be impossible to take care of the transients who may be attracted to Chicago when cold weather comes."[53] In this assertion, relief officials demarcated the boundaries around the humanitarianism and social duty they called Chicagoans to embody.

JERF officials vowed that they could avoid giving relief to outsiders by establishing a clear bureaucracy. At the founding of the GCUR (the first drive), chairman Getz announced that the city's relief agencies would undertake a survey of the city's jobless and register each of them. Registering the unemployed initially just served to inform the committee of the city's need and to facilitate relief giving. On November 13, 1930, the *Tribune* reported the findings of the Chicago subcommittee of the GCUR: "Approximately 37,000 emergency cases were found to exist among the 90,000 unemployed who have registered in Chicago. Relief in those cases was being given as rapidly as possible by turning the registration cards over to the various relief agencies."[54]

Relief workers and the *Tribune* also went on the offensive against transients. In this approach, relief officials drew on a historic tradition of requiring proof of local residency to receive alms, a feature of colonial and eighteenth-century laws that favored local care of the poor. The magnitude of the economic crisis in the 1930s allowed relief officials to define poverty as a tragedy inflicted on a person rather than as a moral failing, but their attention to localism established limits to this charitable culture.[55] As the JERF "announced that Chicago would not be a Mecca for the unemployed of other parts of the country," the *Tribune* sent an "undercover" reporter into transient hangouts to discover the true intentions of the "Hobo Horde." Just as the writer had suspected, he found that the city was "known from coast to coast as a good town. . . . Prospects for the bread lines and free beds pour in on almost every freight train."[56] The *Tribune*'s alarm bell rang in the ears of concerned citizens. Perhaps the most severe recommendation came from the Van Buren Street Improvement Association, a city group that suggested to Chicago mayor Anton Cermak that he take drastic action against out-of-town beggars. In a city cabinet meeting, this group called for the "establishment of a concentration camp for the internment of homeless beggars and peddlers" and proposed that "they be made to work on a rock pile to discourage their staying in Chicago."[57] These suggestions, although certainly on the extreme end of the spectrum, reflected a broad and growing sense of concern: because the city did not have enough funds to secure relief for its own residents, nonresidents threatened the livelihood of the community's true members.

Narratives about residency and relief shifted fluidly between place and propriety. The *Tribune* undercover reporter certainly encouraged the Van Buren Street Improvement Association's worries by offering character sketches of unemployed transients in the city. People from other places, these sketches argued, came to the city because they wanted easy access to food and shelter. In one account of findings from the field, *Tribune* reporter Chesly Manly asked "three loiterers at a lamp post" about getting a job in the city and received confirmation of the nature of drifters: "'A job?' asked one of the men derisively. 'We're looking for a drink and haven't got the money. Just get here? Well, 'sa good town, best in the country. Don't worry about no job though; you can always eat and sleep.'"[58] After interviewing fifty or so men in the breadlines, the reporter informed his readers, "Most of the out-of-towners seemed carefree and confident of a winter that's 'at least better than working.'" The *Tribune*'s story made a point to distinguish between unemployed Chicagoans and drifters: "There were, on the other hand, many hard luck stories from Chicagoans."

Yet Manly's article offered a place for slippage from objective (residency) to subjective (right behavior) measures for legitimacy. The city only gave relief to its residents, Manly implied, because transients were not interested in working and would likely spend relief money on drinking and other unsavory activities. It is unclear whether Manly's account was entirely legitimate—considering the glibness of his jobless "interviewees," it is certainly possible that some of his research was fabricated. Regardless, his discussion of residency modeled a specific way of talking about behavior and legitimacy. The article seemed to imply that the people who deserved funding not only came from a certain place but also behaved in a specific way. The transition from place to propriety made its way into relief-giving policies. The JERF's principal aims, as laid out by organizer Insull Jr., were to "provide work for as many as possible"; "provide food, shelter, and baths for the out of work"; and, significantly, "weed out the worthless and drunken from the worthy and sober."[59] Clearly, in protecting their funds by emphasizing localism, relief officials established that place would be the first marker of potential worth, followed by propriety as a second marker if the first was met. With these guidelines, relief officials delineated the worthy and the unworthy.

In the early 1930s, Chicago's relief officials worked feverishly to raise enough funds to keep the city's unemployed from destitution and to keep its charities from going under. They created a culture of relief giving in the city in which the well-to-do were criticized for stinginess and invited to think of relief as being part of membership within elite society. Relief officials drew on the cultural logics that shaped them: noblesse oblige, welfare capitalism, and localism. These business owners cajoled, admonished, and informed their way into raising millions and millions of dollars for the poor.

Yet these efforts were not enough. Their drives suffered from an economic burden that even the city's most successful philanthropists could not manage. Moreover, their inability to see past old frameworks for public welfare limited the scope of the relief drives and promoted equally old ideas about the poor. As such, their statements and suggestions indicated a desire to maintain a system of charity with which they closely identified: one that was local, that depended on Chicagoans fulfilling their civic and humanitarian obligations, and that maintained social hierarchies. Ultimately, relief officials were forced to turn to the state for help, but they never abandoned their sense that localities, rather than the government, were best suited to administering relief.

Relief officials and philanthropists were not the only Chicagoans who encountered the failure of charity during the Depression. In the 1930s, settlement workers, who had always thought of their efforts as being separate from casework and charity, found themselves distributing more relief and aid than ever before. By joining the world of relief in Depression-era Chicago, settlement workers also exhibited the failure of local charity during this crisis, which only confirmed for them the sense that what unemployed workers needed was relief, certainly, but without ties to charity.

3

Charity and Entitlement

I n 1932, Chicago Commons head resident Lea Taylor described the
Depression's impact on the West Town settlement in distinctly personal terms:

> [This] fifth year of unemployment in our local community left
> in its wake discouraged and disheartened men and women,
> constantly fearful that relief funds will cease; panicky when
> grocery orders are delayed or cut down; faced with continual
> irritation from landlords unpaid for many months and them-
> selves struggling to exist . . . trying to heat a four-room apart-
> ment with a small garbage burner which often also serves as
> a cook-stove.[1]

Chicago Commons workers had watched this slow deterioration. They had seen their neighbors—poor laborers who lived in
West Town and frequented the settlement for gatherings, discussion groups, and casework—lose jobs, spend their savings, and even
(as a last resort) ask for charity. As the jobless dealt with the slide
into indigence, settlement workers were forced to rethink their roles
as "good neighbors." Whereas settlement workers had long prided

themselves on offering friendship rather than alms, the intensity of the Depression ultimately led residents and staff to accept that they now worked in a relief-giving organization. Settlements around the city developed hastily assembled departments for assessing need and distributing aid.

Settlement workers' responses to rising unemployment were reactive, stemming from the emergency in which they found themselves. Yet although Taylor and other settlement workers hardly had the resources to build a fully systematic response to the Depression, through casework and club work, they assembled a new and influential conception of unemployment. While distributing material aid, attending to the psychological stresses of joblessness, and encouraging productive uses of idle time, these social reformers drew on and expanded the ideas presented in the National Federation of Settlements (NFS) study on unemployment. In turn, they constructed a framework for understanding unemployment that would influence them (and their allies) throughout the decade. Unlike the NFS study, caseworkers and group workers in Chicago's settlements did not explicitly propose a way of approaching unemployment; rather, as this chapter examines, their reflections on work reveal how they perceived unemployment and how their thinking evolved because of it. Like the NFS findings, settlement workers in Chicago associated masculinity with employment, called on the government to right the economic crisis, and entitled some poor people to federal subsidies.

Settlement workers' participation in casework, a venture that was pushed upon them by the financial collapse, showed their willingness to be flexible and meet the emerging needs of the neighborhood. Yet they were unprepared for the requirements of casework, institutionally and psychologically. Newly created casework departments had few clear standards for assessing the poor and distributing funds, which left case visitors and caseworkers to determine neediness on their own. These settlement workers, moreover, were not used to viewing their neighbors as clients, and their case records reveal confusion about how to manage the transition. In relief giving, settlement workers insisted on the necessity of material relief, a conviction that also insisted on their neighbors' legitimacy, while employing distinctions between the "worthy" and "unworthy" poor. However, their nonmaterial relief promised to fulfill the settlement workers' mission.

Inspired by social science research on the vulnerability of the family during the Great Depression, settlement leaders attended to the nonmaterial needs of their neighbors. In 1931, Taylor described how in families with unemployment, "anxiety and insecurity are paramount [and] worry takes a toll on health with both men and women."[2] In response, settlement workers expanded clubs, discussion groups, and activities that might ease the pain of unemployment. In noncasework programming, they maintained the dignity of the unemployed, even in a cultural climate that attempted to dethrone jobless men from their posts as breadwinners. At the same time, settlement workers subtly endorsed a definition of masculinity that preserved gender-based family roles and expectations.

In casework and club work, Chicago's settlement workers perhaps unknowingly put together a series of ideas, beliefs, and practices that would serve as the foundation for their emerging embrace of worker entitlement. On the one hand, settlement workers upheld their historic commitment to treating the environmental causes of poverty and offered programs that emphasized their neighbors' lack of blame for their neediness. On the other hand, settlement caseworkers simultaneously held onto traditional ideas about poor families, suggesting that only some deserved full relief. Settlement casework and club work vindicated unemployed men and their families but ultimately reinforced conceptions of worthiness and placed limits around the right to demand employment.

Settling for Charity

It must have seemed strange to Harriet Vittum, the head resident of Northwestern University Settlement House (NUS), when, in 1930, she and other house leaders first appointed caseworkers dedicated solely to distributing relief to the unemployed. Vittum had been there since 1904, a time when those in the settlement movement offered themselves as an antidote to charity workers and promised to treat the urban poor as "neighbors" rather than as "clients." Whereas charity workers necessarily critiqued their clients' behavior and lifestyle, settlement workers argued that good neighbors built relationships instead of judgments. Despite settlement leaders' historic (and persistent) resistance to engaging in charity, during the Great Depression, they had no choice but to undertake charity and relief work. Even as settlement workers decried the kinds of evaluations that came from charity work, they ended up reinscribing such judgments as their duties shifted.

Settlement relief giving in the 1930s was surprising in part because the divisions between settlement work and charity were long-standing, if at times artificial. Since the movement's origins in the nineteenth century, settlement leaders like Harriet Vittum, Jane Addams, and Graham Taylor had positioned themselves against the charity movement, characterizing themselves as "good neighbors" rather than investigators of scientific charity. Addams argued that charity workers preached "'don't give,' 'don't act,' 'don't do this or that'" and gave the poor nothing but advice.[3] In an 1899 article, Addams explained to *Atlantic Monthly* readers that charity visitors, who lived in the world of the rich and hardly understood the poor, could not help but impose "incorrigibly bourgeois" standards on their clients.[4] Settlement workers were suspicious of charity organizations' emphasis on investigation and instead promoted flexibility and the cultivation of relationships in responding to poverty. Graham Taylor, the founder of Chicago Commons, called on his compatriots to offer "not alms but a friend."[5] Further, at their most ideologically pure, settlement workers developed a definition of poverty that was fundamentally at odds with that put forth by charity workers. Whereas the charity movement credited individuals' moral depravity with generating economic destitution and encouraged personal transformation as a solution, settlement workers "believed that the environment, especially the urban environment, was the key to solving social problems."[6]

Certainly, by the 1920s, it was clear that these distinctions were largely artificial, yet many settlement workers were still resistant to being considered charity workers. A visitor's founding philosophy, whether rooted in scientific charity or in neighborliness, likely did not radically affect his or her impact on poor families, and to argue that charity visitors were the only people judging their clients would be to miss moral underpinnings that influenced some settlement programs.[7] Moreover, settlement workers remained tied to the work of charity and welfare in cities like Chicago, where they regularly connected their neighbors to the charities and institutions that might aid them. "By cooperation with every public and private social and philanthropic agency in the city," Vittum told NUS supporters, "the Settlement serves as a switchboard, connecting local problems with city-wide agencies organized for their relief and interpreting the city-wide agencies to those who could learn of them in no other way."[8]

Even in the 1920s, though, as charity work became more professionalized and less voluntary, settlement workers attempted to distance themselves from charity and relief. By then, much of the work formerly undertaken by charity volunteers was being filled by an emerging field of trained social workers, who focused on therapy and emphasized the personal—rather than environmental—changes that might ameliorate family or individual strife. With this approach, social workers and caseworkers adamantly fixed their gaze on the personal and psychological roots of their clients' complaints right before the most severe economic collapse the nation had ever seen, a turn that Robert Halpern calls "one of the ironies of the historical development of supportive services."[9] Settlement workers in Chicago clung to the importance of neighborliness over professionalism. In 1926, Vittum announced that "less and less the Settlement wishes to be considered a charitable institution."[10] This distinction rarely played out as cleanly as settlement leaders would have hoped, but in the 1920s, settlement leaders like Jane Addams, Mary McDowell, Harriet Vittum, and Lea Demarest Taylor hoped that they might preserve the distinctive mission of the settlement movement.[11]

Yet in the 1930s, as their neighbors suffered staggering rates of unemployment, most settlement workers in Chicago found themselves distributing aid. Small settlements—including those that were religiously oriented—were most likely to focus on neighborhood work and charity. These included the Madonna Center, a Catholic settlement located just down the street from Hull House. The center's head resident, Mary Agnes Amberg, acknowledged their neighbors' need for a new kind of settlement: "The function of a Settlement is not, it is true, the work of a Relief Agency, but it *is* its province to aim to secure that relief for its people when needful and possible" (emphasis original).[12]

Even residents and workers in larger settlements soon realized that their neighborhoods could not afford their avoidance of charity. The city's charities and relief system that had traditionally mitigated the problems of family breakdown and financial hardship buckled under the demand of unemployment. Chicago Commons residents in 1932 challenged the legitimacy of a relief system that offered only in-kind relief as opposed to cash; grocery orders, which limited recipients' food options; and especially the countywide prohibition against providing rent subsidies as relief. Lea Taylor also warned of the long-term consequences of poorly administered relief. While unemployment affected each individual, she argued, "the community will eventually pay in prolonged care for the loss in health, in mental poise, in warped child life, and in morale of youth and adults which will be inevitable results of the strain on family and community life."[13] The NUS Neighborhood Service Department had long offered family counseling and sporadic material relief, but Vittum's "Annual Report," written in 1934, struck a different chord than the one published eight years prior: "For five long years the grip of the financial depression and ever increasing unemployment held us to a program of meeting emergencies [and] feeding the hungry whom we knew."[14] Whereas Addams's early writings prioritized community building over relief giving, Depression-era settlements could not ignore the need for charity-like measures in their neighborhoods.

Participating in relief efforts, however, was neither automatic nor easy. Settlement workers were faced with a series of problems. First, more and more of their neighbors required relief and aid, meaning that settlements were overwhelmed with work. In 1932, the Chicago Commons Neighborhood Work Department recorded intakes with three times as many families as it had in 1928–1929, and Commons caseworkers described their work as doubling each year.[15] As it was presented with mounting neighborhood emergencies, Chicago Commons hired an extra assistant to manage the extra relief work.

The second problem was that as the Depression set in, settlements that were largely funded by private donations received fewer contributions and thus had to tighten their budgets and programs. In 1932, Chicago Commons's overall income was 20 percent less than in the years before the stock market crash, and by 1934–1935, the general donations amounted to 54 percent of what they had been in 1927–1928 (dropping from $29,365 to $15,983). Workers at NUS described the same circumstances. Vittum's "Annual Report" for 1930 cast NUS's work in a decidedly gloomy pallor: "The 12 months ending December 31, 1930, have been almost unbelievable in the problems that have accumulated all about us . . . [and] no sorrow that has come to us has been as far reaching, so devastating as this."[16] Vittum described how NUS "found it necessary, as did all agencies which I know, to retrench in every possible way."[17] During the 1930s, NUS staff members were forced to cut their already-meager budget in half and reduce residents' salaries as much as possible. By 1934, the settlement had accrued an overwhelming deficit of more than $13,000, much of which was owed to the staff members.[18] Vittum sacrificed her own pay for at least four months in an effort to preserve the NUS budget.[19]

Finally, settlement workers found themselves battling a culture that dissuaded the newly unemployed from even seeking relief. The underfunded and unnavigable relief system, combined with a general suspicion of charity, functionally discouraged the jobless from applying for relief.[20] A 1931 study of 472 unemployed families known to Chicago Commons found that almost half of unemployed families in the neighborhood had never sought relief from a city agency; that at the time of their first interview, 42 percent had never before contacted a charity or public welfare agency for help; and that only one-fifth of them had been registered with a relief agency prior to 1928. These people were the poor who struggled with a general consensus that relief payments, especially those that guaranteed subsistence, implied laziness and created dependency among recipients. By 1932, only one-fourth of the unemployed received any work relief or direct relief.[21]

Some of the relief that Chicago's settlement workers offered was decidedly temporary, which did not threaten their mission. In 1932, the Madonna Center reported aiding 348 families through medical assistance, relief, and clothing distribution. Chicago Commons distributed milk to homes with needy children, thanks to a milk fund raised at the suburban Lake View High School. And in the same year, Vittum informed NUS supporters that sandwich collections at schools in the northern suburbs had brought in an average of two thousand sandwiches per month to be distributed in the neighborhood.[22] Madonna Center workers reported receiving clothing for needy children from parish members and supporters, allowing them to distribute 3,024 pieces of secondhand clothing. Finally, Vittum described NUS's service to victims of the unstable housing market: "Never a weekend and often for many weeks, never a night without a call to get out cots, make bode and house for a night or two or more some individual or family . . . N.U.S. has been an open door of comfort, of hope and of friendship."[23] Relying on suburban supporters, offering clothing to poor families, and giving milk and crackers to young children were not new strategies for settlement workers, so settlements were well prepared to offer piecemeal forms of relief and aid.

Yet in the early years of the Depression, settlement workers in Chicago also entered uncharted waters, engaging in work that would take them from their mission and reveal the implications of casework. NUS, which has unusually complete case records, offers a clear look into shifting patterns of relief giving.[24] In 1931, Vittum and NUS settlement workers created a distinct Relief Department and corresponding case forms (called the "Special Relief Unemployment Emergency" [SRUE] forms), institutionalizing a shift that had grown over the previous two years. Whereas the long-standing Neighborhood Service Department had traditionally dealt with all cases—most frequently related to domestic discord or juvenile delinquency, but sometimes regarding unemployment or neediness—after 1931, the Relief Department took all cases dealing with unemployment. Among the more than fifty-five case records from 1921–1929, one was related to unemployment and thirty-nine focused solely on domestic issues; yet among the more than sixty Relief Department case records examined from the 1930s, forty-eight dealt with unemployment and relief.[25] Among another thirty-six records from the Neighborhood Service Department, eight focused on unemployment, indicating that joblessness bled into even the department reserved for other issues. Even though Vittum worried that the NUS forms were not as "detailed or as complicated as relief-giving organizations must have," the institutional shift was significant.[26]

Workers in the NUS Relief Department were not all that different from those in the Neighborhood Service Department, but their work did more to shift the settlement from "neighborliness" to casework. Workers in the Neighborhood Service Department and in the Relief Department were trained in social work, so they came from similar backgrounds, and they all took part in interviewing neighbors to gather information. Senior caseworkers in the Relief Department reported a diminished job market, an unnavigable system of city relief, and increasingly intransigent landlords. But these caseworkers often supervised Relief Department visitors, younger and less experienced social workers who were not always residents in the settlement. In the settlement, Relief Department visitors arrived at their neighbors' homes, looked through cupboards, took stock of coal reserves, and made notes of children's attire (or lack thereof). Together, these settlement workers guided clients through the city's relief system and guided their own settlement through the process of distributing material goods.

Just the existence of such a coordinated Relief Department was new to NUS, and caseworkers' increased involvement in doling out money and goods signaled their corresponding responsibility to assess the poor. "Neighborliness" lost some salience when caseworkers found themselves allocating scant resources to too many neighbors. Because caseworkers were required to fully assess need before granting aid, by the 1930s, nearly all casework included a home visit from a settlement staff member or volunteer. These home visits gave caseworkers an intimate look into their neighbors' poverty, but they were also the basis on which caseworkers determined whether to give relief. A home visit might find a neighbor "in wheel chair—cannot walk. House very poor and absolutely no food in home. Emergency food over Sunday very badly needed. Very appreciative of any help," which might result in clothes, a grocery order, rent, or even cash. These visits, however, created for settlement workers not just an opportunity to *assess* need but also a new expectation to *judge* their neighbors and thereby determine their deservedness for receiving aid.[27]

Determining deservedness was not easy, and settlement workers revealed their inexperience in a lack of consistency. Settlement caseworkers, only moderately trained in the profession of social work and without a coherent system for assessing clients, relied on various (and often conflicting) markers to determine need. In one Madonna Center case, family members' insistence that they were too good for relief food clearly annoyed the visitor but also may have established them as not needing traditional aid. M. Mack, the visitor, included detailed notes in the case file:

> This is a Greek family—Frances came in office early in January complaining about the County sending them only Coal and Dry Groceries with no check like the other people in the neighborhood were getting.

"My God, Lady, we can't eat that old dry stuff they put in the boxes—we are not used to eating such stuff."

This child was very impudent and demanding, insisting we get the county to give them money instead of the box of food. She also needed shoes. Shoes and clothing—especially warm underwear were given—talked with C.C.B.P.W. [Cook County Bureau of Public Welfare] about case, who felt family had other resources than what they had told about.[28]

Clearly exasperated, Mack seemed unsure as to whether the family's demands verified their needs or revealed them as living above their means, and she ultimately relied on the Bureau of Public Welfare to make the call. But the conditions that one visitor recorded as intense destitution might show up in another report as impropriety, and it was frequently unclear how a judgment of behavior might affect a client's allocations. This inconsistency was often the case when caseworkers attended to the cleanliness of their neighbors.

A closer look at settlement workers' foray into casework gives a window into why some unemployed workers resisted the relief that came with it: although settlement caseworkers did not rigidly differentiate between "need" and "worth," they regularly relied on the latter to make decisions about allocating aid. This approach becomes clear when examining the NUS attention to cleanliness, which had long been associated with health, honesty, and even good governance. In the 1920s, NUS hosted classes and education on hygiene and proper behavior, and Vittum compelled NUS's neighbors to create cleaner homes, political lives, and even ball games. During the Depression, Vittum still emphasized the relationship between cleanliness and health, arguing that "lessons in health from the standpoint of cleanliness, right feeding, value of rest and relaxation, will, it is believed, last long in the minds of the children, and the practice of the habits taught send them into school better able to meet the strain of winter and of school and of poverty."[29]

While cleanliness was certainly imperative for health in crowded urban neighborhoods, caseworkers who knew that cleanliness mattered in the mission of their settlement had little (if any) instruction in how to carry that aim forward in the Relief Department, and their notes reveal an inconsistency that likely confused and frustrated the unemployed who hoped for their assistance. In sixty case records from the 1930s, caseworkers mention clients' cleanliness, decorum, and friendliness nineteen times. These notes nearly always mix comments about cleanliness with notes on material need, pointing to the caseworkers' confused perception of a relationship between the two. In some cases, evaluating cleanliness was just part of the assessment, as in a note that a visitor filed in 1932: "Nice neat, attractive home. Gas shut off. #1 tells me he works under the name of Stanley Walton as his own is Polish. Both #1 and #2 are very friendly. They tell me [United Charities] has given them no help."[30] This appraisal included a comment on the state of the home but did not assign an explicit value judgment.

In most other cases, however, visitors associated cleanliness with a positive review. In 1931, staff worker G. Law came away from a client's home with these notes: "[Wife] tells me that she is 7 1/2 months pregnant and is attending Inf[ant] Wel[fare] at [Chicago] Commons. She is very nice bright and intelligent woman with a very nice family. [Husband] is very thin and underweight. Home nice and clean." Because this SRUE form included a generally positive evaluation, it reflects that Law (and caseworker H. B. Weston, who wrote the follow-up) seemed to associate cleanliness and friendliness with a family's neediness. The opposite could also be true. In 1935, when NUS neighbors had suffered financial insecurity for nearly seven years, caseworker J. Mazurek described the conditions in one home: "Landlord has been pd rent for last mo, not for this. Dark when entered poor, could be cleaner. Rent received for Sept. to Oct. 25. Would like to have rent pd. for this month." Mazurek's following notes indicate that he recommended allocating funds for this client. Thus, cleanliness seems in these cases to have been a largely unreliable aspect of their casework: to one caseworker, it was a symptom of decorum, but to another, it was part of the slide into poverty and an indicator of need.[31]

In still other cases, though, cleanliness could even arouse suspicion. G. Law (the same visitor who wrote the impartial assessment above) wrote these comments about a home visit:

Home very clean and cozy. Everything very nice. This couple say they are not receiving help from their children, but appearances do not bear this story out. . . . Claim they have no work and can not get help from any one. They say they have nothing, they look as though they have everything. I can not judge.[32]

In this situation, the clean and cozy condition of the clients' home, along with their appearance of having too much, might have worked against them, encouraging Law and caseworker J. Mazurek to withhold relief. More often than not, SRUE visitors and caseworkers identified clients who were clean and "plucky."[33] This example nevertheless demonstrates the ways in which they prioritized settlement ideals regarding cleanliness, but without clear guidelines. Caseworkers at NUS exposed the Relief Department's haphazard nature. Unemployed and poor neighbors, who during the Depression searched for ways to convince caseworkers of their plight, found themselves at the whim of a capricious system of relief giving.

Caseworkers did more than just confusedly use cleanliness to make assessments of how poor a person really was. Their notes indicate that beginning in 1930, these newly minted charity workers repeatedly employed distinctions between "worthy" and "unworthy" in an effort to best allocate shrinking funds to a growing population in want and to make sense of a rate of poverty that defied not only practical experience but also, at times, human imagination. Caseworkers frequently used the term "deserving" (rather than "needy" or "wanting," which would have been less value laden) to describe their clients. Visitors and caseworkers never explicitly defined "deservedness," and although there was little consistency in how they used the term, their notes indicate that a deserving client would likely embody a delicate balance of clean, pleasant, *and* visibly needy. Visitor G. Law's notes about one home visit combined descriptions of need with assessments of worth: "Must meet 1929 and 1930 taxes #1 says no one would give him any help. All his tenants are not paying their rent. Need clothing and shoes for all. Deserving nice worried worthy family." Staff worker H. Klur was more explicit in her assessment of a home visit in the same year: "Home *very* neat. . . . [The mother] seems very much worried over conditions but very pleasant—very desperate—has not heard from UC [United Charities]—gives impression of being very deserving." Klur seems to have written these notes under the assumption that a client keeping her house neat had proven her industry and promised to resist relief-related dependency and apathy.[34]

Settlement leaders like Vittum might have decried the ways in which charity organizations made judgmental distinctions, but as "charity" made inroads into settlement house agendas, settlement caseworkers fell back on those same kinds of distinctions, an irony that the overworked and undertrained caseworkers hardly had time to acknowledge. By sliding between assessments of need and appraisals of worth, settlement caseworkers functionally abandoned their conviction that poverty stemmed from a person's environment, instead suggesting that some poor people, regardless of structural conditions, could make personal adjustments to mitigate the consequences of their poverty.

Settlement workers—from head residents to caseworkers—reflected a broader sense of concern over the effects of the Depression, and they echoed social scientists and researchers who pointed to one site of crisis: the family. While social scientists forewarned of family disintegration and theorized survival strategies, legislators and social commentators chastised employed women for abandoning their posts and stealing jobs from men. Their work, in spite of variation across the political spectrum, suggested that the family was in crisis and needed to be preserved and that the most promising solution involved personal, psychological adjustment.

One place to see the emphasis on family dissolution is among the findings of social scientists who pointed to the Great Depression as a cause for social disorganization and proposed using casework and psychology to redeem floundering families. Sociologist Ruth S. Cavan and psychiatric social worker Katherine H. Ranck, both from Chicago, and New York–based sociologist Mirra Komarovsky looked at the effects of unemployment on social and familial stability.[35] They and others warned of dropping marriage and birth rates and predicted consequences of the marriage deficit that would affect life outside the family unit: population loss, increase in illegitimacy, effects on housing, and expected increase in abortions.[36] Of special concern for Cavan and Ranck were fathers, whose authority and identities were wrapped up in employment and income. An unemployed father's insecurity and feelings of failure could manifest in various ways: the researchers reported fathers who had become irritable, emotional, and depressed due to their lack of work.[37] Without work—his primary responsibility in the family—a husband could scarcely expect his wife to respect him. Unemployed men themselves worried that "when money goes, love flies out the window," revealing a strong sense that their happiness and family stability depended on their ability to provide income. Finally, family patterns combined with unemployment also led to weakened parental control. In turn, Komarovsky urged that fathers maintain calm control over their families, lest they lose authority entirely.[38]

In their study, Cavan and Ranck's underlying argument was that the Great Depression had exacerbated, and made visible, underlying conditions that should be at the heart of casework. The Stevens family was but one example of a family who had "gone through a slow process of disorganization prior to the father's unemployment" and thus responded somewhat ineffectively to the Depression. Although the Stevenses eventually regained economic stability, they suffered an attempted suicide, the removal of one child from the home, and the father's resignation of his authority. In the end, the daughters' behavior exposed the permanent instability of the family. The younger daughter, Cavan and Ranck explained, continued to throw temper tantrums, to which her parents consistently responded with "severe beatings."[39] In turn, Cavan and Ranck argued, the Stevenses' inability to survive unemployment and poverty exposed their true nature. In building their study on the premise that Depression survival depended on preexisting conditions, Cavan and Ranck incorporated a sense of the personal roots of poverty and proposed as the remedy casework at the individual and/or family level.

Even before such researchers as Cavan, Ranck, and Komarovsky sounded their warning cries, settlement workers had expressed concern over family stability, but rarely in conjunction with unemployment. Many settlement workers understood their positions as "good neighbors" to necessarily include counsel and services for struggling families. Throughout the 1920s, Chicago Commons caseworkers in the Neighborhood and Family Work Department kept statistics on the number of broken homes and the causes of family disintegration; in 1928, the list included the death of a parent, desertion, insanity, separation or divorce, a sick parent, or a parent in an institution. Nursery workers, who cared mostly for children from broken homes and single mothers, described the majority of fathers as "dead, has deserted, is incapacitated or [is] insane." Threats to family stability in the 1920s were therefore primarily attributed to the physical removal of a parent (father) or a parent's disability.[40]

During the 1930s, however, unemployment came to be represented as the major threat to families. As early as 1929, caseworkers created a new category of broken home: those suffering from severe unemployment. To settlement workers, a present but unemployed father was as bad as one who had deserted or become incapacitated. Day nursery workers more frequently cared for children who attended because of unemployment—57 percent in 1930. But the author of a report written that year described a group of families with specific kinds of problems present and in need of care. This group—which suffered from "unemployment, unadjustment between parents, truancy of older children, incipient delinquency, health problems, parole, etc."—included families with homes broken by desertion, separation, or illegitimacy; homes with the father in prison or in the hospital; and homes in which the father was unemployed and the mother forced to work. Settlement workers, then, understood unemployment to be potentially as great a threat to family stability as health issues, crime, and desertion.

Settlement programming in the 1930s indicated a commitment to attending to family crises not only by giving material relief but also by offering activities and services that might help recipients manage the emotional strain and stresses that threatened families. The same settlements that gave one family emergency food or coal might offer another family counseling in an attempt to "adjust incipient domestic trouble which is increasing greatly" or develop educational and recreational groups to take a family member's mind off economic hardship.[41] Settlement leaders professed that their clubs and groups ameliorated much of the frustration and isolation that their jobless neighbors felt. "The fellowship of the group," Commons head resident Lea D. Taylor explained, "means much to those under heavy burdens." She continued, "The unburdening of troubles and the feeling that some one does care, are real helps in keeping up morale." So, settlement workers invited unemployed neighborhood residents to join various settlement groups, from classes to sports teams. They saw some encouraging results. Taylor reported hearing one mother comment to a friend, "Just remember that this is Thursday night and club night and on that night we forget our troubles." In offering

programming—clubs, activities, classes, and discussion groups—
settlement workers attempted to preserve families and family members who suffered under the emotional burden of unemployment.[42]

Yet settlement workers rarely dealt with families as a whole. Perhaps as a function of their organizational structure, in which departments' purposes were distinguished by age and gender, settlements
dealt primarily in the framework of individual, gender-based family
roles. Because of departmental limitations and priorities, settlement
workers (perhaps unintentionally) created a program that suggested
the distinctive ways in which men and women experienced, and
should respond to, severe unemployment. The Men's Department
cared for unemployed men and fathers exclusively, while the Wom-
en's Department offered tips for wives and mothers of unemployed
men. In tending to families, settlement workers simultaneously compiled a series of notions about employment, family roles, and ideal relief. Taken together, their programs put into action cultural concerns
about the state of family and gender relations and offered a method
for addressing such concerns.

Redeeming Breadwinners

Men's Department settlement workers, such as Karl Borders, a League
for Industrial Democracy (LID) organizer, built a program of activities and clubs that assumed the centrality of paid labor to masculinity
and thus tended to the emotional stresses that came with unemployed
men's fractured identity. When Men's Department workers offered
dignified ways to pass the time, they saw themselves as maintaining
masculinity by staving off apathy and bolstering self-esteem. These
programs also invited men to assert their identities as workers by discussing the economy, the fate of the unemployed, and the possibilities of collective bargaining. Such activities suggested that, as much
as material aid, jobless men needed help passing the time absent of
productive work and that in the meantime, these workers should look
to the government and union organizing for economic salvation.[43]

Social scientists' research on the Depression proposed that unemployed men were particularly vulnerable to the emotional costs of
joblessness, and settlement workers' neighborhood work fully confirmed such an alarming notion. Caseworkers reported unusually

high frequencies in incidents of domestic dispute stemming from unemployment, and they worried about the collateral damage that it caused. At the Madonna Center, caseworkers took note of the mental stress that was a companion to unemployment. One caseworker, Miss Martin, began a case analysis by describing how the father, a high school graduate and leader of an "over studious" family, was "mentally disturbed because he has been unemployed for so long, about 2 years." Caseworkers looked for a job for him in a Catholic vocational school. In the 1932 Chicago Commons "Annual Report," Lea Taylor expressed concerns similar to those of Miss Martin: "When the patience which has been amazing develops in apathy, there is a loss of initiative and effort towards self-help." Unemployed workers, caseworkers cautioned, suffered from a severely detrimental loss of morale.[44]

These caseworkers, along with settlement workers around the city, had come to embrace a widely held notion that a man's identity was wrapped up in his ability to secure paid labor and earn steady income. In 1928, Lea Taylor was already describing the central issue plaguing West Town as "the unemployment of breadwinners of families," identifying the problem at hand (unemployment) and the people whom the problem hit hardest (family breadwinners). In her choice of terms, Taylor entered a cultural conversation about the fragile state of men's identities as breadwinners, a conversation that firmly linked employment to masculinity. As E. Wight Bakke noted in the years following the Depression:

> The futility of pretending, when the search for a job is extended, that one continues to play the roles designated as respected in the world of labor should be obvious. "A producer," "the holder of a swell job," "a fellow your mates look to," "a good provider," "a man who never lets his family down" are clearly not terms which describe the man who is wandering from gate to gate begging for a chance to work.[45]

In the decade following an amazing surge in feminism and female employment, the sudden precariousness of the labor market encouraged men to hold on tight to their status as workers. In other words, the absence of work itself could increase its value to a man's identity.[46]

In her report, Taylor did not connect breadwinning with masculinity—and indeed, throughout the decade, she discussed female breadwinners—but Commons programming priorities seemed to imply that more often than not, the family father was the breadwinner. Historian Ralph LaRossa contends that the "crisis of masculinity" has been overblown and instead suggests that in the absence of work, many men adopted new identities as participatory fathers. In a way, this assertion seems to have been true, as what were described as the most "successful" families employed flexible strategies, including incorporation of new gender role expectations. Yet settlement programming indicates that men were frequently not encouraged to adopt new roles in the family.[47]

Instead, because most of the people they worked with were newly poor unemployed workers and their families, settlement workers created programs that assumed that men's natural state was productivity and so treated their unemployment as a temporary ill brought on by external forces. To keep unemployed men and boys busy, NUS workers organized drives by which they could deliver donated sandwiches to families in need and created the Unemployed Group, a club of men who gathered to discuss unemployment and relief. In a similar fashion, the Chicago Commons current events discussion group offered unemployed men the space to "talk out their problems, . . . hear plans for relief or adjustment, and get fellowship and recreation so greatly needed." Glenford Lawrence—in charge of adult education—explained the fundamental purpose of Chicago Commons classes and clubs: "In times of unemployment it helps greatly in strengthening morale, creating fellowship, giving a man 'something to do' which is constructive in his enforced idleness, and more important still, giving him something to think about and encouragement in seeking further education." Thus, rather than encouraging Men's Department participants to work—or shaming them for not working, a response to unemployment that, as is explained in Chapter 1, was all too common in the 1920s—these programs aimed to help breadwinners continue in their roles despite major changes in their material conditions and/or the world around them.[48]

Settlement workers' focus on preserving breadwinners' status was most noticeable in their attention to free time. Unemployed men, they sensed, especially needed help in filling time they were not used to having—the kind of time that settlement workers liked to describe as "enforced leisure." This extra time, they argued, was the dangerous commodity of jobless men, a side effect of unemployment that ate away a man's sense of purpose and possibility if he did not know how to fill it. Lea Taylor perhaps surprisingly included "purposeless leisure" in a list of the effects of the Great Depression, an inclusion that indicated the seriousness with which she viewed the problem. Enforced leisure, settlement leaders believed, was free time not asked for and therefore not used with good intention.[49]

Settlement workers undertook an assault on enforced leisure that targeted unemployed men and implied that their joblessness was not something to be ashamed of. In 1931, Vittum of NUS used rather alarming language when she described "hordes of people who are idle and must have something to occupy minds and hands," but she soon offered a solution: at the Lindy Club, a settlement social club, out-of-work men could meet once a week to discuss their problems and the economy. On the city level, settlement leaders like Amberg joined more than thirty Chicagoans working in education and recreation to establish the Leisure Time Committee, a centralized clearing house for information on daytime programs for the unemployed. The committee recruited unemployed "white collar men" as recreation leaders and orchestrated get-togethers for the jobless and their families. These kinds of clubs and activities offered support of a less tangible nature than caseworkers gave: instead of coal or grocery orders, settlement workers hoped to give "fellowship and friendship and wholesome occupation for enforced leisure."[50] Unemployed men in the Lindy Club also received a semblance of dignity. In a culture that chastised men for abandoning their post as breadwinner, such clubs affirmed their fundamental worth and assured them that they were not to blame for their poverty.

Responses to enforced leisure implied that their goal was to manage the time until those without jobs returned to their former, natural state of employment and breadwinning. Settlement workers suggested that men without jobs should get out of the house to avoid the emotional perils of home and the moral perils of loitering on the street. The Chicago Commons Adult Education Department gave them a place to go. In 1932, settlement workers began construction on a space "for the exclusive use of unemployed men, which would open right off the street, and be a place where they could read or work."[51] Organizer Lawrence hoped that with a haven in the settlement, these men would be less likely to loiter outside or, in a fit of frustration, drink their sorrows away. This kind of space also gave such men the license to maintain their family role and a place where they might collectively imagine themselves as future breadwinners.

Beyond filling leisure time to keep up morale, settlement workers aimed to inject a sense of capability into the unemployed in their neighborhoods. In 1932, adult education workers committed to helping the jobless learn about possible measures for relieving unemployment so that they could "realize that they need not be helpless tools of self-seeking politicians." Instead, settlement workers explained, these people could become "effective citizens, working for the adoption of sound measures of relief and action in times of crisis."[52] As their adult education objectives indicate, early in the Depression, settlement workers encouraged unemployed men to think of themselves as political and to have a say in relief and unemployment legislation. This kind of language—a moderate call to politicize the unemployed—carried through settlement workers into unemployed organizing, the focus of Chapter 4. In Men's Department and leisure time programming, settlement workers suggested to unemployed men that they did not deserve to be poor and that their rightful place was back at work.[53]

Women's Work and Working Women

Settlement workers in Women's Departments seemed to have different objectives for women in families with unemployment. In Men's Departments, they encouraged unemployed men to see themselves as "capable citizens" whose identities were threatened by joblessness, but the priorities and activities of settlements' Women's Departments indicate that workers did not see women's identities as being at risk. Instead of charging women with the capability to shape responses to unemployment, settlement workers aimed to help women perform their roles within the constraints of economic hardship. In other words, women in families suffering from unemployment were encouraged to continue their work maintaining the home and family. Departments offered classes that taught women how to cook, shop, and raise families with less money and limited food options. Most importantly, settlement workers planned activities to lift spirits, often by distraction, which meant that they discouraged women from pondering employment issues as members of Men's Departments did. At the same time, they suggested that even during the unemployment crisis, women's identities remained intact, and that women's role in the Depression was to protect their families and their family position.

Settlement workers considered their work with mothers to be of utmost importance, for while unemployed men felt isolated, overwhelmed, and guilty, settlement workers believed, women bore the weight of the whole family's pain.[54] Lea Taylor described to Chicago Commons supporters how the mothers she worked with, who collected and managed the experiences of every family member, served as a barometer for entire families and even the community: "They know how anxious a bread winner is to hold a job. They know what it is to worry about the boy on the street corner. They know how it feels to have to tell a little child that there is little food in the house, or to see it go out in the cold weather poorly clad."[55] Unlike their husbands, mothers carried, and attempted to mitigate, other family members' struggles. Their experience of the Depression was, in fact, everyone else's experiences.

For these women, settlement leaders organized programs that were intended to ease their concerns. As in the men's programs, these activities frequently focused on fellowship and entertainment. Settlement workers from around the city directed mothers to the Chicago Federation of Settlements Mothers' League, which hosted activities and discussions between women from a variety of neighborhoods. And within settlements, mothers were invited to participate in picnics, evenings of games and singing, and dramatic productions.[56] Settlement workers believed that their programs were as crucial as material aid; as Commons worker Martha E. Carris explained, parties and Christmas plays gave mothers "some of the lift that makes it possible for them to weather the many problems that beset them."[57]

Recreation and entertainment could certainly distract mothers from their obligations, but most women's programs centered on enabling mothers to better fulfill their domestic duties, even with reduced income. In the first year of serious unemployment, Vittum proclaimed the NUS Department of Homemaking and Health to be "the hub of our wheel," as "a well-ordered home is the recognized unit in American community life." These programs instructed women in their persistent responsibilities at home and their roles as home managers, despite the crisis. Settlement workers, then, offered a strikingly similar narrative as that articulated by Komarovsky and other social scientists: individual efforts, they suggested, could influence the family's ability to manage unemployment. Much of the effort, their work indicated, should come from the mother.[58]

Although many of the home-centered clubs and classes had an air of middle-class domesticity, they were quite practical, focusing on making the best home environment with limited resources. Clubs instructed mothers in home nursing, making furniture out of boxes, and quilting. Most common were lessons in cooking for a family with only relief grocery orders, which tended to offer limited options and frequently exasperated those on relief. Cooking lessons, demonstrations in meal planning, and talks on health and nutrition all served to aid women in managing life on relief. Working-class mothers in West Town were instructed as part of a massive shift toward thrift and domestic industry. Women around the country learned to can their own foods instead of buying canned goods, initiated a surge in home sewing, and planted gardens. Settlement workers, then, were encouraging their neighbors to take part in what could be a creative and even ingenious endeavor to, as historian Ruth Milkman puts it, "substitute their own labor for goods and services they had formerly purchased."[59]

At the same time, with so many women working to bolster their husband's wages (or lack thereof), settlement programs were especially attentive to working women. Mothers who took their children to the Chicago Commons day nursery were encouraged to also meet with each other on a weekly basis. Together, these working and single mothers were instructed in many of the same skills as mothers who were not employed. The nursery mothers took lessons from an infant welfare nutrition worker, who taught mothers about infant needs and diet. Day nursery workers like Marjorie Ingraham understood these mothers to be no less of home managers but filling their role with a handicap.[60] In so doing, Ingraham and other settlement workers emphasized the rigidness of family roles and their conviction that even a breadwinning woman should be in charge of the home. Caseworkers also met with them to discuss children's behavior and how to treat such problems as delinquency, suggesting that mothering while working, and in a home with unemployment or desertion, put the family at risk for what Taylor described as "the many problems present in such homes."[61]

As early as 1930, settlement workers indicated that, however much they may have endorsed women's homemaking and child rearing, they were also fully aware that many of their neighbors would not have been able to survive the early years of the Depression without their wives and daughters entering the labor market. Ingraham described being a typical working mother in 1932: "Working mothers earned very little this year. One, a skilled worker, was paid $1.25 for two days' work on a dress which sold for $14.95 in a State Street store. Tailor-shop mothers often waited all day for work, and sometimes earned only carfare and lunch money or less." Many of these women were supplying a large portion of their families' incomes. Historian S. J. Kleinberg has estimated that as many as one-third of all married women who worked provided the only income their families would see. In light of this reality, settlement workers funded work projects for men and women. In 1931, Chicago Commons workers organized a garment-making workshop at the settlement. For five months, women gathered in this workshop to make garments out of "old or raw material." In that time, the women made 476 garments and repaired another 506. Taylor emphasized that "one of its major values was the fellowship of the group and the noticeable effects upon the individuals in it, and their attitude toward life."[62]

Yet settlement leaders like Taylor exhibited a tension between the ideal of the breadwinner economic model and the desire to assist their neighbors. Settlement leaders created opportunities for temporary work, but they continued to emphasize (if implicitly) the appropriate family structure and roles. In 1933, the Chicago Commons Girls' Department took a house survey of 182 families in the neighborhood and found that more than half of the families had no employed members. In their description of their findings, presented in an annual report, the settlement workers revealed their assumptions about employment in the Depression. They described how "two-third[s] of the group of gainful workers (excluding mothers) were unemployed, or the proportion of 658 out of 1,000 workers." They continued, "In addition there were 7 mothers working: three steadily and four irregularly—who are not included in the above figures."[63] In other words, working mothers were not counted as employed, and settlement workers perceived unemployment to be a distinctly male problem. In the aforementioned nursery study, the author described families with "serious unemployment of the father, necessitating the finding of work by the mother."[64] Settlement workers did not count these working mothers as employed, as their employment was only out of necessity and was not sufficient for the family or for settlement statistics.

West Town mothers frequenting settlements like NUS soon learned that even though it was admissible that they worked, they still had an obligation to fulfill their roles as mother. Vittum, who could certainly betray her emotions in house meetings, informed the NUS staff of her expectations for some less-involved settlement mothers. In describing the NUS Cooking Class for Women, Vittum complained, "Only 34 women have registered for this class, and it has an average attendance of 20 to 22." Her sense that neighborhood mothers were shirking their duties and taking advantage of the settlement was palpable in her recommendation for action: "If more women do not come," she charged, "we may have to tell them we will have to withhold relief for a while, and if they are not interested in the lessons we give they are not interested in the food we give either."[65] In part, Vittum's concerns likely stemmed from a desire to reserve relief funds for actively participating neighbors. Yet her focus on a women's cooking class hints at the priority that NUS workers gave to women's domestic activities. Mothers who were unwilling to fulfill their social obligations, her comments suggest, should suffer the consequences.

Assembling Entitlement from Casework and Club Work

When Klur, an NUS caseworker, made her rounds on November 24, 1931, she met a woman who almost certainly was ashamed to be failing at her duties: a mother who, having only milk in the house, had to send her children to her sister-in-law for a real meal.[66] The mother had herself been surviving on coffee and crackers for the previous two days and likely felt a strange combination of humiliation and gratitude upon seeing Klur. The caseworker could provide some form of relief, but her material aid might very well come with some judgment and perhaps an admonition to join her at a settlement activity sometime. What neither this mother nor Klur could have realized—in the haze of desperation and scrambling to recover—was that Klur, along with her fellow caseworkers and settlement program organizers, was cobbling together a series of ideas and beliefs about this mother's new and startling poverty.

Settlement workers' ideas began with the notion that for the time being, relief was an unavoidable, necessary part of life, and they included the corollary that many of the people asking for aid were not themselves to blame for their situation. Yet in the process of assessing their neighbors and distributing relief, Klur and her compatriots at times slid into the dangerous practice of treating some petitioners as less deserving of aid than others—dangerous because caseworkers relied on sometimes contradictory indications of need, decorum, and cleanliness. At the same time, Klur's coworkers in the Men's and Women's Departments developed the conviction that *all* unemployed workers deserved to be cared for as innocents in an environmental catastrophe. Their programs in intellectual discussion and recreation suggested to the unemployed that while jobless, they could still maintain their dignity and even offer useful ideas and opinions about the state of labor. Wives, who took cooking classes in the evenings after working, learned that their job was to be unemployed unless absolutely necessary, for their families and homes needed them.

Within a few years, settlement workers and their neighbors had built a framework for understanding and responding to the wave of unemployment, which would come to shape their responses to the Great Depression. In the daily practice of their lives—in visiting neighbors, hosting events, and managing budgets—settlement workers developed the sense that many of the newly poor deserved material assistance, the notion that attention to home and family denoted worthiness, and the conviction that the benefits of full employment belonged to unemployed men. In the same years—1930–1932—unemployed workers and settlement leaders would bring these ideas to early labor organizing, and by 1932, settlement leaders would take them to relief officials in the city, legislators in Springfield, and members of Congress in Washington, DC.

4

Entitled to Relief

"The Chicago situation is very serious," wrote Lea Taylor in early 1932. "Relief funds will be exhausted in February, and even now they are giving such inadequate relief that standards of living are almost dropping out of sight." As the head resident of Chicago Commons and daughter of founder Graham Taylor, Lea Taylor spent her whole life at the near-north Chicago settlement. Thus Taylor was intimately aware of her neighbors' vain attempts at finding work and equally futile efforts at acquiring relief. She described a city "at a standstill, or rather slipping down hill fast."[1] Yet just over a year later, Taylor would express hope, noting "a very strong difference in the general attitude and the intensity of the situation."[2] Unemployed workers, who came to Chicago Commons to fill their free time, were articulating their right to relief during the Great Depression and the federal government's responsibility to provide it.

In the intervening year, Taylor had joined her assistant head resident in founding the Chicago Workers Committee on Unemployment (WCOU) and facilitated a movement that gave voice and relief to Chicago's thousands of unemployed workers. The committee's efforts were perhaps the decisive factor in the change Taylor described. Twenty thousand members strong at its peak, the WCOU called for drastic changes in the relationship between the government—state and, ultimately, federal—and the poor. From 1931 to 1936, the committee, which was made up of workers rendered dependent by the Great Depression, pressured government and philanthropy leaders for more relief funds. Amid widespread suspicion of the dole, the committee claimed that relief and unemployment insurance were workers' right, owed to them by the federal government and free of stigma. And they claimed that although it was the government's responsibility to ensure the well-being of its citizenry, the poor knew best what they needed.

Settlement leaders on the committee—namely, Lea Taylor and Karl Borders of Chicago Commons, Harriet Vittum of the Northwestern University Settlement House (NUS), and Esther Kohn of Hull House—echoed the findings of the National Federation of Settlements (NFS) regarding unemployment. Like the settlement workers on the 1927 Unemployment Committee, and much like settlement leaders at the turn of the twentieth century, members of the WCOU asserted that the jobless were poor because of the economy and not because of their character, making them legitimate recipients of aid. With this belief, they also assured their donors and legislators that the unemployed were neither paupers nor loafers.

Yet while the 1927 campaign proclaimed worker vulnerability during prosperous times, the WCOU emphasized the very present Depression. As such, whereas the NFS unemployment studies focused on social insurance, the WCOU emphasized that relief came first, although unemployment insurance was the long-term goal. The WCOU's main complaints were about the system of casework-based relief that even settlement workers used to distribute funds. Through protesting Chicago's relief system and authoring reports detailing life in the Depression, the WCOU pressured lawmakers to sanction government-funded relief and work programs.

Beginning in 1931 and lasting for more than five years, the WCOU agitated for quality relief. At its inception, the committee brought community members together, and by offering venues for those suffering to understand each other, it encouraged the formation of a movement based on common experiences and desires. In 1931 and 1932, the WCOU became an organized movement that nurtured collective action and exploited fears about radicalism to gain influence.

By utilizing the connections of reformers and the grassroots organizing of laborers, the WCOU developed into a significant poor people's movement. Ultimately, it created building blocks for major New Deal policies that would alter the relationship between the government and its people by articulating workers' right to relief and to social insurance. In 1932, the NFS and settlement workers used their research materials to ensure the passage of Wisconsin's unemployment insurance law (the first of its kind in the nation), and in 1933, Taylor presented WCOU and settlement material at the Illinois legislature's hearing on unemployment insurance. Just two years later, social insurance would be part of the national infrastructure.

Gaining public support for federal relief, however, required a major intellectual shift among unemployed workers as well. At the start of the Depression, most workers tackled the problems associated with their unemployment and subsequent poverty independently or within their families. But testimony from 1932 reveals that these workers were now beginning to see themselves as participants in a city- and even countrywide economic collapse. As the scale of the Depression hit them, unemployed workers became comfortable defining their claims as legitimate and holding state and federal governments responsible. WCOU leaders created the space in which workers could define themselves and unite, but the workers gave the WCOU a movement.

Achieving Cognitive Liberation

Scholars and New Dealers alike have reflected on the Herbert Hoover years as a time when the poor stomached their fate with what David Kennedy calls a "curious apathy." In 1933, journalist Lorena Hickok, sent around the country to report on Americans in the Depression, described unemployed Kentucky miners who took relief cuts without protest. "Little groups of people," Kennedy writes, "many of them illiterate, straggled to closed relief agencies, stared helplessly at written notices announcing the end of aid, and silently shuffled away."[3] In 1933, Hickok herself described miners in West Virginia who, although they had not worked for eight years and suffered under meager relief budgets, voiced "relatively few complaints."[4] But the year before Hickok anxiously asked Eleanor Roosevelt why the poor were not rallying, Chicago's unemployed had begun to see themselves as unified. As members of the Chicago WCOU, they turned despair into frustration and asked senators and even the president what the government was going to do about their situation.

The success of unemployed workers' organizing in the 1930 was not a given, for many of these jobless workers were the kinds of people whom the NFS described as resistant to charity and prone to blaming themselves for unemployment. Before these workers organized collectively, they needed to see themselves as one of many and not at fault for their condition. In this perception, they echoed the beliefs of settlement workers who, years before, had argued that unemployment was not the fault of the worker, and they drew from settlement discussion groups where they discussed employment and social insurance. This shift occurred early in 1932 and was made visible in their report on a series of open hearings in the city.

The WCOU organized in September 1931, when concerned community leaders held a meeting for unemployed men at Humboldt Park United Methodist Church, led by the Reverend W. B. Waltmire. The fifty attendees who came expressed frustration about their poverty and curiosity about the WCOU's proposal that they organize based on their unemployment. The following week, Waltmire hosted an even larger group of unemployed workers, who came to hear local labor activist Borders. Borders was a Chicago Commons resident who organized current events clubs and speakers on labor and politics. At this time, Borders was also serving as the executive secretary of the League for Industrial Democracy (LID), a decades-old organization committed to spreading the tenets of democracy and socialism. In the interwar period, the LID (under the direction of such socialist leaders as Norman Thomas, Upton Sinclair, and Walter Reuther) emphasized the potential for union organizing among workers. As the effects of the Great Depression spread through Chicago, however, Borders turned his attention to a new kind of organizing: among the unemployed. Toward this end, Borders founded the WCOU.

Borders and the Reverend Waltmire were but two of many Chicago liberals, reformers, community activists, and labor leaders who first formed the WCOU. The founders included numerous individuals involved in settlement houses, such as Lea Taylor, the head resident for Chicago Commons and founding member of the NFS unemployment study of the 1920s; Harriet Vittum, who presided over NUS; and University of Chicago economist Paul H. Douglas, who had advised the NFS Unemployment Committee. Many of the WCOU founders had experience in Progressive-Era reform organizations, including the Immigrants' Protective League and the Legal Aid Society. They sat on the National Labor Defense Council, the Chicago Civil Liberties Committee, and the Chicago Forum Council. From their reform-minded roots, WCOU leaders charted a path that was focused on the problems and scale unique to unemployment in the 1930s. For members of the WCOU, the need for relief eclipsed issues related to labor, children's rights, and morality. Moreover, they professed that state and federal governments were responsible for providing relief funds. They were, according to one WCOU member and student, "an imposing letterhead array of Chicago's best known liberals."[5]

In 1931, WCOU leaders pointed out for those remaining skeptics the sheer scope of unemployment in the city. Unemployment, they explained, reverberated throughout Chicago. Families of the unemployed slid into impoverishment, many had no option but to rely on charity for survival, and the city's charities and neighborhood agencies reported a burden that they could not bear. Just one year later, "there were some 624,000 people in the city of Chicago who were unemployed, although they were able and willing to work; . . . the various charities were carrying a load of some 125,000 families; . . . relief funds were being dispensed at the rate of about $100,000 a day, which would mean that the funds available would be exhausted early in February; and . . . the situation seemed to be getting worse all the time."[6]

The founders of the WCOU argued that workers were in the best position to effectively describe their own needs, so most of these "best known liberals" stepped aside to organize themselves as a separate but allied group, which they called the Citizens Committee. As it seemed less radical and more respectable, the Citizens Committee acted as an advisory board and crucially served as a liaison between the unemployed and city elites. Its membership included a wider scope of the political spectrum, from left-leaning WCOU founders like Karl Borders to politically moderate figures like Mrs. Wilbur Fribley, of the Chicago Housewives League. In January 1932, this group of liberals joined WCOU members in hosting a series of public hearings in the city, inviting anyone affected by unemployment to tell their story.

To gather support from jobless workers and publicize their plight, the Citizens Committee and the WCOU first organized seven open hearings around the city during the second week of January 1932. Beginning with the near-north settlement district,[7] Chicagoans affected by the Depression—workers, landlords, grocers, pastors, aid workers, and educators—were invited to "give the members of the communities the opportunity to tell to a wider audience just what ha[d] been happening to them in this period of serious depression."[8] During the hearings, 175 people articulated the major struggles of Chicago's poor and unemployed communities. Their testimony, read closely, offers insight into what these poor workers thought about their poverty and whom they deemed responsible. Citizens Committee members intentionally planned their hearings to reach a broad spectrum of people affected by the crisis, a fact that is confirmed by their decision to hold the January 12 hearing at St. Stephen African Methodist Episcopal (AME) Church, located in Garfield Park, on Chicago's west side. Although this neighborhood in the 1930s was not yet predominantly African American, the AME church was and is a predominantly African American denomination. Yet a look at the report from the hearings indicates that although settlement workers and members of the Citizens Committee were not uninterested in the plight of unemployed African Americans, they were also not interested in discussing racism itself.

The Citizens Committee then compiled the hearings report, intended to convince city leaders that relief efforts were failing and compel them to greater action. The hearings and following report expanded on the NFS research, presenting personal stories as evidence and emphasizing the vulnerability of the poor. Titled *An Urban Famine*, the report likened the Depression to a natural disaster and the unemployed its hapless victims. Much like the authors of the NFS report, the editors of *An Urban Famine* argued that their research was more persuasive than statistical research, which was widely available but had not compelled people to act. As the report explained:

> It was felt that, if the people who were in a position to provide the requisite funds for immediate relief were to be convinced that they must act, and if adequate plans for the prevention of a recurrence of this disaster were to be formulated, then these

statistics would have to be converted into terms of human situations, of personality and community disorganization.[9]

In other words, committee members hoped that these hearings would "put a human face on the Depression," evincing their belief that individual stories rather than cold data were more likely to persuade decision makers. They anticipated that *An Urban Famine* would ultimately prompt relief legislation in Springfield and even in Washington, DC.

As *An Urban Famine* revealed, the hearings also played an important role in enabling Chicago's workers to organize as the WCOU. In the wake of the 1932 hearings, and in the midst of WCOU activities and protests, workers enacted a form of what such social movement theorists as Doug McAdam term "cognitive liberation," or an intellectual ability to see themselves as members of a collective struggle and their claims as legitimate. In other words, over the course of a series of public hearings, the unemployed embraced a sense of entitlement. In the wake of the hearings, WCOU leaders convinced lawmakers and donors of the same.

At the WCOU open hearings, poor Chicagoans described their plight candidly and with anxiety, but largely without self-hate or apologies. They laid out a series of problems that, taken together, made life almost unbearable. Without any real income, these newly unemployed struggled to pay for the basic requirements of urban life: coal, gas for cooking and electricity, food, clothing, rent, and carfare. Case records and interviews indicate that the unemployed went to extreme lengths to survive financial hardship without taking charity. They shut down rooms of their houses to save on coal; they waited outside factories all day in the hopes of getting a job; and they moved in with relatives to save on rent. Those who did finally go to relief stations begged, and even threatened, caseworkers for aid, grocery orders, or coal slips. These individual efforts brought no relief. The economy refused to offer them respite, their elected officials were skeptical of their plight, and even charity (although a last resort) proved unnavigable and underfunded.

If unemployment had brought the speakers to their knees, the relief system left them there. By the time of the hearings, Chicago's charities and relief agencies, coordinated by the Bureau of Public

Welfare, had exhausted their budgets and were preparing to cut food orders by 25 percent. The relief an unemployed Chicagoan could get was highly problematic. Most relief was in-kind rather than in cash, and the grocery orders that the unemployed relied on were meager and overpriced. In the hearings, Chicago's poor described increased evictions and charities refusing to pay rents, a product of a relief system that would only subsidize a first-month's rent. They also faced daylong waits at relief stations, after which they might receive, as one Chicagoan described, "less than a dollar a day (two weeks' grocery order) to feed five, and my boys can eat more than I can."[10] And long lines at charities and medical centers made them almost not worth visiting. One poor parent (witness 147) explained that the delays at the free central dispensary might actually prolong her child's illness: "I wouldn't take a chance of taking him to the dispensary and probably waiting two days. I am hoping he will be better today."[11]

Finally, these workers fought a culture that dissuaded many from seeking aid. The newly impoverished hardly had time to teach themselves about the city's system of relief before they found themselves destitute. "The present system of relief," committee leaders asserted, "reduced every applicant to pauperism before he is given consideration." Moreover, it was a well-known phenomenon that unemployed Americans frequently avoided seeking relief at all costs. Reports of suicide suggested that, at times, even death was preferable to the dole. Chicago workers indicated the same hesitancy. Committee members describe how it was "in desperation" that many unemployed clients came "to the point where all [their] American training has taught [them] it is a disgrace to come, namely, to ask for charity." Finally, as discussed in the previous chapter, the same year saw overworked caseworkers—with as many as six times their usual caseload—employing artificial distinctions between worthy and unworthy clients. What money Chicago's unemployed had was being spent on bad food and moving costs. Relief funds, which were to many a chimera, came with a cultural stigma attached.[12]

Refusing to be thus stigmatized, the unemployed workers who testified in 1932 instead described themselves as victims of a hostile climate. Testimony that depicted hopeless situations, for instance, directed culpability away from the poor themselves. An unemployed and impoverished parent described being trapped by circumstances not under his or her control: "Now, I have two boys to go to work and they haven't been working for two years and two months. . . . [T]hey would like to go and look for a job, but they can't because they haven't any shoes."[13] Moreover, rather than being ashamed (or focusing on her shame), witness 133 asserted that this family's poverty was not for want of initiative. Witness 249 also told his or her story without begging forgiveness of the public:

> Just before New Year's, I was expecting my grocery order of fifteen dollars. I waited for it, and it didn't come. I said, "We will get it by New Year's and eat beans if we don't eat anything else." We had beans left from the County (rations) and had beans for New Year's. I went there Saturday and waited from nine to two. I was handed a ticket and told to come Monday. I went there Monday and got my grocery order, which was cut to twelve dollars.[14]

The distinct lack of shame among these witnesses reallocated responsibility from these struggling laborers onto their society. Sometimes the absence of guilt even rendered formerly shameful acts innovative and entrepreneurial. One witness boldly described his participation in the most disgraceful of bum behaviors: "There is in the neighborhood a public eating place, and sometimes when the hash has been warmed up too many times they cannot very well put it on the table. The fit place for it is in the garbage can, but it is not yet spoiled and they give it to me."[15] This Chicagoan's willingness to make public his begging for and eating old restaurant hash indicated a belief that he was the victim of something beyond individual failings and personal poverty. Moreover, the act of searching for alternative avenues to food could actually prove that an unemployed Chicagoan continued to be productive and independently motivated. This testimony, then, was a public declaration of creative responses to undeserved poverty.

The frustration and creativity expressed by those who testified reflected a commonality in the history of urban poverty: that, as Peter Mandler explains, "at no point did the forms in which charity was offered match the forms in which it was needed." Jobless workers who found themselves with useless or insufficient relief rations also found themselves in the frustrating position of having to make use of relief as it came to them and best fit it to their needs. In Chicago in 1932, this task seemed rather futile.[16]

Frustrated with their lack of options, many abandoned the endless, seemingly pointless days of waiting in relief lines and outside factories. Instead of trying the same thing again and again, these poor workers asserted that they had developed new methods for survival. "I didn't have anything to eat this morning," explained witness 244. "I went to the National Tea and took a loaf of bread, went to another grocery store and got a jar of jam and that is what I had for breakfast this morning. I am not ashamed to say it. As long as I have to have something to eat, I will get it if I have to rob."[17]

With this admission, witness 244 indicated a shift toward what sociologist McAdam terms "cognitive liberation," or the ability of the poor to see their concerns as reasonable and shared. Harold Kerbo and Richard Shaffer further argue that cognitive liberation "allows social movement members to legitimize their demands in their own eyes, and thus makes them feel more justified to act."[18] As the 1932 testimony revealed, Chicago's unemployed determined that their suffering came from an external source rather than laziness or apathy, that they had attempted every strategy by which to escape the Depression (to no avail), and that even neighborhood institutions were unable to survive economic collapse. By (and because of) the 1932 hearings, these poor began the process of becoming a movement. For some unemployed, this cognitive shift allowed them to use illegal means of survival, including theft. Witness 146 defended these new means of survival: "I was brought up with the understanding that honesty was the best policy. I have existed, for the past several months, under a condition where if I were honest it would not be a virtue but a deliberate sin, inasmuch as it would deprive my children of the necessary food."[19]

Cognitive liberation, however, was not limited to the unemployed, for it also served to unite divided communities. *An Urban Famine* revealed that despite putting pressure on the poor, landlords and grocers were not the villains in the Depression but victims of the same external forces. The "haves" in these poor communities explained that they, too, were trapped by the Depression and struggled to offer what little help they could. As relief funds were rarely made available to pay for rent, one landlord explained, he earned nothing from his tenants unless he spent the money for an eviction notice. Before the hearings, organizers explained, poor tenants wondered why their landlords had limited grace. Landlords also felt the divide: "We buy just one bottle of milk a day. The people who live in the house get three bottles of milk a day from the charities."[20] Neighborhood grocers, who extended thousands of dollars in debt to their communities, seemed to be punished for their kindness. "I have a grocery store these ten years. I have now no customers," lamented one grocer. "I can get no help."[21] And relief workers, some of whom had organized the hearings, confessed that their budgets could barely afford to extend relief through the winter. For many unemployed Chicagoans, these were the figures who daily stymied their attempts to endure, but in these hearings, they joined the unemployed in a community's cognitive liberation.

In front of their tenants, customers, and relief recipients, they revealed how the Depression had ruined them and how a larger system of relief, although meant to sustain poor communities, actually added to their burdens. Community grocers explained that the city's grocery slips, through which private agencies paid for food for the poor, could only be used at specific city stores. "We have lost about twenty-five customers," another grocer complained, "through charity slips on the chain stores. When a customer owes you he does not like to come in when he cannot pay you." Grocer number 93 then laid out the implications of the relief system that seemed to offer insufficient aid to the poor while also breaking down the kinds of institutions and relationships that would facilitate survival within a community. Whereas a family in 1931 may have felt resentment toward a seemingly unsympathetic grocer, members of the Citizens Committee described at the hearings how "the grocer and the landlord had a chance to tell their side of the story, charity workers explained the handicaps under which they were working, and many misunderstandings were cleared up."[22]

It was in settlement houses, churches, and Young Men's Christian Associations (YMCAs) that the poor and their landlords, grocers, and relief workers could see each other as having the same goals and the same struggles. They were, the report explained, creating a unified front that might "strengthen the hands of all the agencies working toward amelioration of the tragic conditions."[23] These were the kinds of individual intellectual modifications that allowed the unemployed and their communities to legitimize their struggle for themselves and crystallize their sense that outside figures should be held responsible for their struggles.[24] In the coming years, their participation with the WCOU would encourage many to simultaneously blame and call on the government. As the unemployed and their institutions described the creative measures they had taken to maintain their community, they began to develop the kind of group consciousness that was necessary for movement building.[25]

While most of the 1932 testimony only indicated the beginning of their politicization, at the hearings, some were already looking to the government: "A year or two ago if I had seen somebody holding up somebody else I might have risked my life to stop it," explained one unemployed worker. "Today, I would say, 'I hope he has a big fat politician by the neck and kills him or a big fat banker.'"[26] In this testimony, perhaps more than any other, witness 146 expressed an indignation that had the potential to undergird a movement for change.

Yet the stories told in the hearings were isolated. They indicated individual shifts in consciousness, and even an emerging recognition of shared suffering, but not (yet) a sense of group complaints and goals. It was not until after the hearings, at the urging of WCOU leaders, that the witnesses and their unrecorded neighbors began to think of themselves as part of a larger movement. In response to the hearings, members of the WCOU and their allies began to make new claims for public relief.

The WCOU, the Citizens Committee, and the Protection of Morality

From 1931 until 1934, WCOU members rallied for relief. Their strategies and success evince the kind of movement that relied on the restlessness of the masses and the skills and resources of their leaders. Although unemployed workers built one of the most notable poor people's movements in modern U.S. history, they were bolstered by members of the Citizens Committee—experienced community workers and labor organizers—who had the connections necessary to bring permanent change to state and federal legislatures.[27] Members of the Citizens Committee published and disseminated the hearings report in an effort to persuade legislators and city leaders to take notice of the plight of the unemployed. In their efforts, they crafted a justification of entitlement that rested on the idea that "unwarranted" poverty was bad for the poor, their neighborhoods, and their cities. They warned that joblessness could draw workers into immorality and apathy and offered their demands as the solution.

WCOU and Citizens Committee leaders used the hearings report to lay out a few key demands. In its first years, the WCOU focused solely on relief. As its members pushed for greater relief funds, from any source possible, they targeted three groups: Chicago's major donors, Illinois state legislators, and ultimately the federal government. To settlement workers in 1931, it was clear that the city's charities could not keep up with the rate of unemployment and need. Settlements, as has been discussed, attempted to make up some of the difference, but their meager budgets could only offer so much. Some on the Citizens Committee held out hope that increased funds for private charity would buoy the unemployed. But given the dismal outcomes of the 1931 Chicago relief drive, it became increasingly clear that public relief was more promising.

Thus, settlement workers like Taylor, Vittum, and Kohn saw no other option but to throw their energy into acquiring more state and federal funds for relief and aid. Representatives of the city's major charities, religious institutions, community centers, and labor organizations joined them. Perhaps surprisingly, although the Citizens Committee included a few well-to-do Chicagoans, and although neighborhood charity workers continued to request donations from their standard lists of donors, committee members saw no involvement by any Chicago relief officials. The Citizens Committee and WCOU members daily witnessed unemployed men deserving of work but barely able to acquire charity in the form of coal and food. In the climate of crisis, then, they *both* argued for the obligation of the government to unemployed workers (making claims to a welfare government) *and* treated their regular donors as fundamental to the survival of Chicago's unemployed.

WCOU organizers called on private and public sources for aid, but they also argued that public funds should provide a long-term solution, largely because private campaigns for funding had proven unequivocally unsuccessful. In 1932, for instance, WCOU leaders decried the insufficiency of the Joint Emergency Relief Fund (JERF). To committee leaders, the JERF experience served as evidence of the private sector's inability to meet the great demand for relief. "The resources of private charity, the Joint Emergency Relief Fund, although administered with utmost care, are totally inadequate to meet this disaster," Taylor argued in 1932. "The amounts allocated to each family furnish only the barest amount of food and fuel. The relief is entirely inadequate." Taylor and the WCOU suggested that instead of relying on local donors to rescue the city, "The legislature must find a way to provide immediate revenue."[28] The committee was clear: public funds were crucial to the survival of Chicago's unemployed.

Second, the WCOU requested that new relief be more equitable—that is, in the form of cash relief and applicable toward any rent payments. The committee railed against the fundamental flaws in the city's welfare and relief bureaucracy. They decried the Bureau of Public Welfare's policy to cover rent for the first month but end rent relief after that. The system, committee members charged, actually encouraged the transience that can come with poverty and fostered resentments between community members. Desperate landlords, knowing that their desperate tenants would receive no aid until evicted, were encouraged to look for new tenants from the relief office. Tenants had limited options, and even generous landlords would eventually evict them (as they were also suffering from the consequences of the Depression). The unemployed could move, which, as the hearings report explained, many families had been forced to do repeatedly. Or they could invite family members to move in and share the burden of rent, such as one family who "had to go live with a sister who had five children, which made thirteen children in one place."[29] Finally, Chicago's unemployed at times found that the best option was to resort to unsavory measures to obtain rent money. A desperate Chicagoan declared, "I made up my mind I moved four places already and I won't move again. If I have to go out and rob, I am going to do it."[30]

Third, and related to the second demand, the WCOU asserted that it was fundamentally an organization of *workers*: although unemployed, they aimed to work again and looked for the leaders and legislators who could return them to employment. With this assertion, the committee in essence expanded the category of "employable" to include people who were without work because of the economy. Thus, the mass of jobless in the 1930s could claim themselves as workers first and foremost, regardless of their actual employment status. The committee also favored programs that would return these workers to the job market. Citizens Committee editors described hearing testimony in which a "preference for a *work fund* rather than charity was unanimous."[31] In this goal, the WCOU articulated its priorities: relief first, but work finally.

Much like the NFS Unemployment Committee, the WCOU counted on personal stories, rather than data, to change the way people thought about the crisis. Its members explained that the hearings "resulted from the recognition that there was a certain type of information concerning the situation which was not available, namely an intimate picture of what has been taking place within the communities which have been most seriously affected."[32] WCOU members hoped that if they distributed *An Urban Famine* among policy makers and city leaders, they would expose Chicago's faulty and insufficient system of relief to the people who could improve it. Although they still anticipated receiving assistance from private benefactors, WCOU members ultimately hoped that by publicizing the "face" of the Depression, they could pressure city, state, and federal legislators to provide more relief to Chicago's unemployed workers.

Members of the Citizens Committee understood their job to be to recruit support from political and city leaders, which they did by stressing that some poor communities were trustworthy. They took two steps to do so. First, they joined the unemployed in convincing potential donors and politicians that this kind of poverty was new and that these people belonged to a different, trustworthy, nonapathetic category of poor. *An Urban Famine* editors distinguished those who were recently rendered poor by articulating the environmental roots of poverty, much as their settlement predecessors had. Second, the WCOU had to assure city philanthropists and state legislators that their contributions would not be into a new iteration of the dole. To successfully reshape welfare and the dole, editors articulated a distinction between relief and charity.[33] Thus, they identified this relief as legitimate and temporary and promised (not untruthfully) that its recipients were loath to accept charity.

In this approach, leaders of the Citizens Committee presented an alternative definition of poverty, one that harkened to the Progressive Era and recalled the founding philosophy of the first American settlement workers.[34] As in the first decade of the twentieth century,

Depression-era settlement houses articulated a kind of poverty in which the poor were not paupers but rather victims of the whims of an unpredictable economy, avaricious capitalists, and (at best) clueless politicians. By emphasizing the environmental roots of poverty, settlement workers challenged the popular assumption that the poor were lazy, apathetic, or dishonest and thus unworthy of relief. Their implicit arguments promoted public relief and insurance for the unemployed without alienating legislators or private donors. Just as the unemployed asserted their legitimacy during the hearings, committee leaders used the hearing report to convey the same to readers: policy makers and Chicago elites. The WCOU encouraged elites to rethink the dole and to consider the ways in which the government could return the country to prosperity and order.

In redefining poverty, the editors of *An Urban Famine* capitalized on and overturned American elites' fears of the inevitable slide into pauperism. Their work was largely rhetorical, and the 1932 report nicely laid out their strategy.[35] In Section C of the report, titled "The Breakdown of Personal and Family Morale," the writers made explicit the fact that the Depression was at the root of many Chicagoans' poverty and need. These workers, the WCOU explained, were fundamentally good people. Described as "men and women who have always taken care of themselves," they were trapped in an impossible environment. Even as their "hopes and plans for a better type of life for their children [were] destroyed in a few tragic months," Chicago's unemployed went to great extremes to "maintain their self-respect." But no matter what they did, whether "walking many miles every day and standing outside factories hours on end, day after day," or even looking for charity as a last resort, they saw "no end in sight."[36] One man testified:

I have a big family, seven. I live on the County and the United Charities to pay the rent, but nothing for clothing. I have been out of work for a year. . . . I was three months behind in rent in the place where I used to live. Then, they told me to move out. Now the same thing is happening in the place I am living. I have no money to pay the rent and the charities only pay one month in a new place. They tell you to keep moving. It is too much for a self-respecting man.[37]

Whereas objections to the dole hinged on the sense that handouts
led to apathy, *An Urban Famine* argued that the lack of work and the
stigma attached to relief ruined the morale of the poor.

The structure of the report itself confirmed long-held fears that
poverty and morality were causally related and that a breakdown of
morale and moral standards was the inevitable result of unchecked
poverty. Immediately following the section on morale came Section D, "The Breakdown of Community Moral Standards." When
families and individuals were forced to endure transience, insufficient grocery orders, and life without light, Section D claimed, they
would unavoidably push against the boundaries of moral upright-
ness. The report described behaviors that were "coming to be quite
generally approved in communities where unemployment and suffering are most serious":[38] community members stealing food or
merchandise, forcing reinstatement of gas and electricity, deceiving
caseworkers to receive more aid, and defaulting on loans or other
financial obligations. After poverty and unemployment had led to apathy, the report argued, communities and their members abandoned
their moral moorings. In this way, the report seemed to confirm the
widely held belief that the poor were not to be trusted.

However, the WCOU assuaged its readers against the threat of
pauperism by distinguishing between and connecting individual and
community failings. The structure of the report itself argued that
although individuals sustained a loss in *morale*, communities saw a
decline in *moral standards*. In other words, even though individual
people stole food, moral degradation was in no way a personal failing
but the unavoidable consequence of the passivity of the government.
The report explained, "Riots and much of the petty stealing that goes
on in these neighborhoods are to be interpreted as the inevitable result of a situation in which former, law-abiding citizens have been
forced to desperation through no fault of their own."[39] Unchecked
unemployment led individuals and families toward apathy and desperation and communities toward total breakdown.

While relief officials were attempting to preserve Chicago's local
system of relief and charity, committee members were proposing that
the city's poorly funded system of private relief led to personal apathy
and community degradation and that the solution was to increase
public funds. The report's editors wrote that they "came out of this

experience believing to a last person, First of all, that immediate and adequate relief must be given by state and federal appropriations, and Second, that charity from whatever source and in any amount is not the answer to this last infirmity of a noble nation."[40] With this statement, committee members made a rather specific claim: *private* charity would demoralize the unemployed, but *public* relief would allow them to live as dignified workers.

The WCOU's conviction against private charity rested on the widespread sense that, especially when inadequately funded, charity most significantly instilled a deep shame in its recipients—particularly when those recipients were the victims of an economic downturn, not paupers hoping to get by on the dole. In 1932, the Citizens Committee sent a letter to Governor Louis Emmerson and the Illinois state legislature in Springfield, describing among the unemployed "a sense of shame at having to ask for relief, a sense of injustice in that they are unemployed through no fault of their own, a demand for work, and through it all—restlessness and discouragement which leads toward desperation."[41] In this letter, committee organizers not only confirmed the widespread suspicion of the dole but also used decision makers' suspicions to defend federal funding for relief.

When relief and charity led to shame, committee members and unemployed workers argued, the solution should come from the government and, crucially, should include work. At the public hearings in 1932 and 1933, the Chicagoans who spoke (unemployed workers, teachers, charity workers, and religious figures) voiced a preference for public works projects rather than relief or charity. "The one thing that stood out as prominently in the hearings as anything else," the WCOU report stated, "was the repeated demand for work and the expressed aversion to having to take charity."[42] These appeals for work relief were as much practical as they were political, for they stemmed in part from observations about the deplorable state of relief. By 1932, caseworkers were carrying loads up to six times their normal size. Standards of casework lowered, and families waited longer hours to receive less relief, changes that read like undeserved punishment for legitimate, stand-up families. "Waiting long hours, or even days before a first interview," committee members explained, "is sometimes beyond the patience of a man who has had insufficient food."[43] Work relief, they claimed, would preserve dignity and give the unemployed a chance to earn the money they received. At the same time, the demand for work over charity assured elites that the government would indeed be funding productive members of society.

While members of the Citizens Committee defended their unemployed allies against accusations of pauperism, members of the WCOU staked a claim to better relief from the government while defending themselves against allegations of radicalism. The committee argued that, beyond providing jobs and dignity, public support would free up community organizations like settlement houses to return to their intended purpose: bettering the community. *An Urban Famine* lamented, "With large majorities of the people in these communities unemployed, with individual resources and all available credit eaten up, all agencies within the communities have had to turn their major efforts to basic relief work."[44] The local and private system of relief, they argued, was bad for workers *and* for community agencies. It was right and practical that the government should implement more lasting solutions.

Radicalism and Entitlement

The WCOU relied on the support of its advisory committee and hoped to appeal to legislators and relief officials. As the Communist Party (CP) gained traction in the United States, politicians and relief officials became increasingly wary of radicalism, yet WCOU members sounded a lot like a group they frequently worked with: the CP and its Unemployed Councils (UCs). Yet while members of the UCs and the WCOU frequently worked together, members of the WCOU self-consciously maintained their distance and championed the possibility of a worker-centered capitalism that would allow them full citizenship.[45] For WCOU members, full citizenship included financial security in the form of work or adequate relief and exemption from the humiliating world of casework.

In the first years of the Depression, the WCOU could have easily been perceived as a threat to an already unstable social order, shutting down any appeals to sympathetic legislators and potential donors. The national climate was contentious: in 1930, Cleveland police used a fire hose to battle three thousand unemployed rioters;[46] in 1932, General Douglas MacArthur led his troops to the Anacostia Flats in

Washington, DC, to remove (at the points of bayonets) thousands of protesting World War I veterans; and in the same year, Karl Emil Nygard was elected in Crosby, Minnesota, as the first Communist mayor in the United States.[47] And in Chicago, the CP was organizing jobless workers to protest the apparent failures of capitalism. In 1930s America, the WCOU might have seemed as radical as the Communist Party and as dangerous as food rioters, and it constantly faced the potential of being labeled as such. Its members were most likely to be associated with the CP's UCs, which seemed quite similar in goals and tactics. Both groups frequently made the same demands and even participated in the same acts of resistance.

Moreover, from an outsider's perspective, the UCs and WCOU members seemed like neat allies. The UCs first found shape around 1929 and were by mid-1930 central to the CP's activity. They focused on turning grievances from the unemployed into protests and direct action—for instance, canvassing a block to build support for a family threatened with eviction. The UCs in Chicago had a lot of independence, but the city's CP leaders frequently labored to insert party directives and goals into local work.[48] Their first few years saw rather sparse participation, but by 1932, the UCs boasted a membership of approximately twenty-two thousand members in forty-five local branches. Similarly, the WCOU was founded in 1931. It was also politically oriented to the left, having been founded by socialist members of the LID, but as its work was supported by the Citizens Committee, it perhaps appeared more moderate than its socialist founders. WCOU local branches, like the UCs, nurtured collective support and direct action. By 1932, the WCOU boasted twenty thousand members organized into fifty-two local branches, which would expand to sixty-six by 1934.

Members of the two groups joined forces in the fall of 1932, an especially fraught time for unemployed Chicagoans. The Illinois Emergency Relief Commission had just announced that all two-week grocery orders (which the unemployed had already deemed insufficient) would need to last an entire month. In this atmosphere of desperation, the UCs and the WCOU organized a joint hunger march, in which twenty-five thousand unemployed workers and their communities marched in pouring rain from the Loop to Grant Park. They carried signs that proclaimed, "Don't starve; fight!"[49] Together, the UCs and the WCOU achieved some amazing levels of worker organization in the 1930s, suggesting a solid alliance. Their 1932 march was one of the most successful of a spate of hunger marches around the nation that year. After the march, reports of worker unrest made their way to Springfield, where the state legislature agreed to increase state funds for relief, making Chicago one of the most generous cities of the early Depression. (See Chapter 5 for a discussion of the legislative battle.)[50]

Yet despite these successes, the WCOU and the UCs were as close to enemies as two groups of similarly marginalized protesters working together on a joint hunger march could be. In part, this clash had to do with the Communist International's aversion to forming alliances in the early 1930s (before the establishment of the "popular front") and CP members' conviction that every show of protest should also recruit for the party. But members of the WCOU were also wary of associating with the UCs, which their leaders saw as being kept on a short leash by the CP. WCOU organizers complained about UC members' tendency to mobilize for the CP. Seemingly in confirmation of these fears, at a planning meeting for the hunger march, CP members accused WCOU leader Borders of being a "betrayer of the working class." Ten days before the march, Borders sent a letter to "those organizations interested in making the unemployed demonstration on October 31st a non-political event." In the letter, he pointedly explains: "The Chicago Workers' Committee on Unemployment participated in good faith in the call for a united front movement to defeat the cut rations and raise the present miserable standard of relief in Chicago, but we are unalterably opposed to using the plight of the hungry unemployed workers as material for emotional propaganda for furthering the cause of any political party."[51] WCOU leaders hoped a joint conference would create consensus, but during the march, they were dismayed to see signs and banners in support of the CP. While the march was intended to be cooperative, instead, as Judith Trolander describes, it "left a bitter aftertaste."[52]

WCOU members' work with the UCs only intensified their commitment to acquiring nonradical solutions to unemployment. In part, they recognized that their local branches would likely fall apart under the pressure of Communist organizing.[53] Moreover, throughout the 1930s, the committee consistently advocated for the potential of government to ameliorate the unemployment crisis. Settlement workers, too, encouraged unemployed men to think of themselves as political actors and approach the crisis with "sound measures." In 1932, workers in the Adult Education Department at Chicago Commons described as one of their objectives to "help [the unemployed] realize that they need not be helpless tools of self-seeking politicians."[54] Yet they did not advocate abandoning the political system. Rather, settlement workers organized a letter-writing drive, in which eighteen hundred unemployed men sent postcards to their state representatives, which they hoped would "help political representatives from this district to have a clearer understanding of the needs" of the jobless.[55] In other words, despite their seeming alliance with the UCs, by 1932, WCOU members were advocating for workers' rights in defiance of CP prerogatives—apparently with the aim of preserving American capitalism.

WCOU leaders did, however, exploit elites' fears about radicalism and uprising. In their 1932 report, WCOU leaders warned legislators and Chicago elites that unemployment would lead to lawlessness and resentment: "We now know that there can be an urban famine which can have all the characteristics of a rural famine except one: A rural famine represents a failure of nature and seldom does man show a resentment against nature. An urban famine represents the failure of man and is very likely to arouse resentment."[56] Their warning was confirmed by reports offered in the city's newspapers. A *Tribune* article on January 31, 1932, described how a decent man in Evansville, Indiana, was driven to robbery. "Apologizing for what he proposed to do but explaining his family needed the money," the paper reports, "a middle aged man robbed A. R. Phillips, manager of a grocer here, last night, taking about $125 in cash and $55 in checks."[57] It was clear, the committee argued, that stability was tenuous at best.

In fact, WCOU members positioned themselves as bulwarks against possible revolution. In a January 1932 letter to Illinois governor Emmerson, the Citizens Committee warns, "Riots have already occurred and will occur, for hungry and desperate people cannot suffer too long and remain patient." While the Citizens Committee did not explicitly reference the CP, this statement certainly insinuated the possibility of revolution and likely would have pointed Emmerson to the recent Bolshevik revolution. For all the doom, though, the writers

offered a solution: "The cure is not to be found in forcible maintenance of order, but in *funds* which will allow adequate relief, and in
sound planning against similar disasters in the future."[58] In other
words, the Citizens Committee used the threat of revolution to promote their call for state relief funds—thus, simultaneously asserting
themselves as agitators for increased relief and distancing themselves
from the CP.

Throughout, WCOU members advocated for a specific kind of
capitalism, which would protect and value workers. It looked a bit
like welfare capitalism, except that members of the WCOU wanted a
stake in how it would work rather than reconstituting the paternalistic relationships in welfare capitalism. In this aim, they reflected
a growing sense of entitlement (the idea that the government—not
overthrown!—should and could grant its citizens protection from
unemployment, old age, etc.). Yet in the 1930s, ideas of entitlement
were always shaped by the overwhelming need for relief among jobless workers. Relief was central to WCOU members' daily existence,
and it shows up in virtually every WCOU document or statement.
For that reason, the arguments that members made about relief give
us a greater sense of the kind of capitalism they defended—one in
which workers were protected by the state, rewarded by private industry, and exempt from the humiliation of casework.

WCOU members' rhetoric about relief—which the unemployed
needed and abhorred—was dynamic, and its variations indicated
members' growing sense that workers (regardless of employment
status) were entitled to economic security. Certainly, jobless workers
in the Depression cared about relief and wanted it, especially because
they suffered from a floundering system of relief in Chicago. This
desire became clear in a 1932 Illinois Conference on Unemployment
hosted by the WCOU. The goal of the conference was to coordinate
responses to the crisis, and a substantial part of it was focused on
relief. Of four sessions, the second was focused entirely on "The Need
for Relief in Illinois," a reminder that relief was tantamount to survival during the 1930s.

In the years after the hearings and the hunger march, though,
WCOU flyers and protests began to specifically call for what members saw as their right to "adequate relief" and work. They frequently
described Chicago's relief system as making paupers out of every

applicant.[59] In 1934, the WCOU distributed pamphlets that described a "vicious system of pauper relief" in the city and claimed "the need for decent relief"[60] (see Figure 4.1). And in a November 1934 flyer, the WCOU listed seven demands (see Figure 4.2). Their top demand was "Cash relief; or full time job at union wages," with a total of five of the seven demands dealing with relief. At this point, most workers still received relief boxes (a box filled with specific food and home items) or grocery orders (a form of scrip to be used at the grocery store for purchasing only specific items). Cash relief, committee members argued, would allow jobless workers to control their spending. After a hearing (held one year after the original hearings), Taylor reported that "one woman gave a very good demonstration of what cash relief would mean: she brought in what she had purchased for a certain amount of money in the grocery where she was entitled to buy on a relief order, and then she had borrowed the same amount of money and bought hither and yon in the neighborhood, and brought in the actual food to show the difference in quality and quantity."[61] It was the government's responsibility to ensure their well-being, members of the WCOU argued, but poor families knew best what they needed. To committee members, not all relief was equal, and recipients should have a say in what kind of relief they had access to.

In some senses, the culmination of the WCOU's efforts for good relief came with the creation of New Deal programs like the Federal Emergency Relief Administration (FERA) and the Civil Works Administration (CWA), both created in 1933. The FERA brought the federal government into relief giving, suggesting that Franklin Roosevelt and his cabinet had heard the committee's demands for sufficient and useful relief. Through the FERA, the states had access to federal funds to go toward relieving the financial burden of the unemployed.[62] The CWA, even more importantly, was created by Harry Hopkins to provide *work*, which was vitally important to members of the WCOU. The CWA began hiring workers immediately and within a few months had paid 4.2 million men and women for work. CWA workers were also hired without a means test, which distinguished the program from FERA's and from the kinds of casework-driven relief WCOU members had been fighting against.[63]

New Deal programs promised to bring to fruition the kind of capitalism that WCOU members envisioned, but in reality, their

WHAT'S WRONG WITH RELIEF?

Who is responsible for the vicious system of pauper relief in Chicago today? The Illinois Relief Commission? The Federal Government? Or is the whole economic system?

Can rents be paid? Why is medical care lacking? Why are single men forced into miserable flophouses? Are case-workers needed? Do the unemployed need cash relief?

These are questions we want to ask the people of Chicago. Come to this Public Hearing. Tell your own relief story. Listen to the experiences of others. Help the Workers' Committee to focus attention on the need for decent relief.

Butler House—3212 Broadway
THURSDAY, JUNE 28, at 6:30 o'clock

(One of a series of six city wide Public Hearings sponsored by the
Workers' Committee on Unemployment)

(See other side)

Figure 4.1 In this flyer, WCOU members took aim at what they called the "vicious system of pauper relief in Chicago." Chicago Commons Collection, Box 26, Folder 1, Chicago History Museum, Chicago, IL. Chicago History Museum, ICHi-176380-001.

Nov 1934

For Your Protection
Join

The Workers' Committee

in our fight for—

1. Cash relief; or full time job at union wages
2. A higher budget to meet present higher prices
3. Budget to include:
   Regular payment of rent, light and gas
   Adequate clothing
   Provision for decent burial
4. Adequate medical and dental care
5. More adequate relief for single persons
6. Abolition of the casework system
7. Social or job insurance, (the Lundeen bill).

Distributed by Local...........

G. O. No. 457, 8-2-33.

GROCERY ORDER CUT

Price of Ration box increased
November 1934

— W H Y ? —

No. Pers.	Grocery Order Before	Now	Ration Box Before	Now
1.	$10.18	9.15		
2.	17.75	16.00	5.00	5.59
3.	24.25	21.85	6.76	7.52
4.	29.44	26.50	8.40	9.10
5.	34.64	31.20	10.02	11.04
6.	39.84	35.85	11.83	13.11
7.	45.03	40.55	13.60	15.09
8.	50.88	45.80	16.80	18.20
9.	56.72	51.05	18.60	20.14

Deduction for Monthly Milk at the rate of one quart per day
Before 2.74   Now 3.04   Deduction for flour now; 24 lbs. 90c; 49 lbs. $1.75; 73 lbs. $2.65; 98 lbs. $3.50.

Can you live on this budget?
If you cannot, why don't you ask for an increase.
You are entitled to live.
We want you to help us raise this budget to a living standard.
We can not beg all the time.
We must ask and demand.
Join our demonstration Nov. 24, and raise your voice for decent relief.

Figure 4.2 This 1934 flyer from the WCOU highlights the significance of adequate relief and suggests at WCOU members' frustration with casework. Chicago Commons Collection, Box 26, Folder 1, Chicago History Museum, Chicago, IL. Chicago History Museum, ICHi-176381-002.

insufficiencies only made WCOU members more impatient. Both were underfunded, and the CWA (the most generous of the early works programs) lasted through just one winter, but they seemed to change the rhetoric of the WCOU (see Figure 4.3). While organizing a protest of the closure of the CWA, WCOU members barely masked their anger over the reduction in work relief, saying, "Are you Happy? Are you glad the CWA ended? Glad to be back on relief? ... The H—l You Are!"[64] The WCOU rhetoric here is more complex, and this flyer (see Figure 4.4) really shows what its members called for: an end to relief without dignity (meaning: relief without productive work).

Yet this flyer also highlights the central role that casework played in WCOU members' claims to a worker-centered capitalism. For these jobless workers, it seems the worst part of relief was having a caseworker to "help you bring up your kids and teach you how to spend your money."[65] To the unemployed, their caseworkers embodied the frustration of receiving barely subsistence relief funds and the humiliation of being subjected to the methods of social work that included counseling and, too often, judgment. Settlement workers sat at a liminal place in the casework system, for although settlement houses carried on some casework (and thus settlement workers could be associated with caseworker judgment), they continued to identify themselves as counter to the kind of charity workers whom WCOU members distrusted and offered club work as an antidote to casework (see Chapter 3). Throughout the WCOU's existence, its members targeted the casework system as well as caseworkers themselves, the latter being the individuals who seemed most responsible for their fates and who personified their loss of dignity.

They targeted casework even in direct action. During the early years of the Depression, they set up a grievance committee to receive petitions from disgruntled recipients of relief seeking more humane interactions with the at-times mystifying relief apparatus and always overworked agents of relief. Those on the WCOU grievance committee were tasked with conveying unemployed relief recipients' complaints to members of the relief apparatus, and so they loitered around relief stations to put silent pressure on caseworkers and set up conferences with district administrators over shoddy casework and bureaucratic inconsistencies. And in moments of desperation, the WCOU called on skilled members to mitigate the consequences

HERE'S THE OFFICIAL CHICAGO BUDGET

No. Persons	Total Budget	DEDUCTIONS Ration box
1	$10.18	....
2	17.75	$ 5.00
3	24.25	6.76
4	29.44	8.40
5	34.64	10.02
6	39.84	11.83
7	45.03	13.60
8	50.88	16.80
9	56.72	18.60

(deduct $2.74 per month for 1 qt. milk per day), additional qts. at same rate.
(deduct for extra flour received) 24½ lb.-$.85, 49 lb.1.65, 73½ lb.-$2,50, 98 lb.-$3.30.

IS THIS A NEW DEAL?
Join the Workers' Committee in its demand for Adequate Relief and Cash Relief

Central Office: Harrison 5392   20 WEST JACKSON BLVD.

Above, Figure 4.3 Even after the federal government committed funds to relief, WCOU members asserted their claim to protection by the government and their right to "adequate relief." Chicago Commons Collection, Box 26, Folder 1, Chicago History Museum, Chicago, IL. Chicago History Museum, ICHi-176380-002.

Figure 4.4 In criticizing the closure of the Civil Works Administration, WCOU members revealed their deep disdain for the casework system, and thus distanced themselves from the hallmark of means-tested welfare. Chicago Commons Collection, Box 27, Folder 1, Chicago History Museum, Chicago, IL. Chicago History Museum, ICHi-176382-001.

Are You Happy?

Are you glad the CWA ended?

Glad to be back on relief?

Glad to have a kind case-worker to help you bring up your kids and teach you how to spend your money?

The H--l You Are!

Don't kid yourself!

You'll get just enough to keep you from belly-aching too much—enough so you'll stand for being kicked from a bad job to a worse one, UNTIL——

UNTIL you, Mr. Jobless, and you and you and you get together, gang-up and yell for a decent living.

Why Take a Handout?

The Workers' Committee doesn't.

You won't have to either if you join.

Pick out your Workers' Committee local listed on the other side and let's see you at the next meeting.

of unemployment rather than their caseworkers. Should a WCOU member find that his gas was being turned off, he could call on an unemployed gas man on the committee to rectify the situation. Should a member of the WCOU find that a pipe had burst, she just needed to call on an unemployed plumber on the committee to fix it, free of charge. And should a landlord attempt to force eviction by breaking a door in an apartment, a Chicagoan could count on a carpenter in the local WCOU branch to fix it.

In this approach, members of the WCOU articulated the kind of capitalism they supported: a system that rewarded hard workers, protected them against the vagaries of the market, and kept them from the humiliation of casework. They argued that means-tested relief and charity subjected recipients to investigation and withheld the guarantee of assistance, dependent on behavior, need, and so forth. At the same time, they outlined a distinction between entitlements and means-tested public assistance that many historians of the modern American welfare state have noted. In the end, the workers who joined the WCOU were just the kind of people who would find themselves on the entitlements side of social welfare, largely exempt from means testing and the "pauperizing" tendency of relief.

Less than a year after the hunger march, hundreds of unemployed Chicagoans participated in the committee's second set of hearings. The 1933 hearings placed more emphasis on failing community institutions and the decreasing patience of community leaders. While the 1932 hearings ignited the movement, workers' statements in 1933 "resulted in the welfare board's decision to finally include rent in relief budgets." And the next spring, thousands of WCOU members showed up for mass meetings and a citywide May Day parade. Their protests continued—from picketing the *Chicago Daily Tribune* for advocating for the "disenfranchisement of the unemployed,"[66] to protesting the demise of the federal CWA in 1934.

While participating in the WCOU, unemployed workers articulated their goals as a movement and created strategies for reaching them. More than that, they began the process of understanding themselves as speaking members of the American political system. On flyers posted throughout neighborhood institutions, WCOU members and leaders asserted their participation in policy making and invited poor community members to join them. And in citywide protests, tens of thousands of poor Chicagoans made a claim on state and federal funds. At the same time, these jobless workers positioned themselves against Communism and articulated the capitalist system they were willing to participate in. The failure of capitalism seemed stark amid the collapse of industry and traditional sources of relief. Yet members of the WCOU, while challenging the problems of capitalism, used moments of protest like the hunger march to challenge Communism as well, suggesting their support for using electoral politics to reform U.S. capitalism rather than overthrow it.

In establishing their political capital, though, workers also distanced themselves from the hallmark of means-tested social welfare programs: casework. The Chicago Federation of Settlements (CFS) put it succinctly in a 1932 letter to the Chicago Police Commissioner: "These thousands of law-abiding patriotic citizens [had] thus asserted their just claims to more adequate and certain relief and their right to self-supporting security of livelihood."[67] Put another way, in staking out their claim for federal entitlements, the jobless knew that casework would render them stigmatized.

5

Getting Relief from the Government

n January 1932, Workers Committee on Unemployment (WCOU) organizer Lea Taylor wrote to Anna Ickes, Illinois state representative and wife of Harold L. Ickes. Taylor wrote as a representative of the city's charities and the Joint Emergency Relief Fund (JERF) to offer full support of state tax warrants for unemployment relief. "The Chicago Federation of Settlements," Taylor informed Ickes, "strongly endorses the joint resolution for appointment of committee to consider the ways and means of relieving unemployment, as introduced by you in the legislature."[1] On the same date, it was reported that Joel Hunter, general superintendent of United Charities, wrote to Governor Louis L. Emmerson and the Illinois legislature to urge "immediate action to provide funds to care for the poor."[2] One month later, Hunter traveled to Springfield to be on hand when the legislature considered a series of five bills "which [would] provide for the issuance of between 18 and 19 millions in state tax warrants. . . . The relief stations will close if aid does not come from the assembly, leaders say."[3] On the same day, early in 1932, settlement workers, members of the WCOU, and Chicago's relief officials all turned to the state government for aid. While they would not have called themselves a coalition, their goals aligned, and, for a short while, they worked toward the same cause.

In Springfield, after a prolonged battle, state legislators finally buckled under the pressure and drafted an early version of New Deal–style welfare legislation, a bureaucratic structure that sent state money into localities and thus preserved local systems for distributing aid. These legislators were not proto–New Deal figures—they and their downstate constituents were far from interested in turning state attention to what seemed like a mismanaged and perpetually struggling metropolis. At the urging of Chicago's relief organizers, however, Illinois legislators realized that in the interest of preserving their state's precarious financial situation, they would need to shore up its largest city. Ultimately, this story is one of crisis, unintended consequences, and attempted recovery, led by a coalition of businessmen-turned–relief officials and prompted by the agitation of unemployed workers, such as members of the WCOU. What many legislators and reformers believed was a temporary stopgap on the road back to local charity ended up giving the state and federal governments inroads into their local system of welfare. As federal spending increased, these same men fought a battle—financial and rhetorical—to ensure the lasting place of charity in American welfare.

But Taylor and the WCOU did not stop at the state level, nor did they stop with relief. When state funds proved to be insufficient to support their cities, settlement workers, the unemployed, and relief officials all turned to the federal government for a long-lasting solution: unemployment insurance. With this goal, supporters of worker entitlement bridged a gap commonly described between relief and insurance: whereas relief was commonly associated with the needy and helpless, jobless workers and their supporters simultaneously defined themselves as legitimate and deserving relief recipients and entitled to social insurance. In the federal contest for social insurance, the unlikely coalition faced policy infighting, congressional torpor, and fears of radicalism. In the end, workers and settlement supporters won a partial victory: federal unemployment insurance that was controlled by the states.

The Battle in Springfield

While workers were protesting failures in the relief system, relief officials turned to the state for assistance. In February 1932, the General

Assembly of Illinois passed a series of bills that marked a transition in the role of the state in taking care of its needy citizens. In five bills, the Illinois legislature created and funded the Illinois Emergency Relief Commission (IERC), a state body that from 1933 to 1935 distributed $20 million for relief. The creation of the IERC, which would later channel federal funds (from Herbert Hoover's Reconstruction Finance Corporation [RFC] and, more significantly, Franklin Roosevelt's Federal Emergency Relief Administration [FERA]) and thus become the administrator of federal policies shaping the infrastructure of relief and social welfare, suggested that the government had the greatest capacity to attend to the sufferings of the newly poor. Its emergence was no accident but rather the result of a concerted and labored effort by Chicago's leaders in relief and social charity.

Surprisingly, one year after Chicago relief officials began campaigns to ensure local care for their unemployed, they urged the IERC into existence. As their relief funds ran out, JERF officials lobbied for the creation of state assistance as an emergency stopgap measure. They hit an open nerve in the general assembly: the historic tension between Cook County and the rest of the state. Downstate legislators (representing cities and towns outside Cook County) were hesitant to throw state funds at one unstable city and repeatedly threatened to decree relief a local issue. JERF president Edward Ryerson expressed deep concern about this possibility when he declared that "absolute starvation for hundreds of thousands looms, . . . requiring heroic measures and warranting them" and that "the only remedy is . . . action by the legislature."[4] Ryerson acknowledged that local and private relief groups were ill equipped to shore up the city's unemployed, and thus they needed state assistance. The specter of crisis not only helped relief officials secure aid but also defined the character of legislation. Because everyone involved believed that the emergency would soon end, legislators and relief officials alike were less concerned about its structure than its immediate funding needs. As such, relief officials—who hoped to soon return to a system of largely local charity—stumbled into bills that would legislate state and federal funding for a decade.

Chicago's recently elected mayor, the aggressive and controversial Anton Cermak, took the first of many steps toward acquiring state aid. In the fall of 1931, Cermak filed a petition with the Illinois

Supreme Court, requesting access to $10,000 of unemployment relief reserved for the victims of a 1927 Mississippi Valley flood that was not used to cover flood damage. "Some of the good citizens who so nobly gave to the flood relief fund," Cermak argued, "are now in dire need." By looking to emergency funds, Cermak framed the economic crisis as an emergency on the order of a natural disaster like a flood, not a permanent state of affairs. In fact, in statements to the judiciary, Cermak closed with these words:

> The expressed object for relief of the governor's unemployment fund is so near the original purpose of the donation to the flood relief fund that in equity and good conscience, and in the interest of public welfare, it should be applied and used by the governor's unemployment commission [the GCUR] for the purpose for which it has been appointed and devoted.[5]

Cermak's request for aid was refused, in large part because his predecessor and rival, Mayor William Thompson, challenged the constitutionality of Cermak using funds that he and his administration had raised for Cook County. Regardless of his failure, Cermak established a strategy that relief officials would maintain for years, in which they treated the economic crisis as an emergency that only the government could abate.[6]

By the end of 1931, Chicago's relief officials and residents alike seemed convinced that state assistance would be worth it for the city, so they took on the mantle of attaining aid. Perhaps paradoxically, JERF members hoped that outside assistance would ultimately allow them to return to a system of local charity, so they undertook a two-pronged strategy. First, they contacted state legislators and Governor Emmerson directly, in letters, phone calls, and visits to Springfield. Second, in concert especially with the *Tribune*, the JERF orchestrated a media blitz, calling for public approval of new legislation. From mid-1931 until January 1932, JERF leaders simultaneously petitioned Chicagoans for continued relief donations and began to appeal to the Illinois legislature for supplemental state funds.

A look at JERF leaders' shifting arguments in favor of state assistance reveals the intensity of their efforts. JERF leaders, including president Ryerson, first officially requested funding from the state in December 1931, and they began with a rhetorical strategy that emphasized the social-scientific understanding of the problem.[7] This resolution was their first request for state funds, and the JERF (along with non–Cook County members of the GCUR) evinced a faith that with enough statistics and financial evidence to prove that the need was greater than private donations and charities could manage, legislators would certainly meet their request. The resolution relied on data and a transparent explanation of the gap between funds raised and needed—for instance, a claim that "in Chicago and Cook County $10,500,000 will be provided from local sources for relief, . . . [and] there will be a deficit in the funds needed for relief amounting to $15,000,000."[8] JERF leaders asserted in the *Tribune* that they had done their homework when writing the resolution, relying on "analysis of the budgets and estimates of the private relief agencies" to reach the amount requested. As they made their foray into requesting state funds, relief officials anticipated that sufficient information, in the form of economic projections and expenditures, would be enough to acquire legislative support.

In the same vein, members of the JERF and the GCUR initially believed that if they could secure funds (rather than initiating structural changes), they could appease the legislature *and* preserve local charity. Sensing that legislators' "primary concern was with the source of revenue,"[9] explained relief veteran Frank Glick in 1940, relief officials threw their weight behind several tax-to-relief bills, the most popular of which proposed incurring taxes on motor fuel. Legislators held multiple sessions focused on the possibility of diverting or increasing gas taxes (which were intended to pay for maintaining and building state highways) to pay for relief. Unfortunately for relief officials, even though Chicago had employed such measures to raise money, many of these plans were deemed to be on shaky constitutional ground, weakening their strategy of focusing on sound finances.[10]

Yet even if their numbers did add up, relief officials and Cook County legislators soon realized that they were facing a hostile climate in Springfield. It did not help that Cook County had, for decades, struggled with a crippling financial instability, due to such factors as corruption and unpaid property taxes.[11] This history, along with Chicago's overwhelming need, sparked resistance from "downstate" legislators to any plans (including tax plans) that would benefit Cook County more than the rest of the state. Perhaps paradoxically, legislators also did not seem to believe that Cook County needed assistance from the state. "They had no comprehension of what was needed," Ryerson later explained. "They didn't believe any public money should be used in this way. It should all be left to the private welfare agencies."[12]

The continued resistance of the state legislature led to increased despair on the part of Chicago relief organizers, who shifted their strategy away from the logic of finances. As 1931 came to a close, JERF members went from offering data and requesting assistance to stressing the emergency nature of this crisis. To convince people of the necessity of the unthinkable—using state aid in a local relief crisis—leading intellectuals and JERF officials projected a narrative of impending disaster and the need for government intervention. In the *Tribune*, relief workers reported what unemployed laborers in the WCOU already knew: not only did they not have enough funds to meet the city's needs in the long run; they would soon run out of all relief funds. The "normal relief agencies," such charities as the Salvation Army, Catholic Charities, and United Charities, were unable to meet the growing demand for relief. The city had opened "special relief stations," but those, JERF secretary Franklin D. Loomis explained, would have to close in a matter of weeks. In mid-January 1932, the *Tribune* reported that according to the GCUR, by February 15, "more than 100,000 families will be left without adequate relief," if the state did not produce $15 million in aid.[13]

When relief officials shifted tactics, they also positioned the state as ultimately accountable to poor Chicagoans. In January 1932, JERF president Ryerson led a group of relief officials to Springfield, where they hoped to sway legislators to vote for one of the proposed plans to allocate money for relief. On January 12, two weeks before their voluntarily raised funds would run out and the day before the legislature voted on (and rejected) a bill to divert gas taxes to relief, Ryerson issued a public statement that evinced the JERF's anxiety and expectation that the government would help: "We have struggled to carry [the relief load] thus far, with the expectation that the State Legislature would take some action and make possible the use of public funds." Ryerson's statement, printed in the *Tribune*, identified the current situation as a crisis, in response to which the general assembly needed to overlook historic tensions and stabilize the city.[14]

Yet still the state demurred. On January 21, Cermak and legislators jubilantly announced that they had passed a measure to replace Cook County's taxing machinery, which they hoped would "be the first step in the rehabilitation of Chicago's muddled finances."[15] D. F. Kelly, a past member of Chicago's JERF and one of the authors of the tax bill, made the hopeful announcement that if Cook County citizens paid their 1930 taxes immediately, the money could go toward relief efforts. But to the dismay of relief officials, few Cook County residents wanted or could afford to pay their taxes early, so the bill seemed to put the burden of relief on the people who needed it most. The general assembly, having not successfully passed any relief measures, adjourned until February 2. In Chicago, panic set in, and the city's relief leaders readied themselves for battle.

Relief officials—who for so long had celebrated local, private charity—now evinced an intense faith in the power of the state to assist their city. On the evening of January 22—the day after the general assembly adjourned—relief officials met with Cook County representatives to plead their case. The group called Governor Emmerson directly and, pressing him again about the swiftly dwindling relief funds, convinced him to board a train for Chicago that night. Over the next few days, in Chicago's Stevens Hotel, the governor met with local representatives, JERF officials, Chicago bankers, and newspaper editors. On January 24, their campaign paid off, when Emmerson called the general assembly into an emergency session beginning on January 26. During their meetings, moreover, the group had drafted a series of bills that would structure conversation and legislation at the general assembly's emergency sessions.

Coverage in the *Tribune*, the *Chicago Daily News*, and various national papers rendered the relief crisis a very public concern by inserting relief officials' rhetoric into the public imagination and putting pressure on the general assembly. Chicago papers broadcast the crisis and clearly implicated state legislators for abandoning the city. On January 23, the *Tribune*'s banner headline read, "Relief Crisis to Governor: Chicago Fund Near End; Face an Emergency," and the accompanying article called for an emergency session to reconsider relief bills: "Leaders in the administration of the relief fund emphasized that if the legislature does not meet until Feb. 2 it would be too late to meet the emergency. The suffering of the poor would begin the moment the relief stations now in existence are closed on Feb. 1."[16]

The *Tribune*, describing how lack of relief would put 450,000 individuals "in utter destitution," mobilized the language of crisis and imminent starvation that relief officials had begun to use. The following day, the *Chicago Daily News* employed the same rhetorical strategy. In a front-page article titled "Hunger Calls," the *News* urged a "united front" against suffering.[17] The author (unlisted) declared, "FOUR HUNDRED AND EIGHTY THOUSAND HUMAN SOULS, MEN, WOMEN AND CHILDREN, now dependent upon emergency relief funds for food to keep them alive, are just EIGHT DAYS FROM STARVATION!" The *News* article pointed its finger squarely at the state: "Chicago and Cook county, because of the complete breakdown of taxing machinery and credit, are HELPLESS. The duty of meeting the crisis, therefore, inexorably devolves upon the state."[18] These papers flooded their readers with images of the city on the brink of disaster, but they also positioned the relief crisis as a national concern. On January 24 and 25, the *New York Times*, the *Washington Post*, the *Wall Street Journal*, and the *Atlanta Constitution* all published articles alerting the nation that "Chicago and the rest of Illinois are experiencing one of the gravest financial crises in recent years."[19]

With the nation and city watching, in a JERF statement on the emergency session, Ryerson indicated another rhetorical ramping up, from panicky to apocalyptic. His words positioned the general assembly and the Illinois residents alike as culpable for any catastrophe that might come: "The legislature will gladly and quickly act if its members feel they represent the will of the citizens of the state. Citizens of Illinois, it is more than an emergency. It is a condition unparalleled, appalling, desperate. If it were not no such appeal for public aid as this would be made. But when absolute starvation for hundreds of thousands looms it is like war, requiring heroic measures and warranting them."[20] Ryerson's approach certainly lent credence to the pieces of legislation that state senators and representatives debated in Springfield. For a week beginning on January 26, the legislature battled over the state funding, weighing concerns over local responsibility with threats of starvation and disorder. In these meetings, legislators (eventually) accepted the inevitability of state-administered welfare.

The house first debated five bills, disparate measures that were bundled together to be successfully passed. Taken together, they were intended to direct money toward Cook County and protect the interests of downstate constituents. The first created the IERC, which had the power to distribute relief funds around the state. This bill also appropriated $20 million for the IERC, meaning that it that would funnel relief funds into Chicago. The second and third bills offered the preferred mechanisms with which they might fund the IERC: the second bill authorized the sale of $20 million in state bonds, which would be payable in twenty years; and the third bill created a system with which localities could pay for the bonds by authorizing the state to use motor fuel tax monies, collected over the following twenty years, to pay for them, at a rate proportional per county to how much relief money that county had used. These two bills crucially required approval by a majority of votes cast at the next election, which explains Ryerson's urgency in entreating Illinois citizens (outside the legislature) to support these measures. These three measures might have been enough, but the general assembly added two more that would protect downstate interests should Chicagoans opt not to support the bond issue.[21]

These bills were passed as an emergency measure and were clearly more attentive to financial concerns than to the apparatus that would usher in state relief giving. All parties involved expected that the IERC would be disbanded within the year. Considering the economic crisis, the most pressing matters, moreover, seemed to be economic. So, legislators who gathered in the general assembly on January 26 came prepared to fight over money. Downstate senators and representatives acted defensively, understandably concerned that they would shoulder the burden of Cook County's financial problems. Despite testimonies from Ryerson and Hunter, superintendent of United Charities of Chicago, it would take a persistent battle for the general assembly to finally secure Chicago's relief stations.

This battle involved two major arguments, which bore out the state/local tensions. The argument on the one side, from downstate legislators and conservative Chicagoans, was one of distrust: Cook

County should deal with its own problems, for how could they trust that Cook County's preservation would not come at the expense of the state? Chicago attorney Henry E. Cutler declared, "I should think the law of self preservation would operate there." He continued, "If they vote against [the bond issue] their taxes will be raised." Earl B. Searcy, a Republican representative from Springfield, echoed Cutler's threats: "If they don't, it will be the biggest double-cross ever put over on this assembly." The position of the other side, from Cook County legislators and Chicago relief officials, was equally clear: help. Chicago attorney James G. Condon baldly pleaded, "You don't realize that Chicago is sitting on a volcano. We only ask that you give us what you would give your own city."[22] On February 1, the day that relief funds dried up in Chicago, the house was fifty votes short of the majority needed to pass the relief bills.

While it initially appeared that downstate representatives would opt to protect their own financial stability, the threat of total social upheaval, presented by workers' organizations like the WCOU, persuaded them otherwise. The *Tribune* charged, after the first vote, that "Downstate apparently was turning a deaf ear to Chicago's prayer for aid in feeding its hungry and sheltering its homeless."[23] House Speaker David E. Shanahan stepped in with what would perhaps be the tipping point in the battle: "There is grave danger now. The federal government has already issued the orders necessary to curb disorder if it arises. The mayor of Chicago is on the rostrum here and is undecided whether he should agree to calling out the troops tomorrow morning. The armories are under guard now."[24] Downstate legislators must have known, at that point, that they had no choice but to vote for a bill that would very likely go against their constituents' interests. On February 3, the house achieved the majority necessary to pass the bills. Former Minority Leader Truman A. Snell justified his vote: "There isn't going to be any blood on my hands tonight. I'm going to vote for this bill and sleep with a clear conscience. This is war. This is hell."[25]

The legislation passed in the Illinois statehouse was the result of the escalating crisis rather than a thoughtful move toward state relief. In part, it was the product of the legislature's unsurprising (but short-sighted) attention to statewide fiscal concerns, especially the potential that downstate residents might have to bear Chicago's burden. With these concerns in mind, legislators for months resisted creating new relief measures and, in the end, forced themselves to do so while under duress: hastily and with their eyes turned to money. As Glick would explain eight years later, "The question of how to finance the program seemed so important that the creation of a new and unprecedented state agency with almost unlimited authority to administer relief took place almost as a matter of course."[26] Moreover, legislators functioned under the widespread belief that, however dire the circumstances, the crisis was not likely to last longer than a year. The bill that created the IERC gave it thirteen months of life.

The Illinois Emergency Relief Commission Preserves Local Charity

The IERC was not the only commission to usher in the practice of state funding for relief, but it is representative of a larger shift. At the same time, however, the IERC did not supplant local systems of relief. Instead, despite its significance, the IERC ultimately preserved the system of local charity that Chicago's relief officials had been working so hard to maintain.

The IERC was not the first of its kind but rather one of a dozen state agencies formed prior to federal involvement. In fact, the states' response to the economic crisis was staggering and has been too little studied, overshadowed by the attention that scholarship has given to the federal intervention. But in fact, a number of states responded very quickly, with creative but relatively modest measures intended to assist local relief agencies. During 1930–1931, one of the most popular solutions was something that Chicago's relief officials had called for but failed to achieve (in large part due to the deplorable condition of state and city finances). In those two years, New York, Pennsylvania, Ohio, Indiana, and Minnesota all permitted localities to sell bonds to cover relief or public works, to be repaid through taxes. These early measures suggested that state legislatures were open to new systems for funding relief, even though by maintaining local autonomy over it, they were unable to allocate enough money for the growing numbers of jobless.

In 1931 and 1932, several state governments directly invested in relief. The Northeast was the bulwark for state-financed relief measures. In the beginning of 1931, New Hampshire, Maryland, and Oklahoma became the first states to pass legislation for unemployment relief. Most notably, Oklahoma was the first to fund relief directly, as its state emergency relief board distributed $300,000 for food, clothing, and shelter for the destitute. Also in 1931, New York governor Franklin Roosevelt presided over the largest state emergency commission, the Temporary Emergency Relief Administration (TERA), which began with an allocated $20 million for relief, including work relief. Wisconsin followed New York by mobilizing its Industrial Commission, which had been founded in 1911 to administer unemployment relief and insurance.[27] New Jersey and Rhode Island followed shortly thereafter, and in the final month of 1931, Pennsylvania governor Gifford Pinchot oversaw the passage of the Talbot Act, which distributed $10 million not to a relief commission but to the commonwealth's poor district officers.[28] In 1932, Illinois and Ohio created emergency commissions.

It is of no small significance that states joined in the cause of relief giving, even if reluctantly. "That they were happening at all," Udo Sautter argues, "constituted a change of historic significance."[29] Yet state legislators clearly did not act alone, for state initiatives were bolstered by relief officials and local reformers. From Lea Taylor and Joel Hunter of United Charities in Chicago, to Helen Hall, who sat on Pennsylvania governor Pinchot's unemployment commission, to the Ohio Commission, which drew on research from the National Federation of Settlements (NFS) unemployment study, state involvement in relief stemmed in part from reformers, and most particularly from the work of settlement house advocates and partners. The fact that Hunter became a somewhat regular fixture in the Illinois legislature, and that he and Taylor both appealed to Hoover for funds from the RFC, indicates the extent to which local figures translated city problems to state and federal governments.

In Illinois, the IERC fostered relationships between the city and the state and between the state and the federal government. During its existence, the IERC served as the administering agency for distributing federal money coming from temporary bodies, including the RFC and the FERA, and, significantly, from permanent bodies, including the Social Security Administration (SSA). The Illinois General Assembly created inroads to federal relief in bills that were intended to temporarily shore up local agencies. Legislators certainly did not aim to pioneer policy in the history of public welfare administration in the United States. JERF members, even more so, brought about consequences that they had not anticipated.

The IERC promised to radically change the government's role in the administration of public welfare, as it funneled state and federal funds into Cook County. In practice, the IERC did not seem like a huge change in policy. Because the general assembly had drafted IERC legislation while in crisis, and because relief centers and charities were on the brink of collapse, the IERC's initial purpose was to channel funds into already established systems of relief. Chicago's private agencies had, for the previous few years, assumed responsibility for a large proportion of the city's relief funds. Because the JERF managed the relief infrastructure, IERC allocations initially went through it. From February 1932 until July 1933, JERF agencies received IERC funds to continue their work. A settlement like Chicago Commons, for instance, received slightly less than 10 percent of its 1932 income from the IERC. During this year and a half, the general assembly and the JERF created a system of welfare in which public and private worked in concert—in fact, they were practically inseparable.

At the same time, believing that the economic crisis was temporary, relief officials—who had demanded the creation of the IERC—continued to insist on the necessity of private charity in Chicago. Through the 1932 legislative battles, JERF leaders had simultaneously articulated their failure—the failure of local responsibility for relief—and demonstrated the ability of local leadership to acquire the funds needed for survival. In turn, these local relief officials ran subsequent private charity drives that, again and again, called on the city to support its poor. They developed media-driven narratives that insisted that, even as the IERC stabilized the city year after year, private charity (and not government agencies) should be the future of American relief and welfare.

Most notably, perhaps, New Deal relief and social welfare agencies worked through the IERC instead of creating their own new infrastructure. If nothing else, the IERC demonstrated the government's primacy in rescuing the unemployed from economic crisis. But the IERC's structure—largely because of its hasty creation—at least initially set up a strange marriage of public and private. Beginning in

1933, New Deal programs explicitly distinguished between public and private, but this distinction turned out to be artificial, because private agencies were still able to benefit from FERA and IERC money. Chicago's charities, moreover, refused to cede relevance to the government and continued raising money in the city. And in the media, they strongly argued for the persistent significance of private charity. Their events and advertisements also did the same kind of work that they had before: encouraged a resurgence of philanthropy and shored up social distinctions. In so doing, Chicago's relief officials continued to promote the narratives about charity and localism that they had nurtured in their relief drives (discussed in Chapter 3). The IERC (via the state legislature) and Chicago's charities together created in Chicago a semi-welfare state—preserving the historic messiness between public and private and ensuring that massive changes in the legislation would not result in structural change.

Moreover, relief officials and the IERC initially made a feeble effort to distinguish between public and private. They explained to donors that although private contributions would go to support the "normal" work of charity organizations, IERC funds were reserved strictly for unemployment. In October 1932, relief officials announced yet another private drive for relief funds, called the Emergency Welfare Fund (EWF). This fund, they assured *Tribune* readers, "will be dispensed through 101 welfare organizations, many of which will also receive allocations from the Illinois Emergency Relief commission to pay for the unemployment relief work they are doing."[30] In other words, IERC and EWF leaders developed a mutually agreed upon fiction that they were able to maintain the distinction between public (state) and private funds, but for a while, state funding went directly to the same agencies that received EWF donations. In 1932, the IERC attempted to manage this contradiction by differentiating between types of relief. Unemployment relief, IERC members determined, would be covered by public funds; private welfare agencies would attend to issues concerning families, households, and health— that is, anything not related to unemployment.

Even after 1932, when the IERC became the informal conduit of federal funds, it merely replicated local arrangements. When Hoover made RFC funds available, and Illinois became the first state to receive assistance from it, Governor Emmerson created a formally

distinct branch of the IERC, with three new members, that functioned concurrently to the original commission.[31] As the IERC relief machinery was already in place, federal and state administrators
opted to adjust it accordingly and render it an agent of federal funds.

The messy relationship between state money and Chicago's private agencies was poised to change in 1933. At that time, the IERC
adjusted in anticipation of greater funds from Roosevelt's FERA. The
FERA was the first major New Deal agency to send relief funds directly from the federal government to localities. Federal policy, however, insisted that FERA relief funds must be spent through public
agencies only, at which point IERC members determined that private
agencies should no longer receive public funds. With this ruling, and
with initial FERA funding, it appeared that the city would be moving
toward public welfare.

Even after the FERA shift, however, relief officials, social workers,
and settlement workers joined the federal government and state legislators in engineering what Michael Katz calls a semi-welfare state, in
which the federally sanctioned social welfare apparatus maintained
little separation from private and local charities.[32] Well after FERA
legislation disallowed private agencies from receiving public funds,
such settlements as Chicago Commons, Hull House, and the Northwestern University Settlement House (NUS) benefited from the help
of work relief benefits paid by the IERC. Settlements frequently welcomed work relief recipients from the Civil Works Education Service
and the Children's Leisure Time Service, both New Deal programs
funded through the IERC. It may have been surprising that explicitly
"public" agencies would ultimately assist private charity, but Chicago's relief agencies took advantage of this paradox.[33]

In Chicago, relief officials also worked to maintain the relevance of
private charity after a turn to the state. In the year after the FERA split
public funds from private agencies, relief officials organized to create
a more lasting private drive, managed by a board of directors and, unlike the previous drives, involved with the Council of Social Agencies
of Chicago. The Community Fund, as they called it, was formed "to
assist in the maintenance of charitable institutions, agencies, committees or activities operating primarily for or contributing primarily
to the welfare of the people of Chicago, Illinois."[34] Merely by organizing the Community Fund, relief officials evinced a commitment

to private charity. Indeed, Community Fund members were interested not in supplanting federal or state agencies with private ones but rather in creating a complementary structure between public and private. "The general fundamental idea that must prevail," explained Samuel Goldsmith, the chairman of the Committee on Joint Financing, "is that the [Community] Fund is for the purpose of reconstruction or rehabilitation rather than relief."[35] In other words, he suggested that private agencies were necessary for supporting one kind of relief recipient—specifically, those suffering domestic discord or failing health—while public agencies would attend to those primarily in need of employment. By constructing a difference between the mission of public and private welfare agencies, Goldsmith justified private charity even during a seeming shift toward public welfare. His statement, sent to member agencies of the Community Fund, expressed the internal perspective: from one charity worker to another.

Charity leaders explained this distinction in a public venue, conceding that there was "apparent confusion" regarding the difference between the IERC and the Community Fund. Although the IERC, they explained, had the "particular function of helping the jobless," the Community Fund's duty was to the needy, "the duty of a neighbor to a neighbor less fortunate."[36] Certainly the distinction between the jobless and a neighbor less fortunate was hazy at best, and case records show that they were likely helping the same people. As Chapter 3 explains, unemployed workers and their families commonly suffered the kinds of health and relationship problems with which charities and settlement houses were especially concerned. Yet the distinction proved useful for charity leaders, who needed to demonstrate their relevance if they wanted to continue receiving donations. A year later, relief officials cheered the Community Fund's successes at the kickoff of their 1934 campaign to raise $4 million. Brigadier Louis C. Bennett, head of the Salvation Army's Welfare Department, declared in the *Tribune*, "The public's confidence in private charity has been vindicated by the record of agencies participating in the Community fund."[37] In a time when public funding for relief might have called into question the necessity of private social service agencies, Bennett's triumphant words articulated the continued social necessity of the Community Fund and declared its victory even before the drive had started.

As Community Fund leaders attempted to redeem charity, they turned to stronger narratives that derided government welfare and lifted up the moral potential of charity. In a 1934 article, Albert D. Lasker, a vice president of the Community Fund, argues that government relief could not meet the needs of the poor, and he targets the bureaucracy of public welfare: "There grows up routine, red tape, checks and counter checks, which means that such relief often fails to bring what is needed to the needy." Clarence B. Randall, who chaired the grades and industries division of the fund, concurs: "The government doesn't do this job, and it should not." While some members of the Community Fund stressed that government and private agencies would complement each other, Randall and Lasker place charity at a higher moral position than public welfare. By appealing to morality and human sympathy, these Community Fund leaders also reveal the lasting influence of welfare capitalism and noblesse oblige, but in a world with greater public funding and donors of all means. They also appeal, again, to locality. Lasker concludes: "Keep alive the spiritual flame that makes us want to help others. The feeling of communal obligation gives us a richer sense of helpfulness, because then we give voluntarily and not by taxation. Keep Chicago going as a proud community!"[38]

Lasker and Randall are perhaps the most striking examples of relief officials who began as philanthropic welfare capitalists and, even as they demanded public funding and struggled for relevance alongside the New Deal, stayed that way. Chicago's relief officials established a system of charity and a series of narratives about charity that they would fight to preserve. The same relief officials forced the state legislature to enact public spending measures that would lay the groundwork for New Deal legislation and increased state and federal aid. In the end, their ambivalence toward state funding and inability to function without it fostered the creation of a welfare state based on the entitlement of a specific group of working Americans.

From Entitlement to Social Security

In Chicago, as the federal government made inroads into relief and charity, the city's relief officials expressed a sense of reprieve. The

IERC and the FERA promised to ease the sheer panic that had been afflicting the city's relief centers, allowing officials to turn to the task of recovery. As Ryerson reflected in 1934, "The New Deal was fulfilling the hope of those who had been trying to steer the ship. We now had a chartered course to follow."[39] Their success—in establishing a state commission and then petitioning the federal government to assist in financing relief efforts—came from the surprisingly unified efforts of a disparate group of Chicagoans. When the relief drives failed, unemployed workers protested and even threatened upheaval, settlement workers lobbied city and state leaders for aid, and relief officials finally agreed to abandon localism for the state. Although this awkward coalition indeed achieved its immediate goal of receiving government assistance, in 1934, not all of its members shared Ryerson's optimism.

Workers, such as members of the WCOU, benefited from the immediate impact of state and federal funds, but they continued to rail against a system that subjected them to casework. So even as unemployed workers continued to demand better relief, by 1934, they concurrently supported federal plans for unemployment insurance. As such, their definition of entitlement included public assistance and social insurance, two forms of federal support that are still frequently treated as distinct.[40] Despite their claims for a specific kind of unemployment insurance, reformers and workers faced the reality that the future of social insurance rested in the hands of legislators and social policy experts. So, although settlement workers strove to translate the needs of workers to policy makers, they and the unemployed ultimately accepted a flawed form of social insurance, and thus a flawed form of entitlement.

Unemployment insurance had a long history among reformers and in the states, but by 1934, the policy had moved to the federal level. Settlement workers had long supported state measures for unemployment insurance; they celebrated the passage of Wisconsin's state bill in 1932 (the first of its kind) and offered expertise and encouragement when other states (such as Ohio) began developing their own policies. New York senator Robert F. Wagner had for years proposed that Congress adopt a federal measure, and in 1934, President Roosevelt sent a special message to Congress:

If, as our Constitution tells us, our Federal Government was established among other things, "to promote the general welfare," it is our plain duty to provide for that security on which welfare depends. Next winter we may well undertake the great task of furthering the security of the citizen and his family through social insurance.[41]

Much as settlement workers and the unemployed had been calling for, Roosevelt dedicated the federal government to establishing social insurance.

And yet the federal embrace of social insurance seemed to threaten workers' relief programs. Roosevelt's statement did not explicitly malign relief, but it reflected his long-term priorities, which did not include relief-based structures and thus challenged workers' claims to useful relief and social security. As the president understood it, relief and welfare simply subsidized idleness, whereas social insurance programs (such as unemployment insurance) rewarded industry.[42] The House Ways and Means Committee reported that Roosevelt's bill would dissuade the poor from dependence on the government: "While humanely providing for those in distress, it does not proceed upon the destructive theory that the citizens should look to the government for everything. On the contrary, it seeks to reduce dependency and to encourage thrift and self-support."[43] To settlement workers and members of the WCOU, the plan proposed by the newly formed Committee on Economic Security (CES) threatened to prioritize independence from the government over security from unemployment, so they watched developments at the federal level with a critical eye.

Roosevelt appointed Secretary of Labor Frances Perkins to head the CES, created to examine options and make recommendations for federal social insurance. Its executive director was Edwin Witte, an economics professor from the University of Wisconsin who was also an active member of the American Association for Labor Legislation (AALL). Witte worked with Arthur J. Altmeyer, who served as technical director of the CES, to recommend policy to the president. Finally, an advisory council met several times with the CES to give feedback from a range of interests. It included twenty-three "civic leaders"—academics, corporate executives, labor leaders, and reformers. Among them were a few familiar names, including two members of the NFS Unemployment Committee: Paul Kellogg, editor of *The Survey*, and Helen Hall, president of the NFS and director of the Henry Street Settlement in New York. Joel D. Hunter, the general superintendent of United Charities of Chicago, also sat on the advisory council.

Although federal support for unemployment insurance seemed unwavering, the policy itself would not come so easily. In large part, the battle over unemployment insurance was one that had been waged by policy experts for decades and had now found its way to the CES. Should the federal government favor a plan that would incentivize employers to prevent unemployment and be funded by employer reserves, as proposed by Witte and supported by adherents of Wisconsin's plan for unemployment insurance? Or should it favor a plan that instead would use pooled funds to compensate the victims of unemployment, backed by such longtime experts as Isaac Max Rubinow and Abraham Epstein? As David A. Moss reflects, "The magnitude of the joblessness problem seemed to favor [compensation]," and some liberal members of the CES and the advisory board (including Kellogg and Hall) supported federally funded plans for it.[44] Yet Witte, Altmeyer, Perkins, and the majority of the CES supported prevention, which more closely resembled private insurance.[45] Despite (or perhaps because of) the rift between adherents of prevention and compensation, the CES ultimately proposed a bill that would allow states to determine the particularities of their policies on unemployment insurance, effectively using federalism to punt on the issue of policy. As Edward Berkowitz nicely puts it, the "[planners'] stubborn pride of authorship inhibited creativity."[46]

In January 1935, the CES and President Roosevelt presented to Congress the Social Security Act. Its sections on unemployment insurance came from the Wagner-Lewis Unemployment Insurance Bill of 1934, and Titles III and IX promised federal support "for the purpose of assisting the States in the administration of their unemployment compensation laws." Title III of the act specified how the government would pay states and listed a series of requirements for receiving payments to "insure full payment of unemployment compensation when due." Title IX outlined a plan for funding unemployment insurance centered on a federal tax on employers, which could be offset by contributions to a state unemployment fund. The act indicated that the federal government was committed to having each state offering compensation for unemployment, but it offered no precise definition of unemployment compensation, thus leaving the details up to the states. Unemployment insurance seemed to get short shrift in legislation, in part because many in Congress were most concerned with securing relief and establishing more permanent forms of public assistance (which came through such programs as Aid to Dependent Children).[47] The Social Security Act was signed into law in August 1935.

From the creation of the CES in 1934, it was clear that unemployment insurance would be overseen by Roosevelt, but that did not stop some workers and reformers (including the WCOU) from supporting a more radical congressional proposal: the Lundeen bill. Introduced by Ernest Lundeen, a Farmer-Labor Party representative from Minnesota, the Lundeen bill was presented to Congress at the same time as the Social Security Act.[48] Titled H.R. 2827, the Worker's Unemployment and Social Insurance Bill, its roots were clearly among workers and settlement workers. Lundeen himself was associated with Communist-influenced Unemployed Councils (UCs), and the bill was drafted by Mary van Kleeck, who began her career as a fellow for the College Settlements Association on New York's Lower East Side. As an adviser to the NFS Unemployment Committee, in 1929, she suggested that such research on the unemployed should "get the sense of responsibility for unemployment into the imaginations of employers and the public."[49] Van Kleeck and Kellogg corresponded about industrial planning at the start of the Depression, and together they organized conferences and published articles on unemployment.[50] Van Kleeck's priorities and knowledge, and her involvement with settlement research, imbued the Lundeen bill with a sense that working people were entitled to protection from the federal government.

The Lundeen bill had almost no chance of becoming law (and, in fact, never reached the floor of the House of Representatives), but it saw widespread support among workers and even in the Labor Committee.[51] Unlike Roosevelt's plan, the Lundeen bill provided coverage for all workers, regardless of race or occupation. "The benefits of this Act," the bill stated, "shall be extended to workers, whether they be industrial agricultural, domestic, office, or professional workers, and to farmers, without discrimination because of age, sex, race, color, religious or political opinion or affiliation."[52] As such, Lundeen's bill countered Roosevelt's decision to exclude agricultural workers from the security offered by the Social Security Act, a gesture intended to appease southern Democrats that would exclude from entitlement a vast percentage of workers of color in the United States. While workers in the WCOU and settlement workers said little on the intersecting issues of racism and economic insecurity, their support of the Lundeen bill made overtures toward some form of economic parity for African Americans.

Moreover, whereas the Social Security Act preserved state autonomy, the Lundeen bill called for a federal system for unemployment insurance. State autonomy fit with U.S. federalism and helped to ensure constitutionality, but because southern states were still virulently segregationist, state autonomy almost guaranteed discriminatory implementation of unemployment policy. The Lundeen bill also appealed to unemployed workers, because it promised to begin coverage immediately, whereas the Social Security Act required years to build up funds before actually supporting the unemployed. Perhaps most importantly, van Kleeck's bill was funded by an inheritance tax on upper-middle-class and wealthy individuals and corporations. In this way, it was not actually insurance, because, as van Kleeck expressed, "actuarial insurance . . . applied to unemployment . . . breaks down when unemployment attains mass proportions."[53]

Yet the Lundeen bill was essentially dead on arrival because of its impracticality and its association with radicalism. The bill itself was 392 words long, just about two pages, and failed to detail how it planned to manage funding and distribution. In 1934, *Survey* ran a study of the Lundeen bill for its social work readership, including an opinion piece by Rubinow, who offered a strongly worded argument against it, beginning with this statement: "The Lundeen bill is not a serious legislative proposal, but a soap-box for propaganda directed against the present economic order and against its reform."[54] Moreover, some Roosevelt administration officials characterized it as essentially a Communist plot infiltrating the New Deal, cementing its lack of future. Administration officials worried that its emphasis on benefits for all workers would level a necessary hierarchy. One staff member of the CES fretted, "With one stroke of the pen skilled tool-makers, lawyers, doctors and ditchdiggers are to be treated alike in the matter of family benefits?"[55] Witte was more pointed when he asserted that the bill was "excellent propaganda for the 'front line trenches' in the battle for communism."[56] The American Federation of Labor (AFL), moreover, denounced the bill as, in the words of Witte, "a Communist-sponsored measure designed to block, rather than promote, social security."[57] The congressional narrative about the Lundeen bill was, in sum, that it was too extreme for the New Deal.

Yet even though the Lundeen bill was almost guaranteed to fail in Congress, it had the support of unemployed worker groups, feminist organizations, African American groups, ethnic and mutual aid societies, some labor unions, and the Communist Party USA (CPUSA). The WCOU, for instance, threw its weight behind the bill in its 1934 flyer (see Figure 4.2) as its seventh demand, alongside medical care and abolition of the casework system. Supporters of the bill gathered more than three million signatures, which they presented to Congress on three separate occasions. Moreover, in public surveys, Americans indicated that they embraced the ideas presented in the Lundeen bill: the *New York Post*, for instance, polled its readers and found that 83 percent of them preferred van Kleeck's bill to either the Social Security Act or the Townsend bill.[58] In part, then, its significance lay in the fact that it served as a way for these groups to express the form of entitlement they believed they deserved. To many workers (if not Samuel Gompers of the AFL, then certainly unemployed and unskilled workers), the Lundeen bill articulated that they were entitled to generous security, regardless of their occupation or skill level. As van Kleeck wrote in the bill itself, "In its present form [it] may truly be said to be more of a declaration of principle and policy . . . to define the obligation of government and industry to compensate for losses through unemployment that is beyond the control of the workers, individually or collectively."[59]

The Lundeen bill may have also provided workers with a way of ensuring that the more modest policy established in the Social Security Act would be passed. Federal unemployment compensation was so contentious that, as Suzanne Mettler argues, it "might have been dropped from the bill entirely were it not for the countervailing pressure of an alternative plan far more radical: the workers' bill, otherwise known as the Lundeen bill."[60] From their perspective, then, members of the WCOU likely estimated that their support for a "far more radical" bill would encourage Congress and Roosevelt to see to it that unemployment insurance, as outlined in the Social Security Act, would become federal policy.

Yet the Lundeen bill is also emblematic of the inevitable compromises faced by those calling for worker entitlement. Hall and Kellogg, perhaps more realistic and likely hoping to influence the legislation that was most likely to succeed, instead supported the Social Security Act, but theirs was an ambivalent endorsement. As Hall wrote in 1935, settlement workers in the NFS were uncomfortable with changes made to the bill as it neared passage. In a statement for the CES regarding the Social Security Act, Hall and the NFS declared, "Today we recognize the Wagner-Lewis economic security bill as a great advance over the past in many of its provisions, but we feel that the section dealing with unemployment is a step backward."[61] The NFS resolution lamented what its members saw as minimal national uniformity, which meant that workers were vulnerable to state variations. "So far as the protection of the unemployed themselves is concerned," the resolution stated, "the States are left free to experiment."[62] Specifically, they requested a federal payroll tax of 3 percent on employers plus a matching federal contribution of another 2 percent. Hall held up the specter of relief as a warning to legislators: "Without such standards, we will be forced to combine relief with unemployment insurance in order to meet family need in many cases."[63]

Notably, Hall made a bill for unemployment insurance into a personal affair that threatened the breadwinner family. In an effort to appeal to legislators, she emphasized the effects that the Wagner-Lewis bill would have on the unemployed themselves and, especially, their families. After presenting statistical information on the typical duration of unemployment in good times, Hall closed with this plea: "Once more I urge that in the provisions of the Wagner-Lewis bill the unemployed be given a fuller protection by this Government against a hazard which, more than war itself, menaces family life and casts a shadow of insecurity over the lives of children."[64] Hall used the same arguments that the NFS made in its studies of unemployment, the WCOU made regarding their public hearings, and workers made to relief officials and legislators. She also expressed the bittersweet position that she, Kellogg, and supporters of unemployment insurance found themselves in as the 74th Congressional Session came to a close: they had achieved social insurance for the unemployed, but it was a far cry from what they had for so long been working for.

While members of the WCOU lost the battle for the Lundeen bill and more stringent national standards, some workers won the battle for entitlement. Their unemployment insurance was not as nationalized, immediate, or far reaching as the bill they had supported, but by the 1940s, the idea of unemployment insurance was no longer up for grabs. As scholars of the New Deal have proven, the Social Security Act offered some workers, such as the members of the WCOU, a form of social insurance that exempted them from the kind of means testing they had decried during the Depression. These workers had confirmation that the federal government considered them to be workers—employable—even when they found themselves to be jobless.

Entitlement, however, was only partial at the city, state, and federal levels. The categories created by the Community Fund and intended to preserve private charity also established a hierarchy of poverty that would come to define many federal programs. As settlement workers first articulated (see Chapter 2) and caseworkers and unemployed workers echoed (see Chapters 3 and 4), even before the New Deal, employment was the primary marker of worthiness. The unemployed, described by settlement workers, caseworkers, social scientists, and the jobless themselves as victims of an unpredictable economy, turned to public sources of relief for assistance. These jobless workers became entitled through the Social Security Act. As Berkowitz explains, "Twentieth-century social policy based entitlement to Social Security, the predominant form of public aid, on occupation."[65] The "neighbor less fortunate," on the other hand, was caught in the web of private charity that had long struggled to deal with increased need. While the categories were certainly simplistic and often overlapped, their cultural resonance signified a shift toward what Linda Gordon calls the "two-tier welfare state."[66]

At the federal level, the WCOU and settlement workers lost the battle for the Lundeen bill, and what they got was a much less satisfactory form of unemployment insurance. Although it included unemployment insurance, the Social Security Act offered a limited definition of "worker," excluding agricultural and domestic workers.

Yet of more concern to industrial workers in the urban North was its system of funding. The Roosevelt administration's program was funded by contributions—taxes on employers and optional employee donations—much of which would be determined and administered by the states. Thus, workers still found themselves at the whim of their states and employers, often unemployed or underemployed, and stuck in local systems of relief and welfare. Moreover, workers were concerned that, whereas the Lundeen bill promised to go into effect immediately, the Social Security Act did not appropriate funds until the close of 1936, effectively leaving the jobless to suffer the continued Depression.

Workers and settlement leaders were forced to accept a somewhat unsatisfactory form of unemployment insurance, but they too were complicit in the creation of a partial entitlement. Just as settlement workers and relief officials decried this poverty because these poor workers were hard working and trustworthy, the architects of the Social Security Act excluded temporary workers and relegated women and their children to public assistance, which, although widely embraced in the 1930s, brought with it the stigma of casework. In the chaos and crisis of the Depression, workers and settlement leaders accepted government-funded relief that was functionally local and national unemployment insurance that was controlled by the states. A federal-state program for relief and social insurance utilized an already established bureaucracy, but it also preserved a culture of charity driven by assessment and judgment.

Ironically, workers themselves reflected the persistence of charity and their determination to escape caseworkers and the stigma they brought. It is worth reconsidering the WCOU's response when the federal government shut down the Civil Works Administration (CWA): "Are You Happy?" it asked workers. "Are you glad the CWA ended? Glad to be back on relief? Glad to have a kind case-worker to help you bring up your kids and teach you how to spend your money? The H—l You Are!" After inviting dissatisfied workers to join the WCOU, it promised: "Why Take a Handout? The Workers' Committee doesn't. You won't have to either if you join."[67] The stigma of charity was a fact of life, these workers suggested, but not one that they deserved to endure.

Epilogue

Still Entitled to Relief?

In the 1920s, settlement workers undertook a fairly straightforward project: to prove that unemployment existed even in a prosperous time and to convince Americans that unemployed workers deserved government assistance without the stigma of charity. Certainly, theirs was not an easy task, for reformers and legislators alike had seemingly closed the casket on unemployment insurance at the beginning of the decade. Yet at least the terms of the debate were clear enough: they needed to demonstrate that workers were vulnerable even in a thriving economy, and that the unemployed were not necessarily paupers.

For workers, social insurance remained a crucial solution, and the passage of the Social Security Act indicated that they were entitled to have a say in their own economic well-being. In 1935, Chicago's workers clarified that they understood government assistance to be dependent on mutual accountability by the state and the people. "This is not only a situation calling for increased private charity," the workers' flyer explained, "but one involving social responsibility which should be laid democratically upon the whole possessing populace in accordance with their ability to share."[1] In 1937, Lea Taylor informed Chicago Commons supporters that entitlement had indeed arrived in

Old Town. "As the social security laws have begun to operate through the unemployment insurance act, the old age annuity and the old age pension," Taylor mused, "there has come to each individual a sense that he is joining with government and industry in an effort to build for the future."[2] Contributory social insurance, it seemed, resonated with the unemployed.

Franklin Roosevelt agreed. In crafting the Social Security Act, Roosevelt declared that relief was secondary to insurance. In 1934, he overruled proposals to integrate social insurance with relief, "dovetailing the systems designed to keep workers from falling into poverty," as Daniel Rodgers explains, "with the systems designed to sustain them should the safety net fail to work."[3] The success of the act for social insurance, Roosevelt suggested, instead depended on a rejection of relief.

In the chaos of the Great Depression, though, the settlement workers' campaign for unemployment insurance became more complicated. As settlement neighbors went from financially insecure to financially destitute, unemployment insurance became, in a way, secondary to relief. For the rest of the decade, settlement workers balanced two forms of government support: relief and social insurance. For while they believed that unemployed workers *deserved* unemployment insurance, they knew that workers *needed* relief.

Moreover, the New Deal government had an ambivalent relationship with relief from its inception. Because the New Deal's social insurance legislation was firmly contributory, workers faced delayed payments for unemployment insurance and thus continued to turn to relief agencies for assistance. In other words, insurance would have to wait, and workers remained "reliefers."

Their options for relief were mercurial at best. On the one hand, the cash relief offered by Federal Emergency Relief Administration (FERA) caseworkers looked an awful lot like charity. Because the FERA was run through state and local institutions, such as the Illinois Emergency Relief Commission (IERC), recipients relied on caseworkers to access their relief and thus frequently suffered cutbacks. After 1935, moreover, they were functionally sent back to their local systems for relief. In 1936, four years after Chicago's workers organized a hunger march, Taylor described her neighbors in hardly different terms:

It is mid-summer evening on Grand Avenue and Morgan Street, and our two little new trees which we have watered most carefully are flourishing, and the flowers in our window boxes are blooming.

I wish our neighbors on relief were as well cared for. The greatly reduced relief at present while relief stations are closed, amounts to an average of only $18 per month, per family, most of it in the form of a grocery order. There is no provision for clothing or household supplies, and nothing for rent except in exceptional cases.

And yet, the majority of families have patiently—or apathetically—expected that something would happen to bring more adequate relief.[4]

On the other hand, what Taylor's neighbors likely hoped for was work relief, but programs like the Works Progress Administration (WPA) and the Public Works Administration (PWA) also proved to be unreliable for many workers. These federal programs were perpetually underfunded and suffered challenges from the private sector as well as from the jobless. Even as they offered laborers something more than the "dole," work relief left them in a twilight zone between "reliefer" and "worker."[5] As workers who were still subject to the stigma of relief, laborers also found that, although the government had seemingly bolstered their roles as breadwinner, the low wages of the WPA forced their wives to take jobs in low-paying industries anyway.[6] Even work relief, it seemed, undercut their burgeoning relationship with the federal government.

In a cruel twist of fate, in the years after Congress passed measures for relief and social insurance, the Depression got worse. To the dismay of settlement workers, the Depression that had dragged on for years and finally promised to ease up sunk even lower in 1937. "Reawakened hope killed may make the heart resentful," Harriet Vittum reflected in September 1937, "and there was resentment that had not been evidenced through the eight hard years just passed. Suffering, acute suffering of the body, as well as mind, was everywhere."[7]

Popular support for relief also declined as the extended Depression wore on the sympathies of many Americans. In 1939, in the wake of a cut in WPA funds, Taylor described common responses to workers who were unable to find private employment and so were forced to reapply for relief. "Within the last two weeks," Taylor lamented, "I have heard people 'on the outside' say such things as 'don't you think these people won't work?' and 'it isn't really so bad, is it?'"[8] As James T. Patterson explains, "By the late 1930s popular attitudes seemed harsher. . . . Majorities in polls said that most poor people could get off relief if they tried hard enough. Respondents began to distinguish between the unemployed—perhaps deserving—and 'reliefers,' 'good-for-nothing loafers,' and 'pampered poverty rats.'" Popular jokes suggested that the WPA actually stood for "We Piddle Around" or "We Putter Around" and barbed: "There's a new cure for cancer, but they can't get any of it. It's sweat from a WPA worker."[9]

This was the semi-welfare state in action, which settlement workers and laborers helped create. Until unemployment insurance built up sufficient funds, jobless workers remained on the means-tested side of social welfare, waiting for caseworkers to assess them while fielding judgments from popular culture. In the 1920s, settlement workers had outlined a program for social insurance that emphasized government protection for male heads-of-household who had proven their industry. In the 1930s, when the Depression rendered relief a priority, the workers themselves joined in, and settlement workers and the unemployed demanded fair relief alongside insurance. The Social Security Act, in its final form, entitled some workers to unemployment insurance, and when unemployment rates eased, these workers finally benefited from the settlement campaigns. But the closing years of the Depression indicated that theirs was a limited form of entitlement, as anyone left on relief would suffer from the stigma.

While the battle for entitlement (even partial entitlement) was hard fought and hard won, its rewards were neither universal nor enduring. The champions of social insurance (such as Helen Hall) advocated for it as a way to prevent another Depression from rendering workers destitute. Yet, as Hall and Kellogg predicted, the Social Security Act's commitment to state autonomy has led to wide variation in funding and compensation, as the twenty-first century has confirmed.

The issue of inconsistent funding became especially clear in 2013 (five years after the start of the Great Recession), when all but fifteen states faced insolvency in unemployment insurance funds. The response was often to cut the amount and duration of benefits. A 2014 brief by the Economic Policy Institute found that insolvency was less the result of the recession than a lack of investment in good times. As it states, "It was largely trust fund adequacy before the Great Recession—not significantly less-severe state-level recessions—that differentiated the states with solvent [unemployment] accounts."[10] Just as Hall and settlement workers witnessed, support for unemployment insurance was weaker during times of prosperity, thus rendering the system less prepared for economic crisis.

Patterns of state vulnerability and insufficient funding have extended into the COVID-19 pandemic of 2020. The depth of the crisis has provoked significant federal intervention, but workers (again) are paying for a weakly prepared system of unemployment insurance. States are beyond overwhelmed by unemployment claims (hitting a record thirty million claims filed in the first six weeks of the pandemic), prompting Congress to pass the $2 trillion relief package known as the Coronavirus Aid, Relief, and Economic Security (CARES) Act. Offering $160 billion in unemployment, the CARES Act makes federal protection available to workers in typically unfunded groups (such as self-employed individuals) and extends access to federal benefits from twenty-six to thirty-nine weeks. Like the Social Security Act of 1935, the CARES Act is extremely generous and hampered by what National Public Radio (NPR) describes as "an overwhelmed and creaky unemployment system," leaving many workers unfunded nearly a month after passage.[11]

As the twenty-first century has demonstrated, and as reformers like Hall suspected, support for unemployment insurance during moments of crisis is not a predictor of sustained support, and a lack of sustained support renders the social safety net unprepared for moments of crisis. The close of the Great Depression saw jobless workers (such as members of the Workers Committee on Unemployment [WCOU]) gain the kind of entitlement that promised them protection from the vagaries of the market, while those left uncovered (such as migrant laborers) were relegated to the stigma-filled world of charity and relief.

At the start of what could become a second Great Depression, more Americans are unemployed than have been for almost a century, and they are facing an unprepared social safety net. The nation and world are in a crisis, but perhaps we can learn from settlement workers of the 1930s. Let us conceive of a generous entitlement that encompasses relief and security, and let us take heed of the dangers of taking that entitlement for granted.

Appendices

Appendix 1

Settlements and Other Organizations Cooperating in the
Unemployment Study of the National Federation of Settlements

TABLE A.1			
City	State	Organization	NFS?
Los Angeles	CA	Probation Office	No
Hartford	CT	Hartford Social Settlement	Yes
Washington	DC	Friendship House	Yes
Atlanta	GA	Family Welfare Society	No
Columbus	GA	Family Welfare Society	No
Savannah	GA	Family Welfare Society	No
Chicago	IL	Chicago Commons	Yes
Chicago	IL	Fellowship House	Yes
Chicago	IL	Hull House	Yes
Chicago	IL	Laird Community House	Yes
Chicago	IL	Olivet Institute	Yes
Chicago	IL	South Chicago Center	Yes
Chicago	IL	University of Chicago Settlement	Yes
Indianapolis	IN	Christamore House	Yes
Louisville	KY	Baptist Good Will Center	No
Louisville	KY	Calvary Point Community House	Yes
Louisville	KY	Neighborhood House	Yes
Louisville	KY	Ninth and Hill Center	Yes
Louisville	KY	Plymouth Settlement	Yes
Louisville	KY	Sunshine Center	Yes
Louisville	KY	Wesley Community House	Yes
Louisville	KY	Rose Hudson Community Center	Yes
Lafayette	LA	Home Relief Association	No
New Orleans	LA	Family Service Society	No
New Orleans	LA	Kingsley House	Yes
Boston	MA	Denison House	Yes
Boston	MA	Elizabeth Peabody House	Yes
Boston	MA	Ellis Memorial	Yes
Boston	MA	Good Will Nieghborhood House	Yes

(continued on next page)

City	State	Organization	NFS?
Boston	MA	Jamaica Plain Neighborhood House	Yes
Boston	MA	Lincoln House	Yes
Boston	MA	Little House	Yes
Boston	MA	North Bennett Street Industrial School	No
Boston	MA	North Brighton Community Centre	Yes
Boston	MA	North End Union	Yes
Boston	MA	Robert Gould Shaw House	Yes
Boston	MA	Roxbury Neighborhood House	Yes
Boston	MA	South End House	Yes
Boston	MA	Trinity Neighborhood House	Yes
Cambridge	MA	Cambridge Neighborhood House	Yes
Cambridge	MA	East End Union	Yes
Cambridge	MA	Margaret Fuller House	Yes
Fall River	MA	King Philip Settlement House	Yes
Roxbury	MA	Norfolk House Center	Yes
Detroit	MI	Dodge Community House	Yes
Detroit	MI	Franklin Street Settlement	Yes
Detroit	MI	Highland Park Community Center	Yes
Minneapolis	MN	North East Neighborhood House	Yes
Minneapolis	MN	Pillsbury Settlement House	Yes
Minneapolis	MN	Washington Neighborhood House	Yes
Minneapolis	MN	Wells Memorial House	Yes
St. Louis	MO	Holy Cross Corporation	No
St. Louis	MO	Kingdom House	Yes
St. Louis	MO	Neighborhood Association	Yes
St. Louis	MO	Wesley House	Yes
Omaha	NB	Omaha Social Settlement	Yes
Newark	NJ	Ironbound Community House	Yes
Newark	NJ	Jewish Day Nursery and Neighborhood House	No
Orange	NJ	Orange Valley Social Settlement	Yes
Buffalo	NY	Welcome Hall	Yes
New York City	NY	Christodora House	Yes
New York City	NY	Church of the Sea and Land	No
New York City	NY	College Settlement	Yes
New York City	NY	East Side House	Yes
New York City	NY	Federation Settlement	Yes
New York City	NY	Greenwich House	Yes

City	State	Organization	NFS?
New York City	NY	Haarlem House	Yes
New York City	NY	Hebrew Educational Society	No
New York City	NY	Hudson Guild	Yes
New York City	NY	Neighborhood House of the Central Presbyterian Church	No
New York City	NY	New York Urban League	No
New York City	NY	110th Street Neighborhood Club	Yes
New York City	NY	Recreation Rooms and Settlement	Yes
New York City	NY	Jacob A. Riis Neighborhood House	Yes
New York City	NY	Stuyvesant Neighborhood House	Yes
New York City	NY	Union Settlement	Yes
New York City	NY	Willoughby House Settlement	Yes
Rochester	NY	Baden Street Settlement	Yes
Rochester	NY	Charles Settlement House	Yes
Rochester	NY	Lewis Street Center	Yes
Cleveland	OH	Alta Social Settlement	Yes
Cleveland	OH	Friendly Inn	Yes
Cleveland	OH	Goodrich Social Settlement	Yes
Cleveland	OH	Hiram House	Yes
Cleveland	OH	Merrick House	Yes
Toledo	OH	North Toledo Community House	Yes
Philadelphia	PA	College Settlement	Yes
Philadelphia	PA	House of Industry	Yes
Philadelphia	PA	Neighborhood Center	Yes
Philadelphia	PA	Saint Martha's House	No
Philadelphia	PA	Settlement Music School	Yes
Philadelphia	PA	Southwark Neighborhood House	Yes
Philadelphia	PA	Stanfield Playground	No
Philadelphia	PA	The Lighthouse	Yes
Philadelphia	PA	University House	Yes
Philadelphia	PA	Webster House	Yes
Philadelphia	PA	Workman Place House	Yes
Pittsburgh	PA	Irene Kaufman Settlement	Yes
Pittsburgh	PA	Kingsley House	Yes
Pittsburgh	PA	Woods Run Settlement	Yes
Charleston	SC	Associated Charities	No
Nashville	TN	Martha O'Bryan Community House	Yes
Salt Lake City	UT	Neighborhood House	Yes
Madison	WI	Neighborhood House	Yes

Appendix 2

Partial List of Members of the Governor's Commission
on Unemployment and Relief (GCUR)

Partial list of leaders in labor, churches, and social services:
- A. C. Thayer, superintendent, Urban League
- E. L. Ryerson Jr., president, Council of Social Agencies of Chicago
- John Fitzpatrick, president, Chicago Federation of Labor
- Joel D. Hunter, superintendent, United Charities of Chicago
- Rabbi Louis Mann
- The Reverend Shaller Matthews, president, Chicago Church Federation
- Agnes Nestor, president, Chicago Women's Trade Union league

Partial list of leaders in business:
- Clifford W. Barnes, vice chairman, Chicago Association of Commerce
- W. G. Bierd, president, Chicago and Alton Railway Company
- John Brenza, president, Metropolitan State Bank
- George F. Getz, president, Globe Coal Company
- Samuel Insull Jr., chairman of the board, Peoples Gas Light and Coke Company and Commonwealth Edison Company
- Charles A. McCulloch, capitalist
- Julius Rosenwald, chairman of the board, Sears, Roebuck and Company
- E. V. (Eugene Van Rensselaer) Thayer, chairman of the executive committee and past president of Chase National Bank of New York, Central Trust Company
- William Wrigley Jr., president, William Wrigley Company (and owner of the Chicago Cubs, purchased from Albert Lasker, who would serve as vice president of the Community Fund in 1934)

Notes

Introduction

1. Chicago Workers' Committee, *Pamphlet: We Need You and You Need Us*, November 1934, box 26, folder 1, Chicago Commons Collection, Chicago History Museum (hereafter cited as Chicago Commons Collection).

2. For more on relief and social policy, see Michelle Landis Dauber, *The Sympathetic State: Disaster Relief and the Origins of the American Welfare State* (Chicago: University of Chicago Press, 2013).

3. Settlement workers participated in early conversations about social insurance but ultimately focused on unemployment and thus advocated for unemployment insurance specifically. Because the terminology remained fluid during the early 1930s, I use both terms in this book.

4. One need only take a look at the Franklin D. Roosevelt memorial in Washington, D.C., to get a sense of the extent to which American historical memory lionizes FDR. The memorial, although lovely, tells the widely accepted narrative of the poor as helpless and Roosevelt as their savior. Although most historians offer a more nuanced telling, many still ignore the role of city and state governments in paving the way for New Deal policies. For examples, see David Kennedy, *The American People in the Great Depression: Freedom from Fear, Part 1* (New York: Oxford University Press, 1999); William Edward Leuchtenburg, *Franklin D. Roosevelt and the New Deal, 1932–1940*, The New American Nation Series (New York: Harper and Row, 1963); Paul Conkin, *The New Deal*, The American History Series (Wheeling, IL: Harlan Davidson,

1967); Kirstin Downey, *The Woman behind the New Deal: The Life and Legacy of Frances Perkins—Social Security, Unemployment Insurance, and the Minimum Wage* (New York: Random House, 2009); and Steve Fraser and Gary Gerstle, *The Rise and Fall of the New Deal Order, 1930–1980* (Princeton, NJ: Princeton University Press, 1989).

5. Lea D. Taylor, *Report of the Work of Chicago Commons Association for the Year Ending September 30, 1931*, September 30, 1931, 2, box 5, folder 2, Chicago Commons Collection.

6. See Kennedy, *The American People in the Great Depression*; Leuchtenburg, *Franklin D. Roosevelt and the New Deal*; Conkin, *The New Deal*; Downey, *The Woman behind the New Deal*; and Fraser and Gerstle, *The Rise and Fall of the New Deal Order*.

7. Lizabeth Cohen's landmark study of Chicago workers during the Depression suggests that as workers developed class consciousness during the 1930s, their identities as urban ethnics and relationships with religious and ethnic institutions were subsumed by their participation in labor organizing, a shift that defined New Deal labor policies. Cohen's work misses the ways in which neighborhood and ethnic institutions facilitated increased union organizing. What's more, Cohen (like many labor historians) ignores the ways in which laborers were, during the Depression, welfare recipients—and the role of labor in shaping welfare policies. See Lizabeth Cohen, *Making a New Deal: Industrial Workers in Chicago, 1919–1939* (New York: Cambridge University Press, 2008).

8. Here, they echoed (ever so slightly) Jane Addams, who by 1900 had fully embraced the ethic of pragmatism, a school of thought most famously articulated by John Dewey and William James. For more on pragmatism, see Jane Addams, "The Subjective Necessity of Social Settlements," in *The Jane Addams Reader*, ed. Jean Bethke Elshtain (New York: Basic Books, 2002), 14–28; and Louise W. Knight, *Citizen: Jane Addams and the Struggle for Democracy* (Chicago: University of Chicago Press, 2005), 257, 330, 357–358.

9. Because of the astonishing rates of unemployment and the scope and range of programs that the federal government implemented to combat the Depression, in the 1930s, poverty "came out from hiding" in a way, creating a generational shift in attitudes toward it. See James T. Patterson, *America's Struggle against Poverty in the Twentieth Century* (Cambridge, MA: Harvard University Press, 2000), 48–52.

10. Roy Lubove, *The Professional Altruist: The Emergence of Social Work as a Career, 1880–1930* (New York: Atheneum, 1973).

11. For a sampling, see Allen F. Davis, *Spearheads for Reform: The Social Settlements and the Progressive Movement, 1890–1914* (New York: Oxford University Press, 1967), 231–235; John H. Ehrenreich, *The Altruistic Imagination: A History of Social Work and Social Policy in the United States* (Ithaca, NY: Cornell University Press, 1985), 58–60; Michael Katz, *In the Shadow of the Poorhouse: A Social History of Welfare in America*, 10th anniv. ed. (New York: Basic Books, 1996), 168; Lubove, *The Professional Altruist*, 146–147; Walter Trattner, *From*

Poor Law to Welfare State: A History of Social Welfare in America, 6th ed. (New York: Free Press, 1999), 176; and Judith A. Trolander, *Professionalism and Social Change: From the Settlement House Movement to Neighborhood Centers, 1886 to the Present* (New York: Columbia University Press, 1987), 2.

12. Katz, *In the Shadow of the Poorhouse*, 167. Robyn Muncy has compellingly charted the impact of settlement reformers not in their cities but on federal policy making. Although Muncy makes no claims to the local history of the settlement movement, hers is part of a collection of scholarship suggesting that the most significant parts of the settlement movement occurred outside the settlements themselves. Robyn Muncy, *Creating a Female Dominion in American Reform, 1890–1935* (New York: Oxford University Press, 1991).

13. Jane Addams, foreword to *Religion in Social Action*, by Graham Taylor (New York: Dodd, Mead, 1913), xxx.

14. As Raymond Mohl describes it, early American social welfare "developed in a confused and contradictory ideological context which suggested both that it was a moral responsibility to aid the poor but also that the poor were responsible for their lowly circumstances and should climb out of poverty through their own individual efforts." Raymond A. Mohl, "Mainstream Social Welfare History and Its Problems," *Reviews in American History* 7.4 (December 1979): 471.

15. Florence Kelley, "Minimum Wage Boards," reprinted from *Proceedings of the National Conference of Charities and Correction, June 1911*, quoted in Kathryn Kish-Sklar, "Two Political Cultures in the Progressive Era: The National Consumers' League and the American Association for Labor Legislation," in *U.S. History as Women's History: New Feminist Essays*, ed. Linda Gordon, Alice Kessler-Harris, and Kathryn Kish-Sklar (Chapel Hill: University of North Carolina Press, 1995), 59.

16. Helen Hall, "Introducing Our Neighbors," in *Case Studies of Unemployment, Compiled by the Unemployment Committee of the National Federation of Settlements*, ed. Marion Elderton (Philadelphia: University of Pennsylvania Press, 1931), xxiii.

17. For more on the relationship between public assistance and social insurance, see Edward D. Berkowitz, *America's Welfare State: From Roosevelt to Reagan* (Baltimore: Johns Hopkins University Press, 1991), 3; and David A. Moss, *Socializing Security: Progressive-Era Economists and the Origins of American Social Policy* (Cambridge, MA: Harvard University Press, 1996), 4.

18. Linda Gordon, "Social Insurance and Public Assistance: The Influence of Gender in Welfare Thought in the United States, 1890–1935," *American Historical Review* 97 (February 1992): 20. See also Linda Gordon, *Pitied but Not Entitled: Single Mothers and the History of Welfare, 1890–1935* (New York: Free Press, 1994); Kish-Sklar, "Two Political Cultures in the Progressive Era"; Gwendolyn Mink, *The Wages of Motherhood: Inequality in the Welfare State, 1917–1942* (Ithaca, NY: Cornell University Press, 1995); and Barbara Nelson, "The Origins of the Two-Channel Welfare State: Workmen's Compensation and

Mother's Aid," in *Women, the State, and Welfare*, ed. Linda Gordon (Madison: University of Wisconsin Press, 1990), 123–151.

19. Even though *All in the Family* focuses on the 1960s, Self's depiction of the New Deal consensus resonates with settlement workers in the Depression. Robert O. Self, *All in the Family: The Realignment of American Democracy since the 1960s* (New York: Hill and Wang, 2012).

20. See Clarke A. Chambers, *Seedtime of Reform: American Social Service and Social Action, 1918–1933* (Minneapolis: University of Minnesota Press, 1963); and Davis, *Spearheads for Reform.* The only real study of settlement workers in the 1930s is Judith Trolander's *Settlement Houses and the Great Depression* (Detroit: Wayne State University Press, 1975), which asks why some settlements in this era were more reform-oriented than others.

21. See especially Edwin Amenta, *Bold Relief: Institutional Politics and the Origins of Modern American Social Policy* (Princeton, NJ: Princeton University Press, 1998); Cohen, *Making a New Deal*; Kennedy, *The American People in the Great Depression*; and Christopher L. Tomlins, *The State and the Unions: Labor Relations, Law, and the Organized Labor Movement in America* (New York: Cambridge University Press, 1985).

22. See Ruth Hutchinson Crocker, *Social Work and Social Order: The Settlement Movement in Two Industrial Cities, 1889–1930* (Champaign-Urbana: University of Illinois Press, 1992); and Elisabeth Lasch-Quinn, *Black Neighbors: Race and the Limits of Reform in the American Settlement House Movement, 1890–1945* (Chapel Hill: University of North Carolina Press, 1993).

23. The exclusion of black laborers from the benefits of labor organizing has been well documented. Lizabeth Cohen's study of 1930s-era laborers in Chicago reveals persistent racism among employers and white laborers, and as Judith Stepan-Norris and Maurice Zeitlin highlight, sometimes the antipathy ran both ways, with black laborers being highly suspicious of what they saw as "white-man's trade unions." Later in the twentieth century, Thomas Sugrue has revealed, black workers in the urban North faced systematic exclusion in the workplace, effectively stripping them of the benefits of entitlement. In his landmark study of laborers in the twentieth century, Ira Katznelson succinctly describes such programs as social security as white laborers' version of affirmative action. The exception was the Communist Party USA (CPUSA), which in the 1930s actively recruited among African Americans, considering them to be a dispossessed nation and calling for their social and economic equality. Antiradicalism in the subsequent decades, though, all but guaranteed that the CPUSA would not be able to engineer entitlement for laborers of color. See Lizabeth Cohen, *Making a New Deal: Industrial Workers in Chicago, 1919–1939* (New York: Cambridge University Press, 2008), 205–206; Judith Stepan-Norris and Maurice Zeitlin, *Left Out: Reds and America's Industrial Unions* (Cambridge, UK: Cambridge University Press, 2003), 102; Thomas Sugrue, *The Origins of the Urban Crisis: Race and Inequality in Postwar Detroit* (Princeton, NJ: Princeton University Press, 2005), chap. 4; Ira Katznelson, *When Affirmative*

Action Was White: An Untold History of Racial Inequality in Twentieth-Century America (New York: Norton, 2005); and Randi Storch, *Red Chicago: American Communism at Its Grassroots, 1928–35* (Urbana: University of Illinois Press, 2007), 77–78.

24. For scholarly accounts of the racialization of poverty and the focus on black single-parent families, see Jennifer Mittelstadt, *From Welfare to Workfare: The Unintended Consequences of Liberal Reform* (Raleigh: University of North Carolina Press, 2005); and Jill Quadagno, *The Color of Welfare: How Racism Undermined the War on Poverty* (New York: Oxford University Press, 1994).

Chapter 1

1. Helen Hall to Gifford Pinchot, January 7, 1931, box 40, folder 2, Collection 64, Social Welfare History Archives, University of Minnesota (hereafter cited as SWHA).

2. Clinch Calkins, *Some Folks Won't Work* (New York: Harcourt, Brace, 1930); Marion Elderton, ed., *Case Studies of Unemployment* (Philadelphia: University of Pennsylvania Press, 1931).

3. For more on the role of reformers in policy change, see Miriam Cohen and Michael Hanagan, "Politics, Industrialization and Citizenship: Unemployment Policy in England, France and the United States, 1890–1950," in *Citizenship, Identity, and Social History*, ed. Charles Tilly (New York: Cambridge University Press, 1996), 123.

4. *Unemployment Summary Presented to Executive Committee in Cleveland*, November 10, 1928, 1, box 38, folder 7, Collection 34, SWHA.

5. Daniel Rodgers, *Atlantic Crossings: Social Politics in a Progressive Age* (Cambridge, MA: Belknap Press of Harvard University Press, 1998), 252. The Russell Sage Foundation was especially interested in studying local responses to unemployment during and after the depression of 1920–1921 and funded two notable studies: Leah Hannah Feder, *Unemployment Relief in Periods of Depression: A Study of Measures Adopted in Certain American Cities, 1857 through 1922* (New York: Russell Sage Foundation, 1936); and Philip Klein, *The Burden of Unemployment: A Study of Unemployment Relief Measures in Fifteen American Cities, 1921–22* (New York: Russell Sage Foundation, 1923).

6. Theda Skocpol and G. John Ikenberry, "The Road to Social Security," in *Social Policy in the United States: Future Possibilities in Historical Perspective*, ed. Theda Skocpol (Princeton, NJ: Princeton University Press, 1995), 141.

7. The American Association for Labor Legislation (AALL) supported proposals for unemployment insurance that prioritized voluntary participation on the part of workers and offered financial rewards to employers who worked toward the regulation and humanization of industry, and it ultimately abandoned plans that depended on public funds and compulsory insurance. See Shelton Stromquist, *Re-inventing "The People": The Progressive Movement, the Class Problem, and the Origins of Modern Liberalism* (Urbana: University of

Illinois Press, 2006), 90–92; and Skocpol and Ikenberry, "The Road to Social Security," 150.

8. For more on the history of the settlement house movement, see Walter Trattner, *From Poor Law to Welfare State: A History of Social Welfare in America*, 6th ed. (New York: Free Press, 1999), chap. 8; Michael B. Katz, *In the Shadow of the Poorhouse: A Social History of Welfare in America*, 10th anniv. ed. (New York: Basic Books, 1996), chap. 6; and Allan F. Davis, *Spearheads for Reform: The Social Settlements and the Progressive Movement, 1890–1914* (New York: Oxford University Press, 1967).

9. Helen Hall and Henry Street Settlement, *The Helen Hall Settlement Papers: A Descriptive Bibliography of Community Studies and Other Reports, 1928–1958* (New York: New York School of Social Work, 1959), 5.

10. Minutes of the Meetings of the Board of Directors of the National Federation of Settlements, Inc., June 12–14, 1931, 3, box 118, folder 4, Collection 56, SWHA.

11. "Minutes of the First Meeting of the Board of Directors of the National Federation of Settlements, Inc.," December 7, 1929, 9, box 118, folder 4, Collection 56, SWHA.

12. Minutes of the Meetings of the Board of Directors of the National Federation of Settlements, Inc., June, 1928, 9, box 118, folder 4, Collection 56, SWHA. The National Federation of Settlements (NFS) voted to "enlarge the organization of the Unemployment Committee" in 1931; see Minutes of the Meetings of the Board of Directors of the National Federation of Settlements, Inc., June 14, 1931, 3. Clarke A. Chambers chronicles this shift in priorities among settlement workers, arguing that "the social-reform impulse had not died or even become dormant in these years [after World War I] of reaction." Clarke A. Chambers, *Seedtime of Reform: American Social Service and Social Action, 1918–1933* (Minneapolis: University of Minnesota Press, 1963), 131.

13. Paul Kellogg to Viola Paradise, May 29, 1929, 1, box 38, folder 11, Collection 34, SWHA.

14. Hall, the chair of the committee, was a rising star in the NFS and active on the issue of unemployment. During the 1930s, she worked on the Plan for Philadelphia, a task force that made recommendations for long-term economic planning; advised Pennsylvania governor Gifford Pinchot on increasing unemployment; aided New York senator Robert Wagner in creating programs to prevent unemployment; and sat on President Franklin D. Roosevelt's Committee on Economic Security, which drafted the Social Security Act of 1935. Ethel Dougherty and Lea Taylor were head residents at settlement houses, and Paul Kellogg was the editor of a journal that regularly discussed settlement issues. The Executive Committee put together a field committee of eighteen people to manage case-story submissions in their regions, each of whom worked in settlement houses around the Midwest, the South, and the East Coast, from Ellis Memorial in Boston, to Roadside Settlement in Des Moines. See Megan H. Morrissey, "The Life and Career of Helen Hall:

Settlement Worker and Social Reformer in Social Work's Second Generation" (Ph.D. diss., University of Minnesota, 1996), 151; and *Unemployment Study Committee of the National Federation of Settlements*, January 1929, 1, box 38, folder 9, Collection 34, SWHA.

15. It is notable that the committee solicited stories from numerous non-settlement organizations, including branches of the Young Men's Christian Association (YMCA) and the Red Cross. Of the 104 organizations that contributed case studies to the project, at least 17 (16.3 percent) were not settlement houses. Elisabeth Lasch-Quinn's study of "settlement-like" programs, including churches and YMCAs, accurately lays out the kinds of organizations that Hall would turn to when she wanted a picture of unemployment in the South. See Ruth Hutchinson Crocker, *Social Work and Social Order: The Settlement Movement in Two Industrial Cities, 1889–1930* (Champaign-Urbana: University of Illinois Press, 1992); and Elisabeth Lasch-Quinn, *Black Neighbors: Race and the Limits of Reform in the American Settlement House Movement, 1890–1945* (Chapel Hill: University of North Carolina Press, 1993).

16. Albert J. Kennedy to Helen Hall, January 7, 1929, 3, box 38, folder 9, Collection 34, SWHA; also in *Unemployment Summary*, 1.

17. Calkins, *Some Folks Won't Work*, 92.

18. Ibid.; Elderton, *Case Studies of Unemployment*.

19. For a useful article comparing British and U.S. systems of social insurance, see Theda Skocpol and Gretchen Ritter, "Gender and the Origins of Modern Social Policies in Britain and the United States," *Studies in American Political Development* 5 (Spring 1991): 36–93.

20. Alexander Keyssar, *Out of Work: The First Century of Unemployment in Massachusetts* (New York: Cambridge University Press, 1986), 263; and Roy Lubove, *The Struggle for Social Security, 1900–1935* (Cambridge, MA: Harvard University Press, 1968).

21. William M. Leiserson, "A Federal Reserve Board for the Unemployed. Outlines of a Plan for Administering the Remedies for Unemployment," *Annals of the American Academy of Political and Social Science* 69 (January 1917): 103. For more on Leiserson, see Irving Bernstein, *The Turbulent Years: A History of the American Worker, 1933–1941* (Boston: Houghton Mifflin, 1970), 808n7 and chap. 2; J. Michael Eisner, *William Morris Leiserson, A Biography* (Madison, 1967); and Frank M. Kleiler, "William Morris Leiserson," in *Proceedings*, by Industrial Relations, Research Association (1957), 95–101. For more examples of early-twentieth-century depictions of unemployment, see Sarah Frances Rose, "No Right to Be Idle: The Invention of Disability, 1850–1930" (Ph.D. diss., University of Illinois at Chicago, 2008), 159n1; and John B. Andrews, "Workmen's Compensation in New Jersey—The Wrong Way," *Survey* 22 (March 27, 1915): 696–697.

22. William H. Beveridge, *Unemployment: A Problem of Industry (1909 and 1930)* (London: Longmans, Green, 1912, 1930); William H. Beveridge, *Insurance for All and Everything* (London: Daily News, 1924); William H. Beveridge,

Causes and Cures of Unemployment (London: Longmans, Green, 1931); and William H. Beveridge, *Full Employment in a Free Society, a Report by William H. Beveridge* (London: Allen and Unwin, 1944).

23. Many Americans also evinced a faith in the American economy to maintain employment, and after World War I, it became commonplace to oppose social insurance in favor of what would be called "sound economic thinking." This belief included the idea that private enterprise should control social welfare measures and the sense that the federal government should avoid additional costs in the wake of war. See James T. Patterson, *America's Struggle against Poverty in the Twentieth Century* (Cambridge, MA: Harvard University Press, 2000), 32; and Rodgers, *Atlantic Crossings*, 26, 231–232.

24. "Suggestions as to Focus in Developing Miss Hall's Proposal" (ca. 1931), 1, box 40, folder 4, Collection 34, SWHA.

25. Helen Hall, *Report at International Conference*, 1932, 3, D1 556, SWHA.

26. Michelle Landis Dauber has persuasively argued that the architects of New Deal relief and social security policies drew on a tradition of federal disaster aid, which allowed them to argue that those suffering in the 1930s were victims of a disaster rather than loafers or paupers. As she says, "Descripting the Depression as a disaster . . . locate[d] relief payments in a moral context that would render them necessary as a required response to victims' circumstances." Settlement workers in the 1920s clearly drew on the language of disaster, but they also recognized the dangers in treating Depression-era unemployment as an aberration. Michelle Landis Dauber, *The Sympathetic State: Disaster Relief and the Origins of the American Welfare State* (Chicago: University of Chicago Press, 2013), 10.

27. Paul Kellogg, foreword to *Case Studies of Unemployment, Compiled by the Unemployment Committee of the National Federation of Settlements*, ed. Marion Elderton (Philadelphia: University of Pennsylvania Press, 1931), ix.

28. Ibid., x.

29. Kellogg to Viola Paradise, 1.

30. Helen Hall, "Introducing Our Neighbors," in *Case Studies of Unemployment, Compiled by the Unemployment Committee of the National Federation of Settlements*, ed. Marion Elderton (Philadelphia: University of Pennsylvania Press, 1931), xxiii.

31. Calkins, *Some Folks Won't Work*, 30–45. David Kennedy discusses the plight of agricultural workers in the 1920s and 1930s, and the 1938 *Report on Economic Conditions of the South*, commissioned by President Franklin Roosevelt, offers a glimpse at the many economic problems facing the (largely agricultural) region. David M. Kennedy, *The American People in the Great Depression: Freedom from Fear, Part 1* (New York: Oxford University Press, 1999), chap. 1; and National Emergency Council, *Report on Economic Conditions of the South* (Washington, DC: U.S. Government Printing Office, 1938).

32. Kellogg, foreword to *Case Studies*, viii.

33. Calkins, *Some Folks Won't Work*, 161.

34. Calkins added, "We have with this parallel problem [industrial accidents and industrial unemployment] the parallel possibility of meeting the risks of unemployment as we met the risks of industrial accidents: first, through stabilization that will reduce the intermittency of earnings; second, through some form of protection for families caught by the dislocations of work which we fail to control." Ibid., 159.

35. Hall, "Introducing Our Neighbors," xxxviii.

36. Minutes of the Meetings of the Board of Directors of the National Federation of Settlements, Inc., May 12–15, 1932, 58. Six months later, Hall expressed concern that the outlook for unemployment insurance was not encouraging, and she urged settlement workers to actively work for unemployment insurance in their cities and states. Minutes of the Meetings of the Board of Directors of the National Federation of Settlements, Inc., December 10–11, 1932, 5.

37. Hall, "Introducing Our Neighbors," xl. See also Daniel Nelson, *Unemployment Insurance: The American Experience, 1915-1935* (Madison: University of Wisconsin Press, 1969); and Lubove, *The Struggle for Social Security.*

38. Calkins, *Some Folks Won't Work*, 20–21. For more on this myth, see Udo Sautter, *Three Cheers for the Unemployed: Government and Unemployment before the New Deal* (New York: Cambridge University Press, 1991), 3; and Patterson, *America's Struggle against Poverty in the Twentieth Century*, 31.

39. Morrissey, "The Life and Career of Helen Hall," 134–135n16.

40. Helen Hall to Irene Nelson, December 7, 1928, 1, box 38, folder 10, Collection 34, SWHA.

41. C. H. Bogart to Mrs. S. Max Nelson, February 1, 1929, 1, box 38, folder 10, Collection 34, SWHA.

42. Irene Nelson to Mr. C. H. Bogart, February 4, 1929, 1, box 38, folder 10, Collection 34, SWHA.

43. Calkins, *Some Folks Won't Work*, 140.

44. See especially ibid., 122–130.

45. Irene Nelson to Helen Hall, January 14, 1929, 3, box 38, folder 9, Collection 34, SWHA.

46. "Instructions to Head-Workers of Settlements for Study of Social Effects of Unemployment," December 9, 1928, 1, box 38, folder 8, Collection 34, SWHA.

47. Helen Hall to Lea D. Taylor, January 26, 1929, 2, box 38, folder 9, Collection 34, SWHA.

48. Nelson to Helen Hall, 4.

49. Chad Alan Goldberg has charted the ramifications in the 1930s of the historic suspicion of relief. As he argues, "Paupers forfeited their civil and political rights in exchange for relief." As Goldberg mentions, and as Linda Gordon has shown extensively, the denial of full citizenship to relief (and ultimately welfare) recipients has been historically gendered, but the 1930s were noteworthy for the extent to which they brought working males into the realm of relief recipients. See Chad Alan Goldberg, *Citizens and Paupers: Relief, Rights, and*

Race, from the Freedmen's Bureau to Workfare (Chicago: University of Chicago Press, 2007), 2; and Linda Gordon, *Pitied but Not Entitled: Single Mothers and the History of Welfare, 1890–1935* (New York: Free Press, 1994).

50. Hall to Irene Nelson, 1.

51. Ibid.

52. Ibid.

53. Elderton, *Case Studies of Unemployment*, 1.

54. Ibid., 347.

55. Ibid., 75, 132, 227, and 346.

56. Ibid., 161.

57. This part of their work was unusual in the 1920s and predated a spate of very popular 1930s sociological studies on families enduring unemployment.

58. They certainly echoed maternalist reformers. See Joanne L. Goodwin, "An American Experiment in Paid Motherhood: The Implementation of Mothers' Pensions in Early Twentieth-Century Chicago," *Gender and History* 4 (1992): 321–342; Christopher Howard, "Sowing the Seeds of 'Welfare': The Transformation of Mothers' Pensions, 1900–1940," *Journal of Policy History* 4 (1992): 188–227; Seth Koven and Sonya Michel, eds., *Mothers of a New World: Maternalist Politics and the Origins of Welfare States* (New York: Routledge, 1993); and Robyn Muncy, *Creating a Female Dominion in American Reform, 1890–1935* (New York: Oxford University Press, 1991).

59. Their focus on families often meant a focus on mothers. Hall led her discussion with the University Settlement's Mothers' Club, which tells us something about who they considered to be research subjects—this study was about unemployment, but it frequently focused on mothers as the barometers of difficulty and the bearers of the family story. With this view, the Unemployment Committee predicted what Robert O. Self calls "male breadwinner liberalism," which emerged with the creation of the New Deal and influenced American society and politics through the twentieth century. Robert O. Self, *All in the Family: The Realignment of American Democracy since the 1960s* (New York: Hill and Wang, 2012).

60. Martha May, "The Historical Problem of the Family Wage: The Ford Motor Company and the Five Dollar Day," *Feminist Studies* 8.2 (Summer 1982): 399–401. Laurence B. Glickman proposes using the term *living wage*, which is a broader term than *family wage*, but because *living wage* fails to acknowledge the gendered dimensions of reform work and settlement workers used neither term consistently in the 1920s, I have settled for the term *male breadwinner household*. Laurence B. Glickman, *Living Wage: American Workers and the Making of Consumer Society* (Ithaca, NY: Cornell University Press, 1997), 158.

61. May, "The Historical Problem of the Family Wage," 404. See also Nancy K. Cauthen and Edwin Amenta, "Not for Widows Only: Institutional Politics and the Formative Years of Aid to Dependent Children," *American Sociological Review* 61.3 (June 1996): 427–448, 430–432; Premilla Nadasen, Jennifer Mittelstadt, and Marisa Chappell, *Welfare in the United States: A History with Documents, 1935–1996* (New York: Routledge, 2009), 14–15; Gwendolyn Mink, *The*

Wages of Motherhood: Inequality in the Welfare State, 1917–1942 (Ithaca, NY: Cornell University Press, 1995), vii; and Linda Gordon, "Social Insurance and Public Assistance: The Influence of Gender in Welfare Thought in the United States, 1890–1935," *American Historical Review* 97 (February 1992): 20.

62. Hall, *Report at International Conference*, 6.

63. Elderton, *Case Studies of Unemployment*, 348–349; and Irene Nelson to Helen Hall, ca. May 1929, 1, box 38, folder 11, Collection 34, SWHA.

64. Florence Kelley, "Minimum-Wage Laws," *Journal of Political Economy* 20.10 (December 1912): 1003, as quoted in May, "The Historical Problem of the Family Wage," 404; Nadasen, Mittelstadt, and Chappell, *Welfare in the United States*, 14; and Koven and Michel, *Mothers of a New World*, 2.

65. Martha May, "Bread before Roses: American Workingmen, Labour Unions, and the Family Wage," in *Women, Work and Protest: A Century of Women's Labor History*, ed. Ruth Milkman (New York: Routledge, 2013), 149. See also Maurine Weiner Greenwald, "Working-Class Feminism and the Family Wage Ideal: The Seattle Debate on Married Women's Right to Work, 1914–1920," *Journal of American History* 76 (June 1989): 147; and Jeanne Boydston, *Home and Work: Housework, Wages, and the Ideology of Labor in the Early Republic* (New York: Oxford University Press, 1990), 155.

66. Jane Addams, *Twenty Years at Hull-House* (New York: Macmillan, 1911), 116.

67. Graham Taylor, "'Some Folks Won't Work'—Challenged," *Chicago Daily News*, November 22, 1930, 1, SWDI 555, SWHA.

68. May, "The Historical Problem of the Family Wage," 404.

69. Calkins, *Some Folks Won't Work*, 113.

70. Ibid., 35.

71. Hall, "Introducing Our Neighbors," xxxi.

72. Ibid., 115.

73. Ibid., 151.

74. Paul Douglas, "'Wanted: Work,' Some Folks Won't Work" (no date given—likely 1932), 1, D1 556, SWHA.

75. Fanny Butcher, "Best Books of the Year in Christmas Parade: Fanny Butcher Surveys Work of the Authors, Chicagoans Find Place High on List," *Chicago Daily Tribune*, December 13, 1930, 15.

76. Minutes, June 12–14, 1931, 3.

77. Taylor, "'Some Folks Won't Work,'" 2.

78. "Offers Plans to End Crisis," *Detroit News*, pre–January 22, 1932, 2, box 41, folder 1, SWHA.

79. Meeting Minutes of the Unemployment Committee, February 27, 1931, 1.

80. Sautter, *Three Cheers for the Unemployed*, 256–257.

81. Minutes of the Meetings of the Board of Directors of the National Federation of Settlements, Inc., January 29–30, 1932, 1.

82. As Hall explained, the Ohio plan required much more state control over unemployment insurance than the Wisconsin plan (which was largely run

by employers). Minutes of the Meetings of the Board of Directors of the National Federation of Settlements, Inc., January 29–30, 1932, 1–2. Roy Lubove outlines the debates between advocates of the Wisconsin plan (which relied on employer-funded reserves) and the Ohio plan (which legislated a more comprehensive insurance policy based on employer and employee contributions). See Lubove, *The Struggle for Social Security*, 171–173.

83. Minutes of the Meetings of the Board of Directors of the National Federation of Settlements, Inc., December 10–11, 1932, 7.

84. Hall to Gifford Pinchot, 1.

85. Helen Hall, "Draft of Letter to President Franklin D. Roosevelt, as the Chairman of the Unemployment Division of the National Federation of Settlements," January 23, 1934; and Louis McHenry Howe, "Letter from the Office of the President to Albert Kennedy, Esq, President of the National Federation of Settlements," February 27, 1934, box 42, folders 1–7, Collection 34

86. Muncy, *Creating a Female Dominion in American Reform*; and Chambers, *Seedtime of Reform*. For one of the primary examples of scholarship on settlement houses in the 1930s, see Judith A. Trolander, *Settlement Houses and the Great Depression* (Detroit: Wayne State University Press, 1975). For examples of scholarship that emphasizes settlement workers' shift toward professionalization, see the works recommended in "Introduction," note 11.

87. Minutes of the Meetings of the Board of Directors of the National Federation of Settlements, Inc., January 26–27, 1935, 5.

88. Barbara Nelson, Linda Gordon, and Gwendolyn Mink first theorized and researched the "two-tiered welfare state," a concept that emphasizes the meaningful differences between entitlement programs, such as unemployment insurance, and means-tested ("welfare") programs, such as Aid to Dependent Children. Gordon, for instance, argues that Roosevelt's Social Security Act ultimately bifurcated along class and gender lines, granting some recipients a sense of entitlement and subjecting others to "personal supervision of [their] private lives; and [with it] a deep stigma." Gordon, "Social Insurance and Public Assistance," 20; Gwendolyn Mink, *The Wages of Motherhood*; and Barbara Nelson, "The Origins of the Two-Channel Welfare State: Workmen's Compensation and Mother's Aid," in *Women, the State, and Welfare*, ed. Linda Gordon (Madison: University of Wisconsin Press, 1990), 123–151.

Acknowledgment: This chapter was originally published as Abigail Trollinger, "Revealing the 'Social Consequences of Unemployment': The Settlement Campaign for the Unemployed on the Eve of Depression," *Journal of Social History* 52, no. 4 (Summer 2019): 1250–1280, https://doi.org/10.1093/jsh/shy020.

Chapter 2

1. Cousin Eve, "Crowded, Gay Parties Mark a Holiday Week," *Chicago Daily Tribune*, December 27, 1931, G1.

2. With the 1925 creation of the Cook County Bureau of Public Welfare, which (as its name implied) was a state-funded modern public assistance

agency, social workers and charities had had to manage a balance between privately funded charity and public welfare.

3. *Report of the Work of Chicago Commons for the Year Ending September 30, 1928*, 11, box 5, folder 1, Chicago Commons Collection, Chicago History Museum (hereafter cited as Chicago Commons Collection).

4. Malachy Richard McCarthy, "Which Christ Came to Chicago: Catholic and Protestant Programs to Evangelize, Socialize and Americanize the Mexican Immigrant, 1900–1940" (Ph.D. diss., Loyola University of Chicago, 2002), 303, 384; Illinois Department of Labor, *Labor Bulletin* 12 (January 1933): 131; Lizabeth Cohen, *Making a New Deal: Industrial Workers in Chicago, 1919–1939* (New York: Cambridge University Press, 2008), 217–218; and Dominic A. Pacyga, *Chicago: A Biography* (Chicago: University of Chicago Press, 2009), 251–253.

5. Lorena A. Hickok, *One Third of a Nation: Lorena Hickok Reports on the Great Depression*, ed. Richard Lowitt and Maurine Beasley (Urbana: University of Illinois Press, 1981), 360.

6. *First Annual Report of the Illinois Emergency Relief Commission for the Year Ending February 5, 1933, Issued Jointly with a Report of the Illinois Emergency Relief Commission (Federal) Covering the Period July 27, 1932 through February 5, 1933* (Springfield: State of Illinois, 1933), 4; and Pacyga, *Chicago*, 259.

7. Lyman B. Burbank, "Chicago Public Schools and the Depression Years of 1928–1937," *Journal of the Illinois State Historical Society* 64 (Winter 1971): 368.

8. Pacyga, *Chicago*, 259; Burbank, "Chicago Public Schools and the Depression Years," 367; John F. Lyons, *Teachers and Reform: Chicago Public Education, 1929–1970* (Urbana: University of Illinois Press, 2008), 27–29; and Mary J. Herrick, *The Chicago Schools: A Social and Political History* (Beverly Hills: Sage, 1971), chap. 10.

9. William Edward Leuchtenburg, *Franklin D. Roosevelt and the New Deal, 1932–1940*, New American Nation Series (New York: Harper and Row, 1963), 21.

10. The Illinois state government did set up free employment bureaus, but even though Chicagoans made up 60 percent of applicants for jobs (12,426 out of 22,609), fewer than one-quarter of those found jobs, unlike the two-thirds of downstate applicants who did.

11. The state acquiesced to Cook County's calls for relief in early 1932, after a protracted legislative debate. For more on that process, see Chapter 5.

12. Lea D. Taylor to Helen Hall, January 20, 1931, 1, box 40, folder 2, Collection 34, Social Welfare History Archives, University of Minnesota (hereafter cited as SWHA); and Cohen, *Making a New Deal*, 224.

13. "Workers Ready for $5,000,000 Job Fund Drive," *Chicago Daily Tribune*, November 17, 1930, 6.

14. I use the terms *private* and *public* as members of the relief drives used them, as terms that described who financed and oversaw relief and welfare efforts. "Private" welfare agencies were those that were funded by private (nongovernmental) donations and run by figures totally independent of the government. "Private" agencies were almost always locally run (from Cook

County), and the most referenced private agencies were Catholic Charities of Cook County, United Charities, and the Jewish Service Bureau. The government, on the other hand, funded "public" welfare agencies. The Cook County Bureau of Public Welfare was the only public welfare agency in the county at the time of the first relief drive. These terms, although used regularly, were not so distinct as they might seem, for social workers referred clients to both kinds of agencies, and, as was the case during the Depression, when one sector (public) had financial difficulties, the other bore the extra burden. Despite the almost artificial distinction between public and private in practice, for relief officials, healthy systems of private charity signaled a healthy, civically minded citizenry.

15. Ruth Crocker, "From Gift to Foundation: The Philanthropic Lives of Mrs. Russell Sage," *Charity, Philanthropy and Civility in American History* (New York: Cambridge University Press, 2003), 201.

16. Oscar Hewitt, "Governor's Job Board Tackles Winter Relief, Report Want Among Poor Growing," *Chicago Daily Tribune*, August 18, 1931, 1.

17. Philip Kinsley, "Jimmie Goes without Lunch and Breakfast, That's Why He Lags in School Work," *Chicago Daily Tribune*, October 5, 1931, 1.

18. Kathleen McCarthy, *Noblesse Oblige: Charity and Cultural Philanthropy in Chicago, 1849–1929* (Chicago: University of Chicago Press, 1982), ix, 178, 151.

19. James O'Donnell Bennett, "Millions Asked for Relief, Not a Cent for Dole, Samuel Insull Jr. Tells of Community Effort," *Chicago Daily Tribune*, October 11, 1931, 4.

20. "Governor Names Commission to Find Work for Jobless," *Chicago Daily Tribune*, October 16, 1930, 2. For more on Chicago industry and business and industrial leaders, see Robert D. Lewis, *Chicago Made: Factory Networks in the Industrial Metropolis* (Chicago: University of Chicago Press, 2008); Harold Platt, *The Electric City: Energy and the Growth of the Chicago Area, 1880–1930* (Chicago: University of Chicago Press, 1991); and John F. Wasik, *The Merchant of Power: Sam Insull, Thomas Edison, and the Creation of the Modern Metropolis* (Gordonsville, VA: Palgrave Macmillan, 2006).

21. Samuel Insull Jr., quoted in "Millions Asked for Relief," *Chicago Tribune*, October 11, 1931, 4.

22. Chamber of Commerce's Committee on Business Ethics, quoted in Cohen, *Making a New Deal*, 162. For more on welfare capitalism in Chicago, see Paul Louis Street, "Working in the Yards: A History of Class Relations in Chicago's Meatpacking Industry, 1886–1960" (Ph.D. diss., Graduate School of Binghamton University, 1993).

23. Wasik, *The Merchant of Power*, 180–181. Insull Jr. was the son of the Chicago business magnate and had a real incentive to incur public goodwill. Samuel Insull Sr.'s $500 million empire collapsed after the crash (he was forced to put his companies in receivership and resign in June 1932), wiping out the life savings of six hundred thousand shareholders and influencing the passage

of the Public Utility Holding Company Act of 1935. See "Charles McCulloch: Capitalist Says May Fields of Endeavor Open to Young," *Miami News*, March 13, 1935, 13.

24. Edward L. Ryerson Jr., "Out of the Depression," *Survey* 70.1 (January 1934): 3.

25. Edward A. Ryerson, quoted in Studs Terkel, *Hard Times: An Oral History of the Great Depression* (New York: Pocket Books, 1971), 179.

26. Olivier Zunz, *Philanthropy in America: A History* (Princeton, NJ: Princeton University Press, 2012), 9. Also see Robert A. Gross, "Giving in America: From Charity to Philanthropy," in *Charity, Philanthropy and Civility in American History*, ed. Lawrence J. Friedman and Mark D. McGarvie (New York: Cambridge University Press, 2003), 31.

27. Ryerson, "Out of the Depression," 4.

28. For more on welfare capitalism, see David Brody, "The Rise and Decline of Welfare Capitalism," in *Change and Continuity in Twentieth Century America: The 1920s*, ed. John Braeman, Robert H. Bremner, and David Brody (Columbus: Ohio State University Press, 1968); Stuart Brandes, *American Welfare Capitalism* (Chicago: University of Chicago Press, 1976); Edward Berkowitz and Kim McQuaid, *Creating the Welfare State: The Political Economy of 20th-Century Reform* (Lawrence: University Press of Kansas, 1992); and Cohen, *Making a New Deal*, 160, 184. For an examination of welfare capitalism after the 1930s, see Sanford Jacoby, *Modern Manors: Welfare Capitalism since the New Deal* (Princeton, NJ: Princeton University Press, 1998).

29. Berkowitz and McQuaid, *Creating the Welfare State*, 63.

30. Ibid., 4.

31. This figure actually refers to giving from 1925 to 1929. See McCarthy, *Noblesse Oblige*, 153. See also Robert H. Bremner, *American Philanthropy* (Chicago: University of Chicago Press, 1988); and Zunz, *Philanthropy in America*, chap. 4.

32. "City's Wealthy Must Aid Fund, Clarke Asserts," *Chicago Daily Tribune*, January 22, 1931, 1.

33. The wrestling match was between Jim Londos, heavyweight wrestling champion of the world, and Ed (Strangler) Lewis, former world's champion. See "Londos Is Ready to Meet Lewis in Charity Bout, Asks Only $250,000 Cash Guarantee," *Chicago Daily Tribune*, September 14, 1931, 21; "Tonight: Charity Ball," advertisement, *Chicago Daily Tribune*, November 2, 1931, 27; "Society Plans Tennis Battle for Charities," *Chicago Daily Tribune*, December 22, 1931, 19; "Chevalier Grin, His Songs, Too, Cheer Society, While Also Helping Funds for the Jobless," *Chicago Daily Tribune*, January 25, 1931, 12; and "Spring Horse Show Will Raise Funds for Needy Families," *Chicago Daily Tribune*, March 16, 1932, 17.

34. "Carson Pirie Scott," advertisement, *Chicago Daily Tribune*, December 1, 1931, 13, 16.

35. "Foster Shoes," advertisement, *Chicago Tribune*, November 2, 1931, 10.

36. Cohen, *Making a New Deal*, 161.

37. Cohen, *Making a New Deal*, 167.

38. "Near Half Way Mark in Drive to Aid Jobless," *Chicago Daily Tribune*, December 14, 1930, 24.

39. Oscar Hewitt, "$8,800,000 Set as City's Goal in Relief Drive," *Chicago Daily Tribune*, August 20, 1931, 1.

40. "Personal Gifts Sought Today in Relief Drive, Ask City's Wealthy to Aid Jobless," *Chicago Daily Tribune*, December 4, 1931, 11.

41. "U.S. Gypsum Gift Boosts Relief Drive, Praise Pay-Deduction Plan to Aid Needy," *Chicago Daily Tribune*, December 21, 1930, 19.

42. "Postal Workers Pledge $100,000 to Relief Fund, Charles S. Dewey to Head Industry Drive," *Chicago Daily Tribune*, August 26, 1931, 5.

43. Ibid.

44. Michael Katz, *The Undeserving Poor: From the War on Poverty to the War on Welfare* (New York: Pantheon Books, 1989), 7. See also John P. Bartkowski and Helen A. Regis, *Charitable Choices: Religion, Race and Poverty in the Post-Welfare Era* (New York: New York University Press, 2003), 27; and Bremner, *American Philanthropy*.

45. Edward L. Ryerson Jr., President, *The Joint Emergency Relief Fund, Statement of Receipts and Disbursements, August 14, 1931 to June 15, 1932*, 1, box 25, folder 1, Chicago Commons Collection.

46. "Sure There Are Unemployed, but Idle? Not Many, Thousands Look for Work; Find It," *Chicago Daily Tribune*, April 20, 1932, 4.

47. Hewitt, "Governor's Job Board Tackles Winter Relief," 1.

48. Lea D. Taylor to Helen Hall, January 28, 1931, 1, box 40, folder 2, Collection 34, SWHA.

49. *Report of the Work of Chicago Commons Association for the Year Ending September 30, 1929*, 1, B. 5 F. 1, Chicago Commons Collection; and *Report of the Work of Chicago Commons Association for the Year Ending September 30, 1931*, 2, box 5, folder 2, Chicago Commons Collection.

50. The JERF was "promoted by but independent of the Governor's Commission." Frank Z. Glick, *The Illinois Emergency Relief Commission: A Study of Administrative and Financial Aspects of Emergency Relief* (Chicago: University of Chicago Press, 1940), 14.

51. By 1932, the total would reach 40 percent. Ibid.; and "Fund for Relief Reaches Total of $9,674,123, Contributions of Day are $154,150," *Chicago Daily Tribune*, December 13, 1931, 9.

52. Ryerson was also quoted as saying, "Men who do not live in Chicago are given temporary shelter and food for a day or so and sent on their way." "Shelters to Bar Those Coming to City for Relief, Ryerson Tells Plans to Care for Homeless," *Chicago Daily Tribune*, October 2, 1931, 7.

53. Oscar Hewitt, "Ryerson Tells Need of Bigger Fund for Relief, Must Collect More Than Last Year, He Says," *Chicago Daily Tribune*, August 19, 1931, 3. Ryerson and JERF leaders also stated frankly in their published JERF goals that

their "purpose is to raise $8,800,000 to save the unemployed of *our* community—not tramps from Texas—from starvation this coming winter." Bennett, "Millions Asked for Relief," 4; emphasis original.

54. "Job Board Finds 37,000 Cases for Emergency Aid, Continue Jobless Census Today and Tomorrow," *Chicago Daily Tribune*, November 13, 1930, 12.

55. Bartkowski and Regis, *Charitable Choices*, 30; and Michael B. Katz, *In the Shadow of the Poorhouse: A Social History of Welfare in America*, 10th anniv. ed. (New York: Basic Books, 1996), 10.

56. Chesly Manly, "Chicago's Free Shelters Lure the Hobo Horde, from Far and Wide They're Coming," *Chicago Daily Tribune*, October 1, 1931, 1. There is a rich literature on the tramp, or the hobo, during the Great Depression. See especially Joan M. Crouse, *The Homeless Transient in the Great Depression: New York State, 1929–1941* (Albany: State University of New York Press, 1986); Todd DePastino, *Citizen Hobo: How a Century of Homelessness Shaped America* (Chicago: University of Chicago Press, 2010), chaps. 6–7; and Kenneth Kusmer, *Down and Out, on the Road: The Homeless in American History* (Cary, NC: Oxford University Press, 2001), chap. 10.

57. "Jobless Relief Fund Is Near Halfway Mark, $200,000 Gifts Received in 36 Hours," *Chicago Daily Tribune*, October 31, 1931, 8.

58. Manly, "Chicago's Free Shelters Lure the Hobo Horde," 1.

59. Bennett, "Millions Asked for Relief," 4.

Chapter 3

1. *Report of the Work of Chicago Commons Association for the Year Ending September 30, 1932*, 1, box 5, folder 2, Chicago Commons Collection, Chicago History Museum (hereafter cited as Chicago Commons Collection).

2. "Report of the Work of Chicago Commons for the year ending September 30, 1928," 1, box 5, folder 1, Chicago Commons Collection.

3. Walter Trattner, *From Poor Law to Welfare State: A History of Social Welfare in America* (New York: Free Press, 1999), 87–89. For a nice statement on charity organization, see Josephine Shaw Lowell, *Public Relief and Private Charity* (New York: Putnam's, 1884). For a good overview of the charity organization movement, see Frank Dekker Watson, *The Charity Organization Movement in the United States: A Study in American Philanthropy* (New York: Macmillan, 1922); and Michael B. Katz, *In the Shadow of the Poorhouse: A Social History of Welfare in America*, 10th anniv. ed. (New York: Basic Books, 1996), chap. 3. For discussion of charity organization in specific cities, see Kathleen D. McCarthy, *Noblesse Oblige: Charity and Cultural Philanthropy in Chicago, 1849–1929* (Chicago: University of Chicago Press, 1982); and Francis Herbert McLean, *The Formation of Charity Organization Societies in Smaller Cities* (New York: Charity Organization Department of the Russell Sage Foundation, 1910).

4. Daniel Rodgers, *Atlantic Crossings: Social Politics in a Progressive Age* (Cambridge, MA: Belknap Press of Harvard University Press, 1998), 213.

5. Jane Addams, "The Subtle Problems of Charity," *Atlantic Monthly* 83 (February 1899): 163–179; and Graham Taylor, *Religion in Social Action* (New York: Dodd, Mead, 1913), 39–40.

6. Judith Ann Trolander, *Settlement Houses and the Great Depression* (Detroit, Wayne State University Press, 1975), 14; see also Roy Lubove, *The Professional Altruist* (New York: Atheneum, 1973), 10.

7. Paul S. Boyer, *Urban Masses and Moral Order in America, 1820–1920* (Cambridge, MA: Harvard University Press, 1978), 156. For more on the moralism of settlement workers, see Allen F. Davis, *Spearheads for Reform: The Social Settlements and the Progressive Movement, 1890–1914* (New York: Oxford University Press, 1967); Thomas Philpot, *The Slum and the Ghetto: Immigrants, Blacks, and Reformers in Chicago, 1880–1930* (Belmont, CA: Wadsworth Publishing, 1991); and Ruth Crocker, *Social Work and Social Order: The Settlement Movement in Two Industrial Cities, 1889–1930* (Champaign-Urbana: University of Illinois Press, 1992).

8. Harriet E. Vittum, *The Worn Doorstep . . . Published by Northwestern University Settlement Association*, February 1, 1930, 7, box 5, folder 1, Northwestern University Settlement Association Records, Northwestern University Archives (hereafter cited as NUS Records).

9. Trattner, *From Poor Law to Welfare State*, 213; and Robert Halpern, *Fragile Families, Fragile Solutions: A History of Supportive Services for Families in Poverty* (New York: Columbia University Press, 1999), 73. For an excellent look at the shift from charity to social work, see Elizabeth N. Agnew, *From Charity to Social Work: Mary E. Richmond and the Creation of an American Profession* (Urbana: University of Illinois Press, 2004); McCarthy, *Noblesse Oblige*, 136–137; Trattner, *From Poor Law to Welfare State*, 155; Katz, *In the Shadow of the Poorhouse*, 161; and Lubove, *The Professional Altruist: The Emergence of Social Work as a Career, 1880–1930* (New York: Atheneum, 1973), 18–20.

10. Harriet Vittum, "1926 Annual Report," 13, box 5, folder 1, NUS Records.

11. Clarke Chambers and Judith Trolander offer good research on the role of funding in determining settlement workers' priorities. See Clarke A. Chambers, *Seedtime of Reform: American Social Service and Action, 1918–1963* (Minneapolis: University of Minnesota Press, 1963), 119; and Trolander, *Settlement Houses and the Great Depression*, 23.

12. Chairman, *Report of Social Service Department*, September 1, 1932, 1–2, box 4, folder 1, Madonna Center Papers, Special Collections and Archives, Marquette University (hereafter cited as Madonna Center Papers).

13. I discuss Chicago's poorly functioning relief system in Chapter 2, and I chart city relief officials' attempts at managing the crisis in Chapter 5. In 1931, Illinois legislators lamented (much to the chagrin of Chicago settlement and relief workers) that private funds were sure to "fall far short of meeting the total relief needs of the State during the coming year" and that for localities like Chicago, local funds would not make up the difference. Unknown,

"Relief in Chicago," 5–6, B. 24 F. 2, Chicago Commons Collection; and *Report of the Work of Chicago Commons Association for the Year Ending September 30, 1932*, 4.

14. Harriet Vittum, *Annual Report of 1934*, 2, box 4, folder 7, NUS Records.

15. "Report of the Work of Chicago Commons Association for the year ending September 30, 1932," 8l, box 5, folder 2, Chicago Commons Collection. The report described 1932 as bringing on "four times as many interviews and much more complicated procedure."

16. Harriet Vittum, *Annual Report of the Head Resident of Northwestern University Settlement*, December 31, 1930, 2, box 4, folder 7, NUS Records.

17. Harriet Vittum to Mr. Joseph Hildebrand, July 15, 1939, 2.

18. Harriet Vittum to Mr. Frank D. Loomis, Executive Secretary, Community Fund of Chicago, Inc., October 25, 1934, 1.

19. "An analysis of our salary budget will show you that for four months I have taken no salary at all and that my salary for three months, went back into the house in the wood." Harriet Vittum to Mr. [Donald] Welles, January 14, 1933, 3, box 28, folder 14, NUS Records.

20. Nancy Rose argues that, since the first colonial settlements, poor Americans have had to contend with the "ideology of the dole," or the "widely accepted belief that relief recipients are lazy and do not want to work." Nancy Rose, "Work Relief in the 1930s and the Origins of the Social Security Act," *Social Service Review* 63.1 (March 1989): 65–66.

21. I chart public attitudes toward relief in Chapter 1. *Report of the Work of Chicago Commons Association for the Year Ending September 30, 1931*, 6, box 5, folder 2, Chicago Commons Collection. For information on the great lengths that the unemployed went to in order to avoid accepting relief and the consequences of "complete dependence," see E. Wight Bakke, *Citizens without Work* (New Haven, CT: Yale University Press, 1940), 265; Katz, *In the Shadow of the Poorhouse*, 218.

22. Harriet Vittum, *1932 at N.U.S.*, 1–2, box 4, folder 7, NUS Records; *Report of the Work of Chicago Commons Association for the Year Ending September 30, 1930*, 6, box 5, folder 2, Chicago Commons Collection; and Harriet Vittum, *1932 at N.U.S.*, 1932, 16, box 4, folder 7, NUS Records.

23. *Minutes of Meeting: Board of Directors, Madonna Center*, October 21, 1931, 2, box 1, folder 5, Madonna Center Papers; and Vittum, *1932 at N.U.S.*, 17.

24. This section of the chapter focuses largely on the Northwestern University Settlement House, because its casework records are much more complete than others in the city. As partial case records and minutes from meetings of the National Federation of Settlements indicate, most Chicago settlements were struggling with how best to distribute aid, indicating that the NUS records serve as a representative case study of the city's other large settlements.

25. Harriet Vittum, Staff Meeting Minutes, March 17, 1932, 3, box 60, folder 7, NUS Records.

26. Ibid.

27. In the 1920s, caseworkers' primary responsibilities were to set up interviews for mediating domestic disputes and sending the destitute to Cook County's Bureau of Public Welfare (BPW). Their work rarely required that they themselves assess their neighbors, which allowed them to maintain a measure of what they called "neighborliness," or friendly relations across class and ethnicity. Interview by J. Gagola, visited by M. Markey, Case File 16464, Form: Special Relief, Unemployment Emergency, March 29, 1931, 2, box 67, folder 1, Northwestern University Settlement Association Case Files, Northwestern University Archives (hereafter cited as NUS Case Files).

28. M. Mack, Case file: Angelopulous (1933–1934), 1, box 1, folder 1, Madonna Center Papers. Mack continued to be confused about how to deal with "demanding" clients. In 1931, Mack described a different family with similar language: "Juliana and Margaret join our Sewing and Play classes. This family was brought in by the Musto's and Martino's, as they live in the same family—in the basement. House is in wretched condition—C. C. B. of P. W. have been assisting all through the year 1930. Clothes were given several times to the children, also a pair of shoes for the mother. Bread was given every day to these children during 1931. The children are always shabbily dressed and are not at all careful of their clothes. They are inclined to be very demanding." M. Mack, Case file: Caporele (1931–1933), 1, box 1, folder 4, Madonna Center Papers.

29. Harriet Vittum, *Annual Report of the Head Resident to the Directors and Supporters of NUSA*, 1937, 5, box 4, folder 7, NUS Records. In another report, Vittum celebrated a volunteer who brought cheer and cleanliness to a formerly "slovenly and careless" young woman, suggesting that with personal effort and responsibility, the woman could have overcome her poverty. Harriet Vittum, *1936 at Northwestern University Settlement*, December 1936, 8, box 4, folder 7, NUS Records; and Vittum, *Annual Report* (1937), 14.

30. N. Kliczewski, Case File 16469, Special Relief, Unemployment Emergency Form, January 13, 1932, 2, box 67, folder 1, NUS Case Files.

31. Interviewed by H. B. Weston, visited by G. Law, Case File 16462, Form: Special Relief, Unemployment Emergency, April 20, 1931, 2, box 67, folder 1, NUS Case Files; and Edith Meyer, Case File 18173, Relief Dept Visitor's Report, October 21, 1935, 1–2, box 74, folder 2, NUS Case Files.

32. J. Gagola, Case File 16474, Special Relief, Unemployment Emergency Form, January 7, 1931, 2, box 67, folder 1, NUS Case Files.

33. G. Law, Case File 16450, Visitor's Report, April 1, 1931, 2, box 67, folder 1, NUS Case Files.

34. Interview by J. Gagola, visited by G. Law, Case File 16455, Form: Special Relief, Unemployment Emergency, April 8, 1931, 2, box 67, folder 1, NUS Case Files; and Hannah Klur, Case File 16460, Visitors Report, November 24, 1931, 4, box 67, folder 1, NUS Case Files.

35. Ruth Shonle Cavan and Katherine Howland Ranck, *The Family and the Depression: A Study of One Hundred Chicago Families* (Chicago: University of Chicago Press, 1938); Mirra Komarovsky, *The Unemployed Man and His*

Family: The Effect of Unemployment upon the Status of the Man in Fifty-Nine Families (New York: Dryden Press, 1940); see also Samuel A. Stouffer and Paul F. Lazarsfeld, *Research Memorandum on the Family in the Depression*, Prepared under the Direction of the Committee on Studies in Social Aspects of the Depression (1937); and *White House Conference on Child Health and Protection, 1930, Washington, D.C.* (New York: Century, 1931), sec. 106–107.

36. Samuel A. Stouffer and Lyle M. Spencer, "Marriage and Divorce in Recent Years," *Annals of the American Academy of Political and Social Science* 188 (November 1936): x, 63. Note: Stouffer was at the time a professor of sociology at the University of Chicago, and Spencer was a fellow in sociology at the University of California; Stouffer and Lazarsfeld, *Research Memorandum on the Family in the Depression*, 5. Also see Alice Kessler-Harris, *Out to Work: A History of Wage-Earning Women in the United States* (New York: Oxford University Press, 1982), 252; and Lois Rita Helmbold, "Beyond the Family Economy: Black and White Working-Class Women during the Great Depression," *Feminist Studies* 13.3 (1987): 641–643.

37. Cavan and Ranck, *The Family and the Depression*, 61, 129.

38. Komarovsky, *The Unemployed Man and His Family*, 14, 92–93. This argument is reminiscent of Jane Addams's suggestion that adolescents had natural proclivities toward adventure and that it was up to adults to provide responsible recreation. Jane Addams, *The Spirit of Youth and the City Streets* (New York: Macmillan, 1909). It is interesting to note Komarovsky's assertion that many of these children "had to have some fun."

39. Cavan and Ranck, *The Family and the Depression*, 133–135.

40. *Report of the Work of Chicago Commons Association for the Year Ending September 30, 1929*, September 30, 1929, 13–16, box 5, folder 2, Chicago Commons Collection.

41. In just one Chicago Commons *Annual Report*, Taylor described settlement workers as "tiding over an immediate emergency of food or coal," "advising with the family as to the use of their remaining resources," "explaining to families relief procedure in threatened evictions and other emergencies," "paying gas bills not included in relief provided by some agencies," "trying to make adjustments more possible where mental or nervous conditions are apparent," and "opening opportunities in our educational and recreational groups." *Report of the Work of Chicago Commons Association for the Year Ending September 30, 1931*, 2–3.

42. *Report of the Work of Chicago Commons Association for the Year Ending September 30, 1930*, 2.

43. See Lizabeth Cohen, *Making a New Deal: Industrial Workers in Chicago, 1919–1939* (New York: Cambridge University Press, 2008), 230.

44. M. Mack, Case file: Albano, 1933, 1, box 1, folder 1, Madonna Center Papers. Settlement workers' concerns over restlessness and apathy catalyzed and defended their actions. This quote about apathy in a way secured their position as counselors and advice givers or gave them leeway to opine about right

behavior. And by warning of restlessness, Taylor defended her own political agitating, which (as I discuss in Chapter 4 on the WCOU) they present as an alternative to anarchy/Communism. *Report of the Work of Chicago Commons Association for the Year Ending September 30, 1932*, 2.

45. *Report of the Work of Chicago Commons for the Year Ending September 30, 1928*, September 30, 1928, 1, box 5, folder 1, Chicago Commons Collection; and Bakke, *Citizens without Work*, 252.

46. For more on men's identities as breadwinners in Depression-era culture and society, see Peter G. Filene, *Him/Her/Self: Gender Identities in Modern America* (Baltimore: Johns Hopkins University Press, 1974), 158; Scott Coltrane, *Family Man: Fatherhood, Housework, and Gender Equity* (New York: Oxford University Press, 1996), chap. 2; Robert L. Griswold, *Fatherhood in America: A History* (New York: Basic Books, 1993); Michael Kimmel, *Manhood in America: A Cultural History* (New York: Free Press, 1996); and E. Anthony Rotundo, *American Manhood: Transformations in Masculinity from the Revolution to the Modern Era* (New York: Basic Books, 1993).

47. What is more, LaRossa fails to deal with the fact that—especially in working-class families—money was often perceived as a necessary tool of parenting. Without it, all the fathering in the world would likely have been seen as insufficient to maintaining authority and family cohesion. Ralph LaRossa, *The Modernization of Fatherhood* (Chicago: University of Chicago Press, 1997), 5.

48. Vittum, *1932 at N.U.S.*, 6–7, 10; and *Report of the Work of Chicago Commons Association for the Year Ending September 30, 1931*, 8.

49. Lea D. Taylor, Notes—Quotations on Unemployment, June 1932, 7, box 25, folder 1, Chicago Commons Collection. The most thorough work on enforced leisure is Susan Currell's examination of American culture and leisure-related social policy during the 1930s and the accompanying emasculation of unemployed men. Susan Currell, *The March of Spare Time: The Problem and Promise of Leisure in the Great Depression* (Philadelphia: University of Philadelphia Press, 2005). A few social scientists also published studies on unemployment and leisure. See Jesse Steiner, "Recreation and Leisure Time Activities," in *Recent Social Trends in the United States* (New York: McGraw-Hill, 1933); and Louis Walker, *Distributed Leisure: An Approach to the Problem of Overproduction and Underemployment* (New York: Century, 1931).

50. Unknown, Notes—House Meeting, November 28, 1933, 2, box 55, Chicago Commons Collection.

51. *Report of the Work of Chicago Commons Association for the Year Ending September 30, 1932*, 6.

52. Ibid.

53. The concern with leisure was citywide. On December 16, 1932, the Chicago City Council established the Chicago Recreation Commission, which was charged with coordinating and planning the city's public, private, and commercial recreational facilities. Eighteen months later, the Illinois Emergency Relief Commission (IERC) created the Chicago Leisure Time Service

(CLTS), a program funded by state funds but carried out in local, public, and private institutions, including settlement houses. During its initial year the CLTS engaged sixty thousand children in Chicago. Harriet Vittum, "To Board Members, Supporters, Fellow Workers and Neighborhood Friends," *Central Committee Meetings*, circa December 1939, 1, box 17, folder 11, NUS Records; Harriet Vittum, Notes: House Meeting, September 7, 1937, 1, box 60, folder 7, NUS Records; and Malachy Richard McCarthy, "Which Christ Came to Chicago: Catholic and Protestant Programs to Evangelize, Socialize and Americanize the Mexican Immigrant, 1900–1940" (Ph.D. diss., Loyola University of Chicago, 2002), 326–327.

54. Their focus on mothers is striking. For example, of the six Women's Clubs listed in the 1934 Chicago Commons *Annual Report*, five were explicitly organized for mothers. The six clubs were the Chicago Commons Women's Club, the Chicago Commons Mothers' Club, the Young Italian Mothers' Club, the Thursday Morning Club (for young mothers), Polish Mothers, and Nursery Mothers. *Report of the Work of Chicago Commons Association for the Year Ending September 30, 1934*, September 30, 1934, 8, box 5, folder 3, Chicago Commons Collection.

55. *Report of the Work of Chicago Commons Association for the Year Ending September 30, 1935*, September 30, 1935, 8, box 5, folder 3, Chicago Commons Collection.

56. Recreation and especially drama had long figured as central to settlement house programming, in large part because settlement workers perceived of the city as lacking sufficient play and joy. See especially Shannon Jackson, *Lines of Activity: Performance, Historiography, Hull-House Domesticity* (Ann Arbor: University of Michigan Press, 2000); and Deborah A. Skok, *More Than Neighbors: Catholic Settlements and Day Nurseries in Chicago, 1893–1930* (DeKalb: Northern Illinois University Press, 2007).

57. *Report of the Work of Chicago Commons Association for the Year Ending September 30, 1935*, 9.

58. Harriet Vittum, *Annual Report of the Head Resident*, 1928, 2, box 4, folder 7, NUS Records. In this, Vittum echoed the sense that the imperatives of feminism, widely touted in the 1920s, collapsed during the Depression, as evidenced in campaigns against married women working and the feeling that men's identity was based in breadwinning. See Lois Scharf, *To Work and to Wed: Female Employment, Feminism, and the Great Depression* (Westport, CT: Greenwood Press, 1980), 65; and Winifred D. Wandersee, *Women's Work and Family Values, 1920–1940* (Cambridge, MA: Harvard University Press, 1981).

59. Ruth Milkman, "Women's Work and the Economic Crisis: Some Lessons from the Great Depression," *Review of Radical Political Economics* 8 (April 1976): 82. See also Helmbold, "Beyond the Family Economy," 638.

60. "In eight families the home was broken by desertion, separation or illegitimacy. In two families the father was in prison, and in one he was in the hospital. In fifteen families there was serious unemployment of the father,

necessitating the finding of work by the mother." *Report of the Work of Chicago Commons Association for the Year Ending September 30, 1930*, 16.

61. Ibid.

62. She continued, "The majority of working nursery mothers are in the nut-picking establishments in the neighborhood, and now get five cents a pound for shelling pecans, and can make at most only fifty cents a day." *Report of the Work of Chicago Commons Association for the Year Ending September 30, 1932*, 15; S. J. Kleinberg, *Women in the United States, 1830–1945* (Basingstoke, UK: Macmillan Press, 1999), 246–249; and *Report of the Work of Chicago Commons Association for the Year Ending September 30, 1931*, 9.

63. *Report of the Work of Chicago Commons Association for the Year Ending September 30, 1933*, 5, box 5, folder 3, Chicago Commons Collection.

64. *Report of the Work of Chicago Commons Association for the Year Ending September 30, 1930*, 6.

65. House Meeting Minutes, April 2, 1933, 4, box 60, folder 7, NUS Records.

66. Hannah Klur, Visitors Report, November 24, 1931, 2, box 67, folder 1, NUS Case Files.

Chapter 4

1. Lea D. Taylor to Helen Hall, January 1932, 1, box 41, folder 10, Social Welfare History Archives, University of Minnesota (hereafter cited as SWHA).

2. Lea D. Taylor to Helen Hall, June 21, 1933, 2, box 42, folder 4, SWHA.

3. David M. Kennedy, *The American People in the Great Depression: Freedom from Fear, Part 1* (New York: Oxford University Press, 1999), 170.

4. Lorena A. Hickok, *One Third of a Nation: Lorena Hickok Reports on the Great Depression*, ed. Richard Lowitt and Maurine Beasley (Urbana: University of Illinois Press, 1981), 16.

5. Robert E. Asher, "The Influence of the Chicago Workers' Committee on Unemployment upon the Administration of Relief, 1931–1934" (master's thesis, University of Chicago, 1934), 14.

6. The Chicago Workers Committee on Unemployment (WCOU), *An Urban Famine: Suffering Communities of Chicago Speak for Themselves*, January 5–12, 1932, 3, box 24, folder 2, Chicago Commons Collection, Chicago History Museum (hereafter cited as Chicago Commons Collection).

7. The first hearing was held at Chicago Commons and co-hosted by Onward Neighborhood House and the Northwestern University Settlement House. Subsequent hearings were held in "(2) The Humboldt Park district; (3) Watson Park; (4) The South Side and the West Side Negro districts; (5) The Central Y.W.C.A., at which testimony was given concerning the unemployed, single, young women of the city; and (6) South Chicago." WCOU, *An Urban Famine*, 3.

8. Ibid.

9. Ibid.

10. Ibid., 6.

11. Ibid., 9.

12. Ibid., 2, 20; *Report of the Work of Chicago Commons Association for the Year Ending in September 30, 1933*, September 30, 1933, 5, box 5, folder 3, Chicago Commons Collection.

13. WCOU, *An Urban Famine*, 6.

14. Ibid.

15. Ibid.

16. See Peter Mandler, ed., "Poverty and Charity in the Nineteenth-Century Metropolis: An Introduction," in *The Uses of Charity* (Philadelphia: University of Pennsylvania Press, 1990), 1–3.

17. WCOU, *An Urban Famine*, 12.

18. Harold R. Kerbo and Richard A. Shaffer, "Lower Class Insurgency and the Political Process: The Response of the U.S. Unemployed, 1890–1940," *Social Problems* 39.2 (May 1992): 140. For more on "cognitive liberation," see Doug McAdam, *Political Process and the Development of Black Insurgency: 1930–1970* (Chicago: University of Chicago Press, 1982), 48–51. For more on resource mobilization theory, see Steve Valocchi, "External Resources and the Unemployed Councils of the 1930s: Evaluating Six Propositions from Social Movement Theory," *Sociological Forum* 8.3 (September 1993): 451–470.

19. WCOU, *An Urban Famine*, 12.

20. Ibid., 16.

21. Ibid., 17.

22. Ibid., 5.

23. Ibid.

24. Kerbo and Shaffer, "Lower Class Insurgency and the Political Process," 141.

25. Fredrick C. Harris, "Something within: Religion as a Mobilizer of African American Political Activism," *Journal of Politics* 56.1 (February 1994): 49.

26. WCOU, *An Urban Famine*, 12.

27. Steve Valocchi describes the resource mobilization as happening in one of two ways: "either aggrieved groups using their own resources to launch social protest or as the outcome of external leaders bringing their own resources to mobilize an aggrieved group." Valocchi, "External Resources and the Unemployed Councils of the 1930s," 452. See also Chad Alan Goldberg, *Citizens and Paupers: Relief, Rights, and Race, from the Freedmen's Bureau to Workfare* (Chicago: University of Chicago Press, 2007).

28. Citizens Committee to the Honorable Louis L. Emmerson, January 16, 1932, 2, box 24, folder 2, Chicago Commons Collection.

29. WCOU, *An Urban Famine*, 7.

30. Ibid., 12.

31. Public Hearings by Citizens Committee, January 1932, 2, box 24, folder 2, Chicago Commons Collection.

32. WCOU, *An Urban Famine*, 3.

33. Jeff Singleton, *The American Dole: Unemployment Relief and the Welfare State in the Great Depression* (Westport, CT: Greenwood Press, 2000), 18.

34. Walter Trattner, *From Poor Law to Welfare State: A History of Social Welfare in America*, 6th ed. (New York: Free Press, 1999), 149.

35. *An Urban Famine* was broken into three parts: I. Aim, Method, and Evaluation of the Hearings; II. The Communities Speak for Themselves; and III. An Urban Famine. Much of the analysis here comes from the second part, which was divided into seven sections: A. Lack of Physical Necessities; B. Effects on Physical Health; C. The Breakdown of Personal and Family Morale; D. The Breakdown of Community Moral Standards; E. Effect on Permanent Agencies for Community Betterment; F. The Distribution of the Economic Burden; and G. Inadequacy of Resources to Meet the Situation.

36. WCOU, *An Urban Famine*, 9.

37. Ibid., 10.

38. Ibid., 11.

39. Ibid.

40. Ibid., 21.

41. Citizens Committee, "Letter to the Hon. Louis L. Emmerson, Governor of Illinois, Members of the Senate and House of Representatives, Springfield, Illinois," January 16, 1932, 1, box 24, folder 2, Chicago Commons Collection.

42. WCOU, *An Urban Famine*, 18.

43. "Public Hearings by Citizens' Committee," 2.

44. WCOU, *An Urban Famine*, 15.

45. See Lizabeth Cohen, *Making a New Deal: Industrial Workers in Chicago, 1919–1939* (New York: Cambridge University Press, 2008), 266.

46. "Police Battle 3000 Jobless Rioters at City Hall Door," *Cleveland Press*, February 11, 1930, box 46, folder 7, SWHA.

47. Pamela A. Brunfelt, "Karl Emil Nygard, Minnesota's Communist Mayor," *Minnesota History* 58.3 (Fall 2002): 168.

48. Randi Storch, *Red Chicago: American Communism at Its Grassroots, 1928–35* (Urbana: University of Illinois Press, 2007), 100–107.

49. Cohen, *Making a New Deal*, 264.

50. Warren Phinney, "Relief of Poor Is Planned for New Session," copy of newspaper article, January 27, 1932, 1, box 24, folder 1, Chicago Commons Collection; and Frances Fox Piven and Richard Cloward, *Poor People's Movements: Why They Succeed, How They Fail* (New York: Vintage Books, 1979), 69.

51. Karl Borders to "Those Organizations Interested in Making the Unemployed Demonstration on October 31st a Non-political Event," October 21, 1932, 1, box 25, folder 1, Chicago Commons Collection.

52. Judith A. Trolander, *Settlement Houses and the Great Depression* (Detroit: Wayne State University Press, 1975), 98.

53. Valocchi quotes two works by Roy Rosenzweig, who argued that UCs "invariably frightened off the average worker" and that they "never enlisted even five percent of all the unemployed at any one time." Roy Rosenzweig,

"Organizing the Unemployed: The Early Years of the Great Depression, 1929–1933," *Radical America* 10.4 (July/August 1976); and Roy Rosenzweig, "'Socialism in Our Time': The Socialist Party and the Unemployed, 1929–1936," *Labor History* 20.4 (1979); found in Valocchi, "External Resources and the Unemployed Councils of the 1930s," 461.

54. Lea D. Taylor, *Report of the Work of Chicago Commons Association*, September 30, 1932, 6, box 5, folder 2, Chicago Commons Collection.

55. Ibid.

56. WCOU, *An Urban Famine*, 19.

57. "Bandit Apologizes, Then Robs Manager of Store," *Chicago Daily Tribune*, January 31, 1932, 1, found in box 24, folder 3, Chicago Commons Collection.

58. Citizens Committee, "Letter to Governor Emmerson," 1.

59. WCOU, *An Urban Famine*, 2, 20; and *Report of the Work of Chicago Commons Association for the Year Ending in September 30, 1933*, 5.

60. WCOU, "What's Wrong with Relief?," 1934, box 26, folder 1, Chicago Commons Collection.

61. Taylor to Hall, 1.

62. For more on the FERA, see Chapter 5.

63. Kennedy, *The American People in the Great Depression*, 175.

64. WCOU, "Are You Happy? The H--l You Are!," circa 1934, box 27, folder 1, Chicago Commons Collection.

65. Ibid.

66. Trolander, *Settlement Houses and the Great Depression*, 102.

67. Chicago Federation of Settlements to James P. Allman, Commission of Police of the City of Chicago, November 3, 1932, 1, box 25, folder 1, Chicago Commons Collection.

Chapter 5

1. Lea Taylor to Mrs. Anna Ickes, January 11, 1932, 1, box 24, folder 2, Chicago Commons Collection, Chicago History Museum (hereafter cited as Chicago Commons Collection).

2. "Tells Governor of Urgent Need for Relief Cash," newspaper unknown, January 11, 1932, 1, box 24, folder 2, Chicago Commons Collection.

3. "Relief Work Leaders to Urge Action on State Loan Today," *Chicago Daily Tribune*, February 1932, 1, box 24, folder 3, Chicago Commons Collection.

4. "Relief Fund Leaders Appeal to Illinois Public to Support $20,000,000 Appropriation Plan," *Chicago Daily Tribune*, January 26, 1932, 4.

5. "Cermak Wins 1st Round of Fight for Flood Fund, Seeks $103,000 Balance to Aid Unemployed," *Chicago Daily Tribune*, September 27, 1931, 6.

6. Relief officials also perceived that Chicago was one of many cities dealing with a national crisis, and their turn toward state assistance came in part from seeing themselves as participating in a nationwide urban trend. Ryerson,

190 \ Notes to Chapter 5

of the JERF, collected reports from 332 cities to illustrate to potential donors—residents from Chicago and Cook County—that the group's request for larger donations fit a national trend. Moreover, New York City's state relief body influenced them in asking the Illinois legislature for funds.

7. In the fall, community leaders of Chicago's Edgewater neighborhood sent a telegram to Governor Emmerson, requesting $7 million in a public works program for the city. "Ask Emmerson for $7,000,000 in Public Works," *Chicago Daily Tribune*, October 18, 1931, D2.

8. Frank Z. Glick, *The Illinois Emergency Relief Commission: A Study of Administrative and Financial Aspects of Emergency Relief* (Chicago: University of Chicago Press, 1940), 16; "Ask Assembly for $10,000,000 to Help Needy, Governor's Commission to Push Plan Tomorrow," *Chicago Daily Tribune*, December 6, 1931, 14; and "Governor's Body Asks 20 Million to Aid Jobless, Calls on Assembly for Immediate Aid," *Chicago Daily Tribune*, December 8, 1931, 21.

9. Glick, *The Illinois Emergency Relief Commission*, 17.

10. In 1933, the state supreme court declared a recent sales tax bill unconstitutional, because it assigned the IERC (which was to disburse only public funds) sales tax income. Of course, by the time this decision came down, thousands of shoppers had paid an additional sales tax, which they believed would be turned over to relief efforts. Shoppers were encouraged to return to stores with their receipts and be reimbursed, but a number of large stores committed to donating any unclaimed sales tax funds to the city's Emergency Welfare Fund. "Unclaimed Sales Tax Funds Will Go to Welfare Group," *Chicago Daily Tribune*, May 14, 1933, 18; and "Two More Stores Give Unclaimed Tax to Charity," *Chicago Daily Tribune*, July 9, 1933, 5.

11. Paul M. Green and Melvin G. Holli, eds., *The Mayors: The Chicago Political Tradition* (Carbondale: Southern Illinois University Press, 1987).

12. Edward A. Ryerson, quoted in Studs Terkel, *Hard Times: An Oral History of the Great Depression* (New York: Pocket Books, 1971), 180.

13. "Final Vote in House Defeating Measure for Chicago Relief," *Chicago Daily Tribune*, January 13, 1932, 2.

14. "Relief Fund Leaders Appeal to Illinois Public."

15. Parke Brown, "Chicago Gets Tax Reforms," *Chicago Daily Tribune*, January 21, 1931, 1.

16. "Relief Crisis to Governor: Chicago Fund near End; Face an Emergency," *Chicago Daily Tribune*, January 23, 1932, 1.

17. "Hunger Calls," *Chicago Daily News*, January 23, 1932, 1.

18. Ibid.

19. "All Illinois Urged to Battle Crisis," *New York Times*, January 24, 1932, 5; "Legislature Called to Aid Unemployed," *Washington Post*, January 24, 1932, M11; "Illinois Emergency Session," *Wall Street Journal*, January 25, 1932, 2; and "Illinois Governor Calls Extra Session," *Atlanta Constitution*, January 24, 1932, 11A.

20. "Relief Fund Leaders Appeal to Illinois Public."

21. Legislators were especially concerned that Cook County residents would not vote in support of these bonds, because they had, in the recent past, been resistant to raising taxes to stabilize the county.

22. Percy Wood, "Chicago Relief Bills Advance, but Passage Is Not Assured," *Chicago Daily Tribune*, February 3, 1932, 3.

23. Parke Brown, "20 Million Aid Appropriation Voted by House, Emergency Clause on All Five Bills," *Chicago Daily Tribune*, February 4, 1932, 1.

24. Glick, *The Illinois Emergency Relief Commission*, 26.

25. Ibid.; "20 Million Aid Appropriation Voted by House," 10.

26. Glick, *The Illinois Emergency Relief Commission*, 27.

27. John R. Commons helped establish the Wisconsin State Industrial Commission to administer and adjudicate complaints related to the state's new workers' compensation program, which was the first of its kind in the nation. David A. Moss, *Socializing Security: Progressive-Era Economists and the Origins of American Social Policy* (Cambridge, MA: Harvard University Press, 1996), 69.

28. "Public Documents: Emergency Relief Reports," *Social Service Review* 8.1 (March 1934): 183; and Udo Sautter, *Three Cheers for the Unemployed* (New York: Cambridge University Press, 1991), 286–287.

29. Sautter, *Three Cheers for the Unemployed*, 291.

30. "Form New Body for Cook County Welfare Work, Emergency Fund Headed by R. D. Stuart," *Chicago Daily Tribune*, October 4, 1932, 5.

31. Malachy Richard McCarthy, "Which Christ Came to Chicago: Catholic and Protestant Programs to Evangelize, Socialize and Americanize the Mexican Immigrant, 1900–1940" (Ph.D. diss., Loyola University of Chicago, 2002), 319n65.

32. Michael B. Katz, *In the Shadow of the Poorhouse: A Social History of Welfare in America*, 10th anniv. ed. (New York: Basic Books, 1986). Also see Walter Trattner, *From Poor Law to Welfare State: A History of Social Welfare in America*, 6th ed. (New York: Free Press, 1999).

33. Catholic Charities made perhaps the most brazen attempt at thwarting the 1933 FERA order, claiming that it should have continued access to IERC funds because its volunteer organization guaranteed that it could give aid to more. Until 1935, the commission made an exception only for Catholic Charities. McCarthy, "Which Christ Came to Chicago," 319n66.

34. Frank D. Loomis, Secretary, "By-laws of COMMUNITY FUND for Chicago Charities, Inc.," May 31, 1934, 1, box 26, folder 1, Chicago Commons Collection.

35. Samuel A. Goldsmith, "Joint Funding," April 1933, 2, box 25, folder 2, Chicago Commons Collection.

36. Katherine Kelley, "2 Great Relief Agencies Help Chicago's Poor," *Chicago Daily Tribune*, October 22, 1933, 16.

37. Katherine Kelley, "Salvation Army Tells Value of Community Fund," *Chicago Daily Tribune*, September 27, 1934, 11.

38. "500 Will Carry Community Fund Message to Workers," *Chicago Daily Tribune*, October 11, 1934, 15.

39. Edward Ryerson, "Out of the Depression," *Survey* 70.1 (January 1934): 7.

40. See Edward D. Berkowitz, *America's Welfare State: From Roosevelt to Reagan* (Baltimore: Johns Hopkins University Press, 1991), 3; and Moss, *Socializing Security*, 4.

41. Franklin Delano Roosevelt, "Message to Congress Reviewing the Broad Objectives and Accomplishments of the Administration," June 8, 1934.

42. Berkowitz, *America's Welfare State*, 14.

43. Mr. Doughton, from the Committee on Ways and Means, "The Social Security Bill," 74th Congress, 1st Session, Report No. 615, April 5, 1935.

44. Berkowitz, *America's Welfare State*, 33.

45. Moss, *Socializing Security*, 165; and Edward D. Berkowitz and Kim McQuaid, *Creating the Welfare State: The Political Economy of 20th-Century Reform* (Lawrence: University Press of Kansas, 1992), 113.

46. Berkowitz, *America's Welfare State*, 29.

47. Thomas H. Eliot, General Counsel for the Committee on Economic Security, 1935–1938, "The Legal Background of the Social Security Act," speech delivered at a general staff meeting at Social Security Administration Headquarters (Baltimore, February 3, 1961), found at the VCU Libraries Social Welfare History Project, https://socialwelfare.library.vcu.edu/social-security/legal-background-of-the-social-security-act/.

48. At this time, Congress also considered the Townsend bill, which had gained popularity thanks to the ideas of Dr. Francis Townsend; it proposed to levy a 2 percent tax on all financial transactions to pay for a monthly pension to every U.S. citizen ages sixty-five and over. Recipients would be required to spend their $200 within thirty days, to keep money circulating. At the height of the Townsendite movement, Mary Poole explains, "Congress received 1,500 letters a day from individual supporters and Townsend clubs, and an estimated 20–25 million people signed petitions." Mary Poole, *The Segregated Origins of Social Security* (Chapel Hill: University of North Carolina Press, 2006), 23.

49. Mary van Kleeck to Mrs. Max Nelson, April 9, 1929, 1, box 27, folder 43, Mary van Kleeck Collection, Sophia Smith Collection, and Smith College Archives, Smith College (hereafter cited as van Kleeck Collection).

50. Their most significant conversations centered on a few international labor conferences, such as the World Labor Congress held in Holland in 1933, and on legislation proposed in response to the Depression. In 1931, Kellogg and van Kleeck discussed an article she was writing for *Survey*, regarding economic planning for the jobless. "The people who are close-in to the problems have not only a stake in shaping any schemes for national economic planning," Kellogg counseled, "but they have as rightful a footing as the bankers and the engineers and the lawmakers in insisting that these schemes promote standards of life in

the people as a whole." Paul Kellogg to Mary van Kleeck, December 7, 1931, 2, box 26, folder 45, van Kleeck Collection.

51. Arthur J. Altmeyer, *The Formative Years of Social Security* (Madison: University of Wisconsin Press, 1966), 31.

52. House Committee on Labor, Hearings on Unemployment, Old Age, and Social Insurance, 74th Cong., 1st sess., February 4, 1935, 1–2, quoted in Suzanne Mettler, *Dividing Citizens: Gender and Federalism in New Deal Public Policy* (Ithaca, NY: Cornell University Press, 1998), 134.

53. Mary van Kleeck, quoted in Linda Gordon, *Pitied but Not Entitled: Single Mothers and the History of Welfare, 1890–1935* (New York: Free Press, 1994), 239.

54. I. M. Rubinow, "Thoughts on the Lundeen Bill," *Survey* (1934): 377–378.

55. Alex Nordholm, quoted in Poole, *The Segregated Origins of Social Security*, 22.

56. Edwin Witte, quoted in ibid., 25.

57. Witte, like many anti-radicals in the New Deal administration, frequently equated the American Federation of Labor with labor, even though Samuel Gompers denounced any unemployment insurance as the "dole" throughout the 1920s. Edwin Witte, "Organized Labor and Social Security," in *Labor and the New Deal*, ed. Milton Derber and Edwin Young (Madison: University of Wisconsin Press, 1957), 245, 254.

58. Poole, *The Segregated Origins of Social Security*, 21–23; and Mettler, *Dividing Citizens*, 133–135.

59. As quoted in Gordon, *Pitied but Not Entitled*, 240.

60. Mettler, *Dividing Citizens*, 133.

61. Helen Hall, "Statement for the Economic Security Act," in *Report to the President of the Committee on Economic Security* (Washington, DC: U.S. Government Printing Office, 1935), 767.

62. Ibid., 768.

63. Ibid.

64. Ibid., 770.

65. Berkowitz, *America's Welfare State*, 6.

66. Linda Gordon, "Social Insurance and Public Assistance: The Influence of Gender in Welfare Thought in the United States, 1890–1935," *American Historical Review* 97 (February 1992). For more on the two-tiered welfare state, see Gwendolyn Mink, "The Lady and the Tramp: Gender, Race, and the Origins of the American Welfare State," in *Women, the State, and Welfare*, ed. Linda Gordon (Madison: University of Wisconsin Press, 1990), 92–122; Barbara J. Nelson, "The Origins of the Two-Channel Welfare State: Workmen's Compensation and Mothers' Aid," in *Women, the State, and Welfare*, ed. Linda Gordon (Madison: University of Wisconsin Press, 1990), 123–151; and Virginia Sapiro, "The Gender Basis of American Social Policy," *Political Science Quarterly* 101.2 (1986): 221–238.

67. Workers Committee on Unemployment, "Handout" (date unspecified), 1, box 27, folder 1, Chicago Commons Collection.

Epilogue

1. Workers Committee on Unemployment, "Hunger and Want, a Flyer" (1935), 1, box 26, folder 3, Chicago Commons Collection, Chicago History Museum (hereafter cited as Chicago Commons Collection).

2. Lea D. Taylor, *Report of the Work of Chicago Commons Association*, September 30, 1937, 1, box 5, folder 4, Chicago Commons Collection.

3. Daniel Rodgers, *Atlantic Crossings: Social Politics in a Progressive Age* (Cambridge, MA: Belknap Press of Harvard University Press, 1998), 444.

4. Lea Taylor to Chicago Commons Trustees, August 6, 1936, 1, box 26, folder 3, Chicago Commons Collection.

5. Chad Goldberg argues, "By positioning WPA workers in an ambiguous and contradictory ways, between relief and employment, New Deal policy makers inadvertently encouraged an intense political struggle over their status, identity, and rights within the emerging New Deal welfare state." Chad Alan Goldberg, "Contesting the Status of Relief Workers during the New Deal: The Workers Alliance of America and the Works Progress Administration, 1935–1941," *Social Science History* 29.3 (Fall 2005): 360.

6. Taylor, *Report of the Work of Chicago Commons Association*, 5.

7. Harriet Vittum, *Report of the Head Resident of Northwestern University Settlement*, September 1937, 2, box 4, folder 7, Records of the Northwestern University Settlement House Association, Northwestern University Archives (hereafter cited as NUS Records).

8. Lea Taylor, "Relief Situation," May 1939, 1, box 27, folder 2, Chicago Commons Collection.

9. James T. Patterson, *America's Struggle against Poverty in the Twentieth Century* (Cambridge, MA: Harvard University Press, 2000), 45.

10. Josh Bivens, Joshua Smith, and Valerie Wilson, "State Cuts to Jobless Benefits Did Not Help Workers or Taxpayers," *Economic Policy Institute Briefing Paper #380*, July 28, 2014, 3.

11. Scott Horsley, "A Staggering Toll: 30 Million Have Filed for Unemployment," *NPR's Morning Edition*, April 30, 2020; and Katie P. Reed and Monica Schulteis, "President Trump Signs into Law the Coronavirus Aid, Relief, and Economic Security (CARES) Act," *National Law Review*, March 29, 2020.

Bibliography

Primary Sources

Manuscript Collections
Benton House Records. Chicago History Museum, Chicago
Chicago Commons Collection. Chicago History Museum, Chicago
Helen Hall Collection. Social Welfare History Archives, University of Minnesota
Madonna Center Papers. Special Collections and Archives, Marquette University
Mary van Kleeck Collection, Sophia Smith Collection, and Smith College Archives. Smith College
Northwestern University Settlement Association Records. Northwestern University Archives

Periodicals
Atlanta Constitution
Chicago Daily News
Chicago Daily Tribune
Detroit News
Labor Bulletin of the Illinois Department of Labor
Miami News
Neighborhood
New York Times
Social Service Review
The Survey

Survey Graphic
Wall Street Journal
Washington Post

Published Sources

Abbot, Grace. *From Relief to Social Security.* Chicago: University of Chicago Press, 1966.

Addams, Jane. *The Spirit of Youth and the City Streets.* New York: Macmillan, 1909.

———. "The Subjective Necessity of Social Settlements." In *The Jane Addams Reader,* edited by Jean Bethke Elshtain, 14–28. New York: Basic Books, 2002.

———. "The Subtle Problems of Charity." *Atlantic Monthly* 83 (February 1899): 163–179.

———. *Twenty Years at Hull-House.* New York: Macmillan, 1911.

Addams, Jane, and Graham Taylor. *Religion in Social Action.* New York: Dodd, Mead, 1913.

Andrews, John B. *Practical Program for the Prevention of Unemployment in America.* New York City: American Association on Unemployment, 1914.

———. "Workmen's Compensation in New Jersey—The Wrong Way." *Survey* 22 (March 27, 1915): 696–697.

Armstrong, Barbara Nachtrieb. *Insuring the Essentials: Minimum Wage Plus Social Insurance—Living Wage Program.* New York: Macmillan, 1932.

Asher, Robert E. "The Influence of the Chicago Workers' Committee on Unemployment upon the Administration of Relief, 1931–1934." Master's thesis, University of Chicago, 1934.

Beveridge, William H. *Causes and Cures of Unemployment.* London: Longmans, Green, 1931.

———. *Full Employment in a Free Society, a Report by William H. Beveridge.* London: Allen and Unwin, 1944.

———. *Insurance for All and Everything.* London: Daily News, 1924.

———. *Unemployment: A Problem of Industry (1909 and 1930).* London: Longmans, Green, 1912, 1930.

Brown, Edwin A. *"Broke": The Man without the Dime.* Boston: Four Seas, 1920.

Calkins, Clinch. *Some Folks Won't Work.* New York: Harcourt, Brace, 1930.

Cavan, Ruth Shonle, and Katherine Howland Ranck. *The Family and the Depression: A Study of One Hundred Chicago Families.* Chicago: University of Chicago Press, 1938.

Cousins, Norman. "Will Women Lose Their Jobs?" *Current History and Forum* 14 (1939): 14.

Doughton, Mr., from the Committee on Ways and Means. "The Social Security Bill." 74th Congress, 1st Session, Report No. 615, April 5, 1935.

Douglas, Paul H., and Aaron Director. *The Problem of Unemployment.* New York: Macmillan, 1931.

Elderton, Marion, ed. *Case Studies of Unemployment, Compiled by the Unemployment Committee of the National Federation of Settlements*. Philadelphia: University of Pennsylvania Press, 1931.

Eloit, Thomas H., General Counsel for the Committee on Economic Security, 1935–1938. "The Legal Background of the Social Security Act." Speech delivered at a general staff meeting at Social Security Administration Headquarters, Baltimore, February 3, 1961.

Feder, Leah Hannah. *Unemployment Relief in Periods of Depression: A Study of Measures Adopted in Certain American Cities, 1857 through 1922*. New York: Russell Sage Foundation, 1936.

First Annual Report of the Illinois Emergency Relief Commission for the Year Ending February 5, 1933, Issued Jointly with a Report of the Illinois Emergency Relief Commission (Federal) Covering the Period July 27, 1932 through February 5, 1933. Springfield: State of Illinois, 1933.

Hall, Helen. "Statement for the Economic Security Act." In *Report to the President of the Committee on Economic Security*. Washington, DC: U.S. Government Printing Office, 1935.

Hall, Helen, and Henry Street Settlement. *The Helen Hall Settlement Papers: A Descriptive Bibliography of Community Studies and Other Reports, 1928–1958*. New York: New York School of Social Work, 1959.

Kelley, Florence. "Minimum-Wage Laws." *Journal of Political Economy* 20.10 (December 1912): 999–1010.

Klein, Philip. *The Burden of Unemployment: A Study of Unemployment Relief Measures in Fifteen American Cities, 1921–22*. New York: Russell Sage Foundation, 1923.

Komarovsky, Mirra. *The Unemployed Man and His Family: The Effect of Unemployment upon the Status of the Man in Fifty-Nine Families*. New York: Dryden Press, 1940.

Leiserson, William M. "A Federal Reserve Board for the Unemployed. Outlines of a Plan for Administering the Remedies for Unemployment." *Annals of the American Academy of Political and Social Science* 69 (January 1917): 103–117.

Lowell, Josephine Shaw. *Public Relief and Private Charity*. New York: Putnam's, 1884.

Lundberg, George, Mirra Komarovsky, and Mary McInerney. *Leisure: A Suburban Study*. New York: Columbia University Press, 1934.

National Emergency Council. *Report on Economic Conditions of the South*. Washington, DC: U.S. Government Printing Office, 1938.

Roosevelt, Franklin Delano. "Message to Congress Reviewing the Broad Objectives and Accomplishments of the Administration." June 8, 1934.

Rubinow, I. M. *Social Insurance, with Special Reference to American Conditions*. New York: Holt, 1916.

———. "Thoughts on the Lundeen Bill." *The Survey* (1934): 377–378.

Ryerson Jr., Edward L. "Out of the Depression." *The Survey* 70.1 (January 1934): 3–7.

Steiner, Jesse. "Recreation and Leisure Time Activities." *Recent Social Trends in the United States.* New York: McGraw-Hill, 1933.

Stouffer, Samuel A., and Paul F. Lazarsfeld. *Research Memorandum on the Family in the Depression.* Prepared under the Direction of the Committee on Studies in Social Aspects of the Depression. 1937.

Stouffer, Samuel A., and Lyle M. Spencer. "Marriage and Divorce in Recent Years." *Annals of the American Academy of Political and Social Science* 188 (November 1936): 56–69.

Taylor, Graham. *Religion in Social Action.* New York: Dodd, Mead, 1913.

Walker, Louis. *Distributed Leisure: An Approach to the Problem of Overproduction and Underemployment.* New York: Century, 1931.

White House Conference on Child Health and Protection, 1930, Washington, D.C. New York: Century, 1931.

Williams, Whiting. *What's on the Worker's Mind: By One Who Put on Overalls to Find Out.* New York: Charles Scribner's Sons, 1920.

Witte, Edwin. "Organized Labor and Social Security." In *Labor and the New Deal,* edited by Milton Derber and Edwin Young, 239–275. Madison: University of Wisconsin Press, 1957.

Secondary Sources

Adams, Stephen B., and Orville R. Butler. *Manufacturing the Future: A History of Western Electric.* New York: Cambridge University Press, 1999.

Agnew, Elizabeth N. *From Charity to Social Work: Mary E. Richmond and the Creation of an American Profession.* Urbana: University of Illinois Press, 2004.

Altmeyer, Arthur J. *The Formative Years of Social Security.* Madison: University of Wisconsin Press, 1966.

Amenta, Edwin. *Bold Relief: Institutional Politics and the Origins of Modern American Social Policy.* Princeton, NJ: Princeton University Press, 1998.

Badger, Anthony. *The New Deal: Depression Years, 1933–1940.* New York: Hill and Wang, 1989.

Bakke, E. Wight. *Citizens without Work.* New Haven, CT: Yale University Press, 1940.

Barrett, James. *Work and Community in the Jungle: Chicago's Packinghouse Workers, 1894–1922.* Urbana: University of Illinois Press, 1987.

Bartkowski, John P., and Helen A. Regis. *Charitable Choices: Religion, Race and Poverty in the Post-welfare Era.* New York: New York University Press, 2003.

Benson, Susan Porter. "Living on the Margin: Working-Class Marriages and Family Survival Strategies in the United States, 1919–1941." In *The Sex of Things: Gender and Consumption in Historical Perspective,* edited by Victoria de Grazia and Ellen Furlough, 212–243. Berkeley: University of California Press, 1996.

Berkowitz, Edward D. *America's Welfare State: From Roosevelt to Reagan.* Baltimore: Johns Hopkins University Press, 1991.

Berkowitz, Edward, and Kim McQuaid. *Creating the Welfare State: The Political Economy of 20th-Century Reform.* Lawrence: University Press of Kansas, 1992.

Bernstein, Irving. *The Turbulent Years: A History of the American Worker, 1933–1941.* Boston: Houghton Mifflin, 1970.

Berry, Mary Frances. *The Politics of Parenthood: Child Care, Women's Rights, and the Myth of the Good Mother.* New York: Viking, 1993.

Bivens, Josh, Joshua Smith, and Valerie Wilson. "State Cuts to Jobless Benefits Did Not Help Workers or Taxpayers." *Economic Policy Institute Briefing Paper #380,* July 28, 2014.

Boydston, Jeanne. *Home and Work: Housework, Wages, and the Ideology of Labor in the Early Republic.* New York: Oxford University Press, 1990.

Boyer, Paul S. *Urban Masses and Moral Order in America, 1820–1920.* Cambridge, MA: Harvard University Press, 1978.

Brandes, Stuart. *American Welfare Capitalism.* Chicago: University of Chicago Press, 1976.

Bremner, Robert H. *American Philanthropy.* Chicago: University of Chicago Press, 1988.

Brody, David. "The Rise and Decline of Welfare Capitalism." In *Change and Continuity in Twentieth Century America: The 1920s,* edited by John Braeman, Robert H. Bremner, and David Brody, 147–178. Columbus: Ohio State University Press, 1968.

Brunfelt, Pamela A. "Karl Emil Nygard, Minnesota's Communist Mayor." *Minnesota History* 58.3 (Fall 2002): 168–186.

Buder, Stanley. *Pullman: An Experiment in Industrial Order and Community Planning, 1880–1930.* New York: Oxford University Press, 1967.

Burbank, Lyman B. "Chicago Public Schools and the Depression Years of 1928–1937." *Journal of the Illinois State Historical Society* 64 (Winter 1971): 365–381.

Burner, David. *Herbert Hoover: A Public Life.* New York: Knopf, 1979.

Carlson, Allan C. "The Family Wage Problem, 1750–1940." In *The Family Wage: Work, Gender, and Children in the Modern Economy,* edited by Bryce Christensen, 9–32. Rockford, IL: Rockford Institute, 1988.

Cauthen, Nancy K., and Edwin Amenta. "Not for Widows Only: Institutional Politics and the Formative Years of Aid to Dependent Children." *American Sociological Review* 61.3 (June 1996): 427–448.

Chambers, Clarke A. *Seedtime of Reform: American Social Service and Action, 1918–1963.* Minneapolis: University of Minnesota Press, 1963.

Cohen, Lizabeth. *Making a New Deal: Industrial Workers in Chicago, 1919–1939.* New York: Cambridge University Press, 2008.

Cohen, Miriam, and Michael Hanagan. "Politics, Industrialization and Citizenship: Unemployment Policy in England, France and the United States,

1890–1950." In *Citizenship, Identity, and Social History*, edited by Charles Tilly, 91–130. New York: Cambridge University Press, 1996.

Coltrane, Scott. *Family Man: Fatherhood, Housework, and Gender Equity*. New York: Oxford University Press, 1996.

Conkin, Paul. *The New Deal*, The American History Series. Wheeling, IL: Harlan Davidson, 1967.

Crocker, Ruth. "From Gift to Foundation: The Philanthropic Lives of Mrs. Russell Sage." In *Charity, Philanthropy and Civility in American History*, edited by Lawrence J. Friedman and Mark D. MacGarvie, 199–216. New York: Cambridge University Press, 2003.

———. *Social Work and Social Order: The Settlement Movement in Two Industrial Cities, 1889–1930*. Champaign-Urbana: University of Illinois Press, 1992.

Crouse, Joan M. *The Homeless Transient in the Great Depression: New York State, 1929–1941*. Albany: State University of New York Press, 1986.

Currell, Susan. *The March of Spare Time: The Problem and Promise of Leisure in the Great Depression*. Philadelphia: University of Philadelphia Press, 2005.

Dauber, Michelle Landis. *The Sympathetic State: Disaster Relief and the Origins of the American Welfare State*. Chicago: University of Chicago Press, 2013.

Davis, Allen F. *Spearheads for Reform: The Social Settlements and the Progressive Movement, 1890–1914*. New York: Oxford University Press, 1967.

Demos, John. "The Changing Faces of Fatherhood: A New Exploration in Family History." In *Father and Child: Developmental and Clinical Perspectives*, edited by Stanley Cath, Alan Gurwitt, and John M. Ross, 425–445. Boston: Little, Brown, 1982.

DePastino, Todd. *Citizen Hobo: How a Century of Homelessness Shaped America*. Chicago: University of Chicago Press, 2010.

Downey, Kirstin. *The Woman behind the New Deal: The Life and Legacy of Frances Perkins—Social Security, Unemployment Insurance, and the Minimum Wage*. New York: Random House, 2009.

Ehrenreich, John H. *The Altruistic Imagination: A History of Social Work and Social Policy in the United States*. Ithaca, NY: Cornell University Press, 1985.

Eisner, Michael. *William Morris Leiserson, a Biography*. Madison: University of Wisconsin Press, 1967.

Fausold, Martin L. *The Presidency of Herbert C. Hoover*. Lawrence: University of Kansas Press, 1985.

Filene, Peter G. *Him/Her/Self: Gender Identities in Modern America*. Baltimore: Johns Hopkins University Press, 1974.

Fitzpatrick, Ellen. *Endless Crusade: Women Social Scientists and Progressive Reform*. London: Oxford University Press, 1994.

Fraser, Steve, and Gary Gerstle. *The Rise and Fall of the New Deal Order, 1930–1980*. Princeton, NJ: Princeton University Press, 1989.

Galbraith, John Kenneth. *The Great Crash, 1929*. Boston: Houghton Mifflin, 1972.

Glick, Frank Z. *The Illinois Emergency Relief Commission: A Study of Administrative and Financial Aspects of Emergency Relief.* Chicago: University of Chicago Press, 1940.

Glickman, Laurence B. *Living Wage: American Workers and the Making of Consumer Society.* Ithaca, NY: Cornell University Press, 1997.

Goldberg, Chad Alan. *Citizens and Paupers: Relief, Rights, and Race, from the Freedmen's Bureau to Workfare.* Chicago: University of Chicago Press, 2007.

———. "Contesting the Status of Relief Workers during the New Deal: The Workers Alliance of America and the Works Progress Administration, 1935–1941." *Social Science History* 29.3 (Fall 2005): 337–371.

Goodwin, Joanne L. "An American Experiment in Paid Motherhood: The Implementation of Mothers' Pensions in Early Twentieth-Century Chicago." *Gender and History* 4 (1992): 321–342.

Gordon, Linda. *Pitied but Not Entitled: Single Mothers and the History of Welfare, 1890–1935.* New York: Free Press, 1994.

———. "Social Insurance and Public Assistance: The Influence of Gender in Welfare Thought in the United States, 1890–1935." *American Historical Review* 97 (February 1992): 19–54.

Gorn, Elliott J. *Mother Jones: The Most Dangerous Woman in America.* New York: Hill and Wang, 2001.

Green, Paul M., and Melvin G. Holli, eds., *The Mayors: The Chicago Political Tradition.* Carbondale: Southern Illinois University Press, 1987.

Greenwald, Maurine Weiner. "Working-Class Feminism and the Family Wage Ideal: The Seattle Debate on Married Women's Right to Work, 1914–1920." *Journal of American History* 76 (June 1989): 118–149.

Griswold, Robert L. *Fatherhood in America: A History.* New York: Basic Books, 1993.

Gross, Robert A. "Giving in America: From Charity to Philanthropy." In *Charity, Philanthropy and Civility in American History,* edited by Lawrence J. Friedman and Mark D. McGarvie, 29–48. New York: Cambridge University Press, 2003.

Halpern, Robert. *Fragile Families, Fragile Solutions: A History of Supportive Services for Families in Poverty.* New York: Columbia University Press, 1999.

Harris, Fredrick C. "Something within: Religion as a Mobilizer of African American Political Activism." *Journal of Politics* 56.1 (February 1994): 42–68.

Helmbold, Lois Rita. "Beyond the Family Economy: Black and White Working-Class Women during the Great Depression." *Feminist Studies* 13.3 (1987): 629–655.

Herrick, Mary J. *The Chicago Schools: A Social and Political History.* Beverly Hills: Sage Publications, 1971.

Hickok, Lorena A. *One Third of a Nation: Lorena Hickok Reports on the Great Depression.* Edited by Richard Lowitt and Maurine Beasley. Urbana: University of Illinois Press, 1981.

Horsley, Scott. "A Staggering Toll: 30 Million Have Filed for Unemployment." *NPR's Morning Edition*, April 30, 2020.

Howard, Christopher. "Sowing the Seeds of 'Welfare': The Transformation of Mothers' Pensions, 1900–1940." *Journal of Policy History* 4 (1992): 188–227.

Hoy, Suellen. *Chasing Dirt: The American Pursuit of Cleanliness*. Cary, NC: Oxford University Press, 1996.

Jackson, Shannon. *Lines of Activity: Performance, Historiography, Hull-House Domesticity*. Ann Arbor: University of Michigan Press, 2000.

Jacoby, Sanford. *Modern Manors: Welfare Capitalism since the New Deal*. Princeton, NJ: Princeton University Press, 1998.

Johnson, Joan Marie. *Southern Women at the Seven Sister Colleges: Feminist Values and Social Activism, 1875–1915*. Athens: University of Georgia Press, 2008.

Karger, Howard Jacob. *The Sentinels of Order: A Study of Social Control and the Minneapolis Settlement House Movement, 1915–1950*. Lanham, MD: University Press of America, 1987.

Katz, Michael B. *In the Shadow of the Poorhouse: A Social History of Welfare in America*. 10th anniv. ed. New York: Basic Books, 1996.

———. *The Undeserving Poor: From the War on Poverty to the War on Welfare*. New York: Pantheon Books, 1989.

Katznelson, Ira. *When Affirmative Action Was White: An Untold History of Racial Inequality in Twentieth-Century America*. New York: Norton, 2005.

Kennedy, David. *The American People in the Great Depression: Freedom from Fear, Part 1*. New York: Oxford University Press, 1999.

Kerbo, Harold R. and Richard A. Shaffer. "Lower Class Insurgency and the Political Process: The Response of the U.S. Unemployed, 1890–1940." *Social Problems* 39.2 (May 1992): 139–154.

Kessler-Harris, Alice. *In Pursuit of Equity: Women, Men, and the Quest for Economic Citizenship in 20th-Century America*. Oxford: Oxford University Press, 2001.

———. *Out to Work: A History of Wage-Earning Women in the United States*. New York: Oxford University Press, 1982.

Keyssar, Alexander. *Out of Work: The First Century of Unemployment in Massachusetts*. New York: Cambridge University Press, 1986.

Kimmel, Michael. *Manhood in America: A Cultural History*. New York: Free Press, 1996.

Kish-Sklar, Kathryn. "Two Political Cultures in the Progressive Era: The National Consumers' League and the American Association for Labor Legislation." In *U.S. History as Women's History: New Feminist Essays*, edited by Linda Gordon, Alice Kessler-Harris, and Kathryn Kish-Sklar, 36–62. Chapel Hill: University of North Carolina Press, 1995.

Kleiler, Frank M. "William Morris Leiserson." *Industrial Relations Research Association, Proceedings*, 95–101. September 1957.

Kleinberg, S. J. *Women in the United States, 1830–1945*. Basingstoke, UK: Macmillan Press, 1999.

Knight, Louise W. *Citizen: Jane Addams and the Struggle for Democracy*. Chicago: University of Chicago Press, 2005.

———. *Jane Addams: Spirit in Action*. New York: Norton, 2010.

Koven, Seth, and Sonya Michel, eds. *Mothers of a New World: Maternalist Politics and the Origins of Welfare States*. New York: Routledge, 1993.

Kraut, Alan M. *Silent Travelers: Germs, Genes, and the Immigrant Menace*. Baltimore: Johns Hopkins University Press, 1995.

Kusmer, Kenneth. *Down and Out, on the Road: The Homeless in American History*. Cary, NC: Oxford University Press, 2001.

LaRossa, Ralph. *The Modernization of Fatherhood*. Chicago: University of Chicago Press, 1997.

Lasch-Quinn, Elisabeth. *Black Neighbors: Race and the Limits of Reform in the American Settlement House Movement, 1890–1945*. Chapel Hill: University of North Carolina Press, 1993.

Leuchtenburg, William Edward. *Franklin D. Roosevelt and the New Deal, 1932–1940*. The New American Nation Series. New York: Harper and Row, 1963.

Lewis, Robert D. *Chicago Made: Factory Networks in the Industrial Metropolis*. Chicago: University of Chicago Press, 2008.

Lubove, Roy. *The Professional Altruist: The Emergence of Social Work as a Career, 1880–1930*. New York: Atheneum, 1973.

———. *The Struggle for Social Security, 1900–1935*. Cambridge, MA: Harvard University Press, 1968.

Lyons, John F. *Teachers and Reform: Chicago Public Education, 1929–1970*. Urbana: University of Illinois Press, 2008.

Mandler, Peter, ed. "Poverty and Charity in the Nineteenth-Century Metropolis: An Introduction." In *The Uses of Charity*, 1–37. Philadelphia: University of Pennsylvania Press, 1990.

Masters, Charles. *Governor Henry Horner, Chicago Politics, and the Great Depression*. Carbondale: Southern Illinois University Press, 2007.

May, Martha. "Bread before Roses: American Workingmen, Labour Unions, and the Family Wage." In *Women, Work and Protest: A Century of Women's Labor History*, edited by Ruth Milkman, 1–21. New York: Routledge, 2013.

———. "The Historical Problem of the Family Wage: The Ford Motor Company and the Five Dollar Day." *Feminist Studies* 8.2 (Summer 1982): 399–424.

McAdam, Doug. *Political Process and the Development of Black Insurgency: 1930–1970*. Chicago: University of Chicago Press, 1982.

McCarthy, Kathleen. *Noblesse Oblige: Charity and Cultural Philanthropy in Chicago, 1849–1929*. Chicago: University of Chicago Press, 1982.

McCarthy, Malachy Richard. "Which Christ Came to Chicago: Catholic and Protestant Programs to Evangelize, Socialize and Americanize the Mexican Immigrant, 1900–1940." Ph.D. dissertation, Loyola University of Chicago, 2002.

McElvaine, Robert. *Down and Out in the Great Depression.* Chapel Hill: University of North Carolina Press, 1983.

McLean, Francis Herbert. *The Formation of Charity Organization Societies in Smaller Cities.* New York: Charity Organization Department of the Russell Sage Foundation, 1910.

Melvin, Bruce Lee, and Carle Clark Zimmerman. *Rural Poor in the Great Depression: Three Studies.* New York: Arno Press, 1971.

Mettler, Suzanne. *Dividing Citizens: Gender and Federalism in New Deal Public Policy.* Ithaca, NY: Cornell University Press, 1998.

Milkman, Ruth. "Women's Work and the Economic Crisis: Some Lessons from the Great Depression." *Review of Radical Political Economics* 8 (April 1976): 71–97.

Mink, Gwendolyn. "The Lady and the Tramp: Gender, Race, and the Origins of the American Welfare State." In *Women, the State, and Welfare,* edited by Linda Gordon, 92–122. Madison: University of Wisconsin Press, 1990.

——. *The Wages of Motherhood: Inequality in the Welfare State, 1917–1942.* Ithaca, NY: Cornell University Press, 1995.

Mittelstadt, Jennifer. *From Welfare to Workfare: The Unintended Consequences of Liberal Reform.* Raleigh: University of North Carolina Press, 2005.

Mohl, Raymond A. "Mainstream Social Welfare History and Its Problems." *Reviews in American History* 7.4 (December 1979): 469–476.

Mohl, Raymond A., and Neil Betten. *Steel City: Urban and Ethnic Patterns in Gary, Indiana, 1906–1950.* New York: Holmes and Meier, 1986.

Morrissey, Megan H. "The Life and Career of Helen Hall: Settlement Worker and Social Reformer in Social Work's Second Generation." Ph.D. dissertation, University of Minnesota, 1996.

Moss, David A. *Socializing Security: Progressive-Era Economists and the Origins of American Social Policy.* Cambridge, MA: Harvard University Press, 1996.

Muncy, Robyn. *Creating a Female Dominion in American Reform, 1890–1935.* New York: Oxford University Press, 1991.

Murphy, Mary. *Mining Cultures: Men, Women and Leisure in Butte, 1914–1941.* Urbana: University of Illinois Press, 1997.

Nadasen, Premilla, Jennifer Mittelstadt, and Marisa Chappell. *Welfare in the United States: A History with Documents, 1935–1996.* New York: Routledge, 2009.

Nelson, Barbara. "The Origins of the Two-Channel Welfare State: Workmen's Compensation and Mother's Aid." In *Women, the State, and Welfare,* edited by Linda Gordon, 123–151. Madison: University of Wisconsin Press, 1990.

Nelson, Daniel. *Unemployment Insurance: The American Experience, 1915–1935.* Madison: University of Wisconsin Press, 1969.

Nelson, Otto M. "The Chicago Relief and Aid Society, 1850–1874." *Journal of the Illinois State Historical Society* 59 (1966): 48–66.

Olney, Martha L. *Buy Now, Pay Later: Advertising, Credit, and Consumer Durables in the 1920s.* Chapel Hill: University of North Carolina Press, 1991.

Pacyga, Dominic A. *Chicago: A Biography*. Chicago: University of Chicago Press, 2009.

Patterson, James T. *America's Struggle against Poverty in the Twentieth Century*. Cambridge, MA: Harvard University Press, 2000.

Philpot, Thomas. *The Slum and the Ghetto: Immigrants, Blacks, and Reformers in Chicago, 1880–1930*. Belmont, CA: Wadsworth Publishing, 1991.

Piven, Frances Fox, and Richard Cloward. *Poor People's Movements: Why They Succeed, How They Fail*. New York: Vintage Books, 1979.

Platt, Harold. *The Electric City: Energy and the Growth of the Chicago Area, 1880–1930*. Chicago: University of Chicago Press, 1991.

Poole, Mary. *The Segregated Origins of Social Security*. Chapel Hill: University of North Carolina Press, 2006.

Porter, Eduardo. "Come the Recession, Don't Count on That Safety Net." *New York Times*, February 20, 2018.

Quadagno, Jill. *The Color of Welfare: How Racism Undermined the War on Poverty*. New York: Oxford University Press, 1994.

Reed, Katie P., and Monica Schulteis. "President Trump Signs into Law the Coronavirus Aid, Relief, and Economic Security (CARES) Act." *National Law Review*, March 29, 2020.

Roberts, Patrick S. *Disasters and the American State: How Politicians, Bureaucrats, and the Public Prepare for the Unexpected*. New York: Cambridge University Press, 2013.

Rodgers, Daniel. *Atlantic Crossings: Social Politics in a Progressive Age*. Cambridge, MA: Belknap Press of Harvard University Press, 1998.

Romasco, Albert U. *The Poverty of Abundance: Hoover, the Nation, the Depression*. New York: Oxford University Press, 1965.

Romer, Christina D. "The Great Crash and the Onset of the Great Depression." *Quarterly Journal of Economics* 105.3 (1990): 597–624.

Rose, Nancy. "Work Relief in the 1930s and the Origins of the Social Security Act." *Social Service Review* 63.1 (March 1989): 63–91.

Rose, Sarah Frances. "No Right to Be Idle: The Invention of Disability, 1850–1930." Ph.D. dissertation, University of Illinois at Chicago, 2008.

Rosenzweig, Roy. "Organizing the Unemployed: The Early Years of the Great Depression, 1929–1933." *Radical America* 10.4 (July/August 1976): 37–62.

———. "'Socialism in Our Time': The Socialist Party and the Unemployed, 1929–1936." *Labor History* 20.4 (1979): 485–509.

Rotundo, E. Anthony. *American Manhood: Transformations in Masculinity from the Revolution to the Modern Era*. New York: Basic Books, 1993.

Sapiro, Virginia. "The Gender Basis of American Social Policy." *Political Science Quarterly* 101.2 (1986): 221–238.

Sautter, Udo. *Three Cheers for the Unemployed: Government and Unemployment before the New Deal*. New York: Cambridge University Press, 1991.

Scharf, Lois. *To Work and to Wed: Female Employment, Feminism, and the Great Depression*. Westport, CT: Greenwood Press, 1980.

Schlesinger, Arthur M., Jr., *The Crisis of the Old Order*. Boston: Houghton Mifflin, 1957.

Schwarz, Jordan A. *The Interregnum of Despair*. Urbana: University of Illinois Press, 1970.

Self, Robert O. *All in the Family: The Realignment of American Democracy since the 1960s*. New York: Hill and Wang, 2012.

Singleton, Jeff. *The American Dole: Unemployment Relief and the Welfare State in the Great Depression*. Westport, CT: Greenwood Press, 2000.

Skocpol, Theda, and G. John Ikenberry. "The Road to Social Security." In *Social Policy in the United States: Future Possibilities in Historical Perspective*, ed. Theda Skocpol, 136–167. Princeton, NJ: Princeton University Press, 1995.

Skocpol, Theda, and Gretchen Ritter. "Gender and the Origins of Modern Social Policies in Britain and the United States." *Studies in American Political Development* 5 (Spring 1991): 36–93.

Skok, Deborah A. *More Than Neighbors: Catholic Settlements and Day Nurseries in Chicago, 1893–1930*. DeKalb: Northern Illinois University Press, 2007.

Smith, Carl. *Urban Disorder and the Shape of Belief: The Great Chicago Fire, the Haymarket Bomb, and the Model Town of Pullman*. Chicago: University of Chicago Press, 1995.

Sobel, Robert. *The Great Bull Market: Wall Street in the 1920s*. New York: Norton, 1968.

Stearns, Peter N. "Fatherhood in Historical Perspective: The Role of Social Change." In *Fatherhood and Families in Cultural Context*, edited by Frederick W. Bozett and Shirley M. H. Hanson, 28–52. New York: Springer, 1991.

Stein-Roggenbuck, Susan. *Negotiating Relief: The Development of Social Welfare Programs in Depression-Era Michigan, 1930–1940*. Columbus: Ohio State University Press, 2008.

Stepan-Norris, Judith, and Maurice Zeitlin. *Left Out: Reds and America's Industrial Unions*. Cambridge, UK: Cambridge University Press, 2003.

Stoddart, Jess. *Challenge and Change in Appalachia: The Story of Hindman Settlement School*. Lexington: University Press of Kentucky, 2002.

Storch, Randi. *Red Chicago: American Communism at Its Grassroots, 1928–35*. Urbana: University of Illinois Press, 2007.

Street, Paul Louis. "Working in the Yards: A History of Class Relations in Chicago's Meatpacking Industry, 1886–1960." Ph.D. dissertation, the Graduate School of Binghamton University, 1993.

Stromquist, Shelton. *Re-inventing "The People": The Progressive Movement, the Class Problem, and the Origins of Modern Liberalism*. Urbana: University of Illinois Press, 2006.

Sugrue, Thomas. *The Origins of the Urban Crisis: Race and Inequality in Postwar Detroit*. Princeton, NJ: Princeton University Press, 2005.

Terkel, Studs. *Hard Times: An Oral History of the Great Depression*. New York: Pocket Books, 1971.

Tomlins, Christopher L. *The State and the Unions: Labor Relations, Law, and the Organized Labor Movement in America*. New York: Cambridge University Press, 1985.

Tonn, Mari Boor. "Radical Labor in a Feminine Voice: The Rhetoric of Mary Harris 'Mother' Jones and Elizabeth Gurley Flynn." In *The Rhetoric of Nineteenth-Century Reform*, edited by Martha S. Watson and Thomas R. Burholder, 224–253. East Lansing: Michigan State University Press, 2008.

Trattner, Walter. *From Poor Law to Welfare State: A History of Social Welfare in America*. 6th ed. New York: Free Press, 1999.

Trolander, Judith A. *Professionalism and Social Change: From the Settlement House Movement to Neighborhood Centers, 1886 to the Present*. New York: Columbia University Press, 1987.

———. *Settlement Houses and the Great Depression*. Detroit: Wayne State University Press, 1975.

Valocchi, Steve. "External Resources and the Unemployed Councils of the 1930s: Evaluating Six Propositions from Social Movement Theory." *Sociological Forum* 8.3 (September 1993): 451–470.

Wandersee, Winifred D. *Women's Work and Family Values, 1920–1940*. Cambridge, MA: Harvard University Press, 1981.

Wasik, John F. *The Merchant of Power: Sam Insull, Thomas Edison, and the Creation of the Modern Metropolis*. Gordonsville, VA: Palgrave Macmillan, 2006.

Watson, Frank Dekker. *The Charity Organization Movement in the United States: A Study in American Philanthropy*. New York: Macmillan, 1922.

Weir, David R. "A Century of U.S. Unemployment, 1890–1990: Revised Estimates and Evidence for Stabilization." *Research in Economic History* 14 (1992): 301–346.

Wenger, Beth S. *New York Jews and the Great Depression: Uncertain Promise*. Syracuse, NY: Syracuse University Press, 1999.

Wilson, John Hoff. *Herbert Hoover: Forgotten Progressive*. Boston: Little, Brown, 1975.

Zunz, Olivier. *Philanthropy in America: A History*. Princeton, NJ: Princeton University Press, 2012.

Index

Van Buren Street Improvement Association (Chicago), 68–69
Van Kleeck, Mary, 145–147
Vittum, Harriet, 9, 73–78, 80, 83, 89, 91, 94, 97, 100, 108, 153
Voluntarism, 52, 56–57, 62, 64–65, 130, 141

Wagner bill (1931), 45–46
Wagner-Lewis Unemployment Insurance Bill (1934), 144, 148
Wagner, Robert, 47, 142
Wald, Lillian, 25
Waltmire, Rev. W. B., 99
Washington DC, 9, 95, 102, 115
Welfare, 2–4, 11–12, 41, 54, 61, 63, 65, 74, 109–110, 123, 139, 141; American welfare policy, 5, 11, 13, 20, 126–128, 132–133, 137–140, 143, 149–150 (*see also* FERA; Welfare state); means-tested welfare, 122–124, 154 (*see also* Casework); private welfare agencies, 51, 56, 58, 64, 130, 137–141, 175n14 (*see also* Charity; Capitalism: welfare capitalism); public welfare agencies, 2–4, 51, 54, 70, 77, 137–141, 175n14 (*see also* Cook County: Bureau of Public Welfare); two-tiered system, 11, 13, 18, 48
Welfare capitalism. *See* Capitalism: welfare capitalism
Welfare state, 11, 13, 48, 108, 123, 138–139, 141, 149, 154

Wisconsin, 143; Madison, 46; relief policies, 46, 48, 98, 136, 142, 144
Wisconsin Unemployment Compensation Law of 1932, 46, 98, 142
Witte, Edwin, 143–144, 147
Women: female dependency, 22–23, 38–39, 41, 44; feminism, 87, 147; settlement house Women's Departments, 11, 86, 90–95; "true womanhood," 39, 41; as workers, 11, 22–23, 38–44, 87–88, 92–94; as workers, criticism of, 40–44, 83. *See also* Motherhood; Unemployment, consequences of: effects on women and feminine identity
Workers Committee on Unemployment (WCOU), 1, 15, 47, 96–98, 99–102, 107–126, 130, 134, 142–143, 145–150, 155; founders, 99–100; frustration with limited relief, 103–106, 108, 113, 118–119; public hearings, 100–107, 123 (see also *An Urban Famine*); use of radicalism, 97, 114–118; views on casework, 15, 97, 114, 118–124, 142, 147 (*see also* Capitalism: worker-centered capitalism)
Works Progress Administration (WPA), 153–154
World War I, 7, 25, 115
Worthy poor. *See* Deserving poor

Young Men's Christian Association (YMCA), 106

Abigail Trollinger is an Associate Professor of History at St. Norbert College in De Pere, WI.